CONSTRUCTING THE GERMAN
WALT WHITMAN

CONSTRUCTING THE GERMAN

Walt Whitman

. . . .

BY WALTER GRÜNZWEIG

UNIVERSITY OF IOWA PRESS  IOWA CITY

University of Iowa Press, Iowa City 52242

Printed in the United States of America

Design by Richard Hendel

Printed on acid-free paper

Library of Congress Cataloging-in-Publication Data

Grünzweig, Walter.

Constructing the German Walt Whitman /

by Walter Grünzweig.

p. cm.

Includes bibliographical references (p.) and index.

ISBN 0-87745-481-7 (cloth), ISBN 0-87745-482-5 (paper)

1. Whitman, Walt, 1819–1892—Appreciation—Europe, German-speaking. 2. Whitman, Walt, 1819–1892—Criticism and interpretation—History. 3. Criticism—Europe, German-speaking—History. I. Title.

PS3238.G78 1994 94-30024

811′.3—dc20 CIP

01 00 99 98 97 96 95 C 5 4 3 2 1

01 00 99 98 97 96 95 P 5 4 3 2 1

To

my brother

WERNER,

another

Whitmanite

CONTENTS

ACKNOWLEDGMENTS

This book would not have been possible without the support of many colleagues, friends, and institutions on both sides of the Atlantic. The extent and quality of this support prove that there really *is* a Whitman community on which individual Whitman researchers can and must depend.

Early assistance and encouragement came from Gay Wilson Allen, the father of modern Whitman research, and Hans Galinsky, one of the great researchers in German-American studies of our century. Throughout my many years of research, I drew on the expertise and friendship of Betsy Erkkila (Philadelphia), Ed Folsom (Iowa City), and Hans-Joachim Lang (Hamburg) for aid in collecting, assembling, and analyzing my material and for the critical evaluation of my manuscript. For effective help with the manuscript, I would also like to thank James E. Knowlton (Sherman, Texas), Anne Ulmer (Northfield, Minnesota), and especially my copy editor, Kathy Lewis.

Philip G. Furia (Minneapolis), Arthur Golden (New York/Ljubljana), Dietmar Goltschnigg (Graz), Larry Meredith (Stockton), Christopher Müller (Berlin), Marianne Müller (Berlin), Paul Raabe (Wolfenbüttel), Gerhard Rothbauer (Leipzig/Bamberg), James R. Thompson (Athens, Ohio), Frank Trommler (Philadelphia), and Larry D. Wells (Binghamton) have given me important advice and help on individual questions relating to my research.

Financial support for my research was generously given by the American Council of Learned Societies, the Austrian-American Educational Commission (Fulbright Commission), and the German Humboldt Foundation.

A large number of libraries and archives have allowed me access to much hitherto-unexplored material. In Germany, special thanks go to the Deutsche Literaturarchiv, Marbach, especially Winfried Feifel and Ingrid Grüninger; the Staatsbibliothek Preußischer Kulturbesitz (Berlin); and the Johannes Schlaf Archive in Querfurt, especially Ingolf Schnittka and Joachim Hartmann. In the United States, I would like to express special appreciation to the University of Pennsylvania's Van Pelt Library, above all the Special Collections staff; Christa Sammons of Beinecke Library, New Haven; and Charles Kelly and Michael McElderry at the Library of Congress.

For intellectual inspiration, I am especially obliged to my colleagues in the Department of American Studies at Karl-Franzens-Universität Graz, especially Jürgen Peper, long-term chair and my principal advisor, and my friend Roberta Maierhofer. Special thanks for covering my prolonged absences are due to departmental manager Sonja Hanauer and its present chair, Arno Heller. Several generations of students, on both sides of the Atlantic, have also significantly contributed to the character of the book.

Much of the book's substance has emerged from long-term professional dialogues and collaboration with Margaret Cotroneo (Philadelphia), whose theologically based humanism has provided me with new perspectives required for an understanding of many of the Whitmanites discussed in this book, and Eva Manske (Freiburg), whose enthusiasm for the avant-garde has taught me new ways to read and appreciate literature.

Finally, I would like to acknowledge more indirect but decisive impacts on my work. My parents, Franz and Elfriede Grünzweig, have provided the background for my definition of and devotion to cultural studies; my German-American wife, Brunhild Fölsch, has shaped my intercultural perspective; and my brother Werner, a musicologist in Berlin, has helped me to take a comprehensive view of cultural processes.

ABBREVIATIONS

F	Johannes Schlaf. *Frühling.* Leipzig: Insel, n.d. [1894].
FB	Johannes Schlaf. "Walt Whitman." *Freie Bühne für den Entwickelungskampf der Zeit* 3 (1892), 977–988.
FWL	Franz Werfel. *Gesammelte Werke: Das lyrische Werk,* ed. Adolf Klarmann. Frankfurt/M.: Fischer, 1967.
GL	Gustav Landauer. "Walt Whitman," in Gustav Landauer, *Der werdende Mensch: Aufsätze zur Literatur,* ed. Gerhard Hendel, pp. 85–97. Leipzig and Weimar: Kiepenheuer, 1980.
HR1, HR2	Walt Whitman. *Walt Whitmans Werk in zwei Bänden,* trans. Hans Reisiger. 2 vols. Berlin: S. Fischer, 1922.
KK	Karl Knortz. *Walt Whitman: Vortrag gehalten im Deutschen Gesellig-Wissenschaftlichen Verein von New York am 24. März 1886.* New York: Bartsch, 1886.
KR	Walt Whitman. *Grashalme: Gedichte,* ed. and trans. Karl Knortz and T. W. Rolleston. Zurich: Verlags-Magazin Schabelitz, 1889.
LG	(with English quotations) Walt Whitman. *Leaves of Grass: Comprehensive Reader's Edition,* ed. Harold W. Blodgett and Sculley Bradley. New York: New York University Press, 1965.
LG	(with German quotations) Walt Whitman. *Grashalme,* trans. Johannes Schlaf. Stuttgart: Reclam, 1986 (original publication 1907).
MiE	Heinrich Lersch. *Mensch im Eisen: Gesänge von Volk und Werk.* Berlin and Leipzig: Deutsche Verlangsanstalt, 1925.
PB	Johannes Schlaf. *Peter Boies Freite.* Leipzig: Seemann, 1903.
Ph	Arno Holz. *Phantasus* (1898–1899). Stuttgart: Reclam, 1968.
TWR	T[homas] W[illiam] Rolleston and H[enry] B[ernard] Cotterill. *Ueber Wordsworth und Walt Whitman: Zwei Vorträge gehalten vor dem Literarischen Verein zu Dresden.* Dresden: Tittmann, 1883.

WM Eduard Bertz. *Whitman-Mysterien: Eine Abrechnung mit Johannes Schlaf.* Berlin: n.p., 1907.

YH Eduard Bertz. *Der Yankee-Heiland: Ein Beitrag zur modernen Religionsgeschichte.* Dresden: Reissner, 1906.

INTRODUCTION

I heard that you ask'd for something to prove this puzzle the New World,
And to define America, her athletic Democracy,
Therefore I send you my poems that you behold in them what you wanted.
Whitman, "To Foreign Lands"

Walt Whitman's reception in the German-speaking countries forms a radical and revolutionary tale. Since 1868, when Ferdinand Freiligrath came out with the first small translation, Whitman has excited some of the finest and most unorthodox minds in Germany, Austria, and Switzerland. His *Leaves of Grass* was an important factor in the modernist revolution in German poetry starting in the first decade of the twentieth century,[1] but its influence has not been limited to the realm of literature. From gay liberationists to anarchists, countless groups have turned the white-maned patriarch into a champion for their causes.

A study that seeks to do justice to the history of this multifaceted reception must posit a very broadly based notion of culture, embodying a wide variety of elements such as high-brow literature, politics, youth movements, sexuality, and various subcultures. Although Germans traditionally differentiate meticulously between literary and popular culture, the reception of Whitman frequently clouds this distinction, suggesting how the American's democratizing force works even in a foreign culture.

Whitman is central to an understanding of German culture between 1890 and 1933. Given the richness of the material Whitman's German reception has produced, the theoretical questions regarding the validity of reception and of "influence" studies in general might be disregarded altogether. From a pragmatic point of view, the very quantity of these findings proves the importance of reception studies for an understanding of the processes of intercultural diffusion.

Still, a theoretical note regarding reception studies in the context of American literary criticism is necessary. In an interesting article on comparative criticism and theory, the champion of reception theory in the United States, the Germanist Robert C. Holub, has pointed out that this German-based theory never really caught on in the United States because it was not considered a sufficient break with traditional theories and methods of criticism: "it has never been perceived as a radical departure from more familiar approaches. . . ."[2]

Although Holub's commentary concerned reception theory and *Rezeptionsästhetik* (especially the work of Wolfgang Iser and Hans Robert Jauß), it might well be extended to reception history. From the point of view of American scholarship, which has traditionally seen the place of the academy at the cutting edge of intellectual/scientific development,[3] reception history, too, appears to be a tedious Germanic exercise in meticulous collecting, classifying, and interpreting along the lines of traditional hermeneutics.

Reception history might be considered a particularly dubious project, because it would seem to disregard the poststructuralist, deconstructive messages stressing the heterogeneous and unstable quality of a text. The present investigation, although of Central European origin, attempts neither to classify reception documents into appropriate and inappropriate reactions to a given text nor to collect critical views in order to arrive at some comprehensive "superinterpretation." Rather, the emphasis is on the question of the German *construction* of Walt Whitman as author and personality.[4]

German, Austrian, and Swiss reactions to Whitman amount to social and literary constructions of an author; these many different constructions, taken together, finally make up the idealized mythical German "Whitmann" presented in this book. In studying Whitman's social and literary construction in the German-speaking countries, we are looking at exchange processes between Central European and American constructions of the author; in this way this book also becomes a study of reciprocal intercultural processes.

In the past decade, "interculturality" has become a catchword in such disciplines as sociology, international education, and communication. In Germany, a Society for Intercultural German Studies (Gesellschaft für Interkulturelle Germanistik) was founded in an attempt to challenge the monocultural traditions and practices of the literary discipline by highlighting its multicultural context.

"Inter-" in "international" usually means "in between" or "beyond." Sometimes it even has a confrontational connotation, as in "international politics." In the present study, "intercultural" describes a *collaborative* phenomenon.[5] The notion of interculturality implies that all contacts between foreign cultures amount to an ongoing dialogue in the course of which the partners in that dialogue mutually affect one other.

Such a conception requires a modification of traditional reception models. The reception of an author in a foreign culture is usually considered a phenomenon which is part of the receiving culture. Quite in contrast to such one-sided patterns (implying, of course, notions of textual intentionality), my model highlights the *interaction* and *exchanges* between the cultures involved. Whitman's reception is not just an American product left to German-speaking translators and readers for further processing. This study chronicles the "Whitman propaganda" produced by such "disciples" as William D. O'Connor and Horace Traubel (and even by Whitman himself) from 1868 until the beginning of World War I, as it enters into and interacts with the activities of German Whitman enthusiasts. Often, as in the case of German-American mediators, it is even difficult to differentiate between source and target culture; the reception documents offer a continuous spectrum of individuals and groups engaged in transcultural activities.[6]

There is a second aspect to the intercultural quality of Whitman's reception which necessitates a departure from the traditional model. Reception studies in comparative literary research usually investigate the response of an audience in one culture to an author or a group of authors from a different culture. Whitman's German reception, however, is in many ways connected to the larger European context. While my main focus is of course on the relationship between German and American culture, the multicultural network of relationships among the Whitmanites from several countries is also considered. Ultimately, once Whitman's relationship to a variety of national literatures is recognized and understood, a multiculturally oriented study of Whitman's global reception will become feasible.[7]

Whitman's reception in the German-speaking countries may serve as a paradigm for German-American cultural relations. Whenever Whitman's works were read, they were understood as representative of American literature and, indeed, as genuine cultural expressions of the New World. The history of his reception is part of the history of the German image of America, a version of the encounter between the Old World and the New, and such a history can help us to understand the dynamics of this relationship.

In my German study *Walt Whitmann: Die deutschsprachige Rezeption als interkulturelles Phänomen,*[8] I focused on the effects of Whitman reception in German-language literatures and cultures, considering in detail German texts of all kinds. The focus, therefore, was on the reception documents. Here, taking into account the interests of readers who are not Germanists, my emphasis is on the construction of Whitman as a cultural artifact.

Carelessly speaking, the question might be worded as "What in Whitman has impressed Europeans?" By this, I do not mean some mystical "German" quality that has made Whitman particularly interesting to German readers. I do not believe that there is a "Germany in Whitman" (through his own familiarity with German idealistic philosophers, German Romantic poets, or the Nibelungen sagas) which is in some way responsible for Whitman's great success in the German-speaking world. Whitman's creative reception *of* German literature is an important question in itself but is not dealt with here.

Since the bi- and multicultural interaction constructs a new Whitman and a new kind of discourse *about* Whitman, the task of this book is not to discover Whitman's ontological center—his "whatness"—but rather to analyze how the various constructions of Whitman function in a German and intercultural context.

PREVIOUS RESEARCH

While my investigations are the first to deal comprehensively with the topic and to evaluate it as a cultural and intercultural phenomenon, there has been some previous research on Whitman in Germany. Whitman became an academic subject at German universities as early as 1910–1911, when an American guest professor in Berlin gave lectures on him.[9] In 1914, an American student wrote the first Ph.D. thesis on Whitman at a German university.[10] At the turn of the century, histories of German literature started mentioning Whitman as a significant force in German literature, although there was often a nationalistic tone coupled with disparaging remarks on American culture.

The first comprehensive evaluation of the phenomenon was undertaken by an American, Edward Thorstenberg, who recognized what he called a "Walt Whitman Cult in Germany" as early as 1911.[11] Thorstenberg and Grace Delano Clark, who wrote on Whitman several years later,[12] limited themselves to a summary of individual statements on Whitman. In contrast to such diagnostic articles, Anna Jacobsen, calling Whitman's German reception "a chapter in comparative literature,"[13] stressed Whitman's significance for German literature and culture. Specifically, she mentioned German expressionist poets, the homosexual discussion, and, most importantly, Whitman's influence on working-class culture. Eleven years later, Gay Wilson Allen, then at the beginning of his career, joined Jacobsen by claiming that "Whitmanesque thought was nothing new in 1855; it was an old story in Germany, France, and Scandinavia. . . . He simply became a link in the chain of proletarian writers—but a very important link, as it will be found when the history of the proletarian literature of the world is finally written."[14] East European criticism before 1989 excepted, such leftist evaluations of Whitman have become rare in contemporary scholarship.

A series of Ph.D. theses by Americans studying in Europe deal with the subject of Whitman's reception in general, the merit of Whitman translations, and the "influence" of Whitman and Whitman's works on modernist German poetry, especially expressionism. However, ideological prejudice or methodological shortcomings prevent these studies from being useful contributions to the topic.[15]

Monika Schaper, an Americanist focusing on German translations of Whitman, has provided a more convincing study.[16] In radical contrast to most of the previous works, her historical approach leads her to view translations as documents of reception, although her analyses of the translations themselves are less than satisfactory. My own work incorporates and builds on the findings of her study.

A number of studies deal with Whitman's German reception in a more tangential fashion, but identify significant impulses and furnish valuable information. These include a chapter on Whitman in world literature in the English edition of Frederik Schyberg's Whitman study, Gay Wilson Allen's sections on German Whitman reception in the various editions of his *Walt Whitman Handbook*, and Marianne Misgin-Müller's dissertation on the treatment of American literature in German Social Democratic periodicals.[17] Of great importance in a different way is Betsy Erkkila's book on Whitman in France,[18] which constitutes a valuable state-of-the-art study of a parallel intercultural phenomenon.

The first part of this investigation characterizes the various German Whitman translations in their respective historical contexts. Translators are, of course, the basic and most important "mediators" for a literary work entering another culture, so it is important to understand their backgrounds, interests, and motivations as well as their abilities. Although it is difficult, in a study written in English, to assess specific linguistic characteristics of German Whitman translations, I attempt to show how the various translations reflect the intentions and the background of the translators.

On the basis of this overview, I discuss the different interest groups who found Whitman important to their work and aims. This categorization of groups does justice to the large variety of responses to Whitman in the areas of literature, politics, and sexuality. That the reaction was strongest on the part of literary critics and authors, both in critical statements and in creative works, is hardly surprising. Yet the nonliterary varieties of reception are equally illuminating.

The final chapter of the book presents a brief summary and evaluation of the results of the intercultural processes described in the preceding chapters. The European projections of Whitman, and the modifications of his work that occur in the course of complex processes of critical and creative reception, prove that

Whitman's German reception is a small but significant and revealing chapter in the large volume of European-American cultural relations.

A NOTE ON PATHOS

One interesting question of comparative poetics must be dealt with in this introduction because it has consequences for the terminology used throughout this study. There is a general consensus among German-speaking readers that Whitman's poetry displays an extraordinary amount of what in German is referred to as *Pathos.* This is one of the few virtually untranslatable German literary terms. M. H. Abrams's *Glossary,* in its thorough fashion, records the original Greek meaning of "the passions, or suffering, or deep feeling generally. . . . "[19]

Today's use of the term in English-language criticism, however, is markedly different. In modern use, "Pathos," according to Abrams, evokes "feelings of tenderness, pity, or sympathetic sorrow."[20] W. V. Ruttkowski and R. E. Blake, in their *Glossary of Literary Terms in English, German, and French,* fail to give an English equivalent for German *Pathos,* although they suggest that the English term "bathos" is simply "pathos" exaggerated to the point of the ridiculous. But the German meaning of *Pathos,* "a stylistic form connecting passionate literary presentation of a subject with high moral and ethical claims,"[21] is more closely related to the meaning of the original Greek term. Often, however, this *Pathos* turns into a *hohles Pathos* (hollow pathos[22]), and then may appear *pathetic* to the ears of English speakers.

One needs to be careful in using these different meanings of an etymologically related word as a starting point for an inquiry into national stereotypes or even characteristics. Applied to Whitman, however, this difference does say something about the American poet's German reception: the serious approach to his works predominates; only a very few German-speaking readers have discerned a humorous or ironic side of Whitman. Whitman was read with sympathy, passion, excitement; his poetry was placed in a context of deep movement and profound emotion, and there was an aura of ceremony connected with the reading of his texts—an altogether serious business.

As I argue in the conclusion of this study, *Pathos* as employed by German writers (and as admired in Whitman's poetry) is a lyrical expression of a desire for totality in human life. This is what the Austrian writer Stefan Zweig meant when he introduced the first edition of the expressionist journal *Das neue Pathos* (*New Pathos*) with an article of the same title in 1913. In this article he claimed that a new *Pathos* manifested itself when even "the churches resound with Walt Whitman's verses, with an American consciousness."[23] This "American consciousness" represents a hoped-for solution to the general feeling of alienation, isolation, and frustration that modern German writers experienced and lamented around the turn of the century. Virtually all of Whitman's addresses to individuals, groups of individuals, or even nonhuman entities were, to German-speaking readers, expressive of an extreme *Pathos* attempting to bridge gaps, invocating desired states of society, redeeming humankind and promising a new totality. A few sample phrases picked at random from "Starting from Paumanok" provide examples for each category: "Democracy!"; "Whoever you are, to you endless announcements!"; "Here for you! and here for America!"; "O camerado close!"

Modern Germans, Austrians, and Swiss, living, as they do, in a postmodern, medialized society, are as little given to *Pathos* as their present-day American counterparts. With the disappearance of the German Democratic Republic, the last (already very weakened) bastion of German *Pathos* was destroyed—and even there *Pathos* had come to look quite pathetic. The false Nazi *Pathos* of German virtue and greatness which translated into the extermination of millions has finished off any real possibility for renewed *Pathos* in the foreseeable future.

But this should not blind us to the fact that there was another, quite different *Pathos* prior to the Third Reich which, when connected with Whitman, Emile Verhaeren, or the German expressionists, promoted progress and change, as well as intellectual and spiritual growth. It was a way of reading Whitman which differed from the mainstream American reception of Whitman. Therefore, this study cannot do without the term, and it is italicized throughout to suggest the German use of *Pathos* in a nonpathetic way, if such a thing be possible.

TRANSLATIONS

The general knowledge of English in the German-speaking countries is a post–World War II phenomenon. Prior to 1945, the knowledge of foreign languages was largely limited to an elite who had attended the *Gymnasium*, the eight- or nine-year secondary school leading to the university. Even there, English was in fierce competition with French and the classical languages.

For this reason, and because of the paucity of texts in the original languages, foreign literature was generally consumed in translations. Throughout the nineteenth century, German-speaking readers were readily supplied with translations from French, Italian, English, and Russian and also from non-European languages. Frequently, translators worked under the exploitative and dehumanizing conditions of an increasingly industrialized book production. Much of popular American literature was translated by low-paid individuals who did not necessarily identify with or bring much empathy to the books they translated.

In the case of poetry, and of Whitman in particular, the situation was quite different. In spite of the comparatively greater interest nineteenth-century readers took in the genre, poetry was hardly an important commercial factor in the emerging industrialized book trade. Whitman, especially, found translators who not only took great interest in his poetry and his person, but who were in a position to use their personal authority and connections in order to propagate the American's works in German-speaking countries. By and large, these men and women were themselves established authors or active members of the German and international cultural scene. Thus, each translation of Whitman's poetry is not only unique in style and selection, but also has a specific sociocultural context, its own "story" within German political and cultural history, and forms a part of the evolution of German-American cultural relations. The following chapters tell the stories of the origins of the various translations and their reception by the German reading public.

CHAPTER ONE

FERDINAND FREILIGRATH, ADOLF STRODTMANN, AND ERNST OTTO HOPP

The life of Whitman's first translator, Ferdinand Freiligrath (1810–1876), tells us much about the character of the society which would prove such fertile ground for Whitman's poetry. Freiligrath was a revolutionary and a poet. In Germany and Austria of the 1830s and 1840s, this was a dangerous combination. The period of liberalism during and shortly after the Napoleonic wars had long passed, and Austria's State Chancellor Metternich ruled all German states with an iron fist from his Viennese center of power. Freedom of expression was possible neither in the autocratic Austrian Empire nor in most of the duchies, principalities, and kingdoms which at that time made up Germany. Poverty and starvation were widespread and, especially during the 1840s as a result of poor harvests, the number of emigrants to the United States increased sharply.

Censorship was strict and unrelenting. The much-celebrated "apolitical" Biedermeier culture, which really lasted until the revolutions of 1848, was much more than a way of life or a style of furniture and decoration. With its philistine emphasis on simplicity and sentimentality, it often represented an elegant but desperate form of escapism for the cultural elite. As always, however, censorship and suppression of intellect and the arts produced strong countercurrents. Especially in Germany, the call for democracy and social justice combined with demands for a removal of the many feudalist parasites and for a unification of Germany. Artists, especially writers, played an important role in this movement.

In 1831, the most famous of these revolutionary authors, Heinrich Heine

(1797–1856), went to Paris, where he lived for the rest of his life, first as a voluntary and later as an involuntary exile. His colleague Freiligrath's fate was similar. A personal friend of Karl Marx (with whom he later disagreed), he was repeatedly forced into British exile because of his subversive activities aimed at the overthrow of the feudal aristocratic power and the establishment of a bourgeois democracy. One coincidence sheds a characteristic light on the political situation in Europe: one of Freiligrath's friends in the London exile of the late 1840s was a radical youth named Jakob Schabelitz, who some forty years later would become the publisher of the first book-length selection of *Leaves.* The political foreground of the German Whitman reception was long in the making.

For a short while, in 1848–1849, it looked as though a general European revolution might bring about much-desired change. Freiligrath did not know Whitman at the time, but Whitman's poem "Europe" might very well have been written with Freiligrath's situation in mind:

> Suddenly out of its stale and drowsy lair, the lair of slaves,
> Like lightning it le'pt forth half startled at itself,
> Its feet upon the ashes and the rags, its hands tight to the throats of kings.
>
> O hope and faith!
> O aching close of exiled patriots' lives!
> O many a sicken'd heart!
> Turn back unto this day and make yourselves afresh.[1]

However, the revolutionaries failed miserably, in part because the weak German and Austrian bourgeoisie was not ready to opt unequivocally for democracy; its eventual compromise with the feudalist forces allowed the reactionary regime to continue.

A large number of revolutionaries, the so-called Forty-Eighters, joined the ranks of exiles in England, the United States, and elsewhere. Individuals like Freiligrath had to face long periods away from home. In order to earn his living, he worked for the London branch of a Swiss bank while keeping up his literary activity and engaging in translations of international poetry.

Sometime in 1868, he must have discovered William Rossetti's semiauthorized edition of Whitman's poetry, *Poems by Walt Whitman.*[2] Judging by the first words of his characterization of Whitman, the first words ever written about Whitman in German, he was quite taken by the book:

> WALT WHITMAN! Who is Walt Whitman?
>
> The answer is, a poet! A new American poet! His admirers say, the first, the only poet America has as yet produced. The only American poet of specific

> character. No follower in the beaten track of the European muse, but fresh from the prairie and the new settlements, fresh from the coast and the great watercourses, fresh from the thronging humanity of seaports and cities, fresh from the battle-fields of the South, and from the earthy smells in hair and beard and clothing of the soil from which he sprang.[3]

This passage is part of an introduction to Whitman's life and work printed in the *Augsburger Allgemeine Zeitung*, then Germany's leading daily, published by Cotta, Goethe's publisher. It appeared in the widely read weekly edition of 24 April 1868. In two installments, the paper later published Freiligrath's first German translations of Whitman's poetry, all from *Drum-Taps*.[4]

For an introductory Whitman sampler, this choice may seem surprising. To understand this selection, we must consider the specific historical context. Ever since James Fenimore Cooper, German readers had looked to American literature (or German literature about America) for reports from the New World. With the Civil War just three years past, the events that had given rise to *Drum-Taps* were still fresh in most German readers' minds; the publisher calculated that public interest in these poems would be accordingly great.

With Whitman (and Marx), Freiligrath considered the American Civil War essentially an antifeudal war of liberation, a revolutionary struggle against the Southern oligarchy and against slavery. He hoped its example might renew the fervor of the Germans, whose antifeudal revolution had failed just twenty years earlier.

There was also a domestic factor. By 1868, the nationalistic urge in the German-speaking countries had increased (and in part supplanted the revolutionary impetus). This resulted in the establishment of the German Reich under Prussian hegemony and subsequently led to the Franco-Prussian War. Before all of this could happen, the multicultural Austrian Empire, which dominated all German states, needed to be pushed out. This occurred in the Austrian-Prussian War of 1866, which left Prussia the strongest power in Germany. Whitman's *Drum-Taps* poems, emerging from the American Civil War and written out of a deep and fervent desire to maintain the integrity of the Union, were therefore of great interest to Freiligrath. The American Civil War was perceived as very similar to the "fratricidal" war between Austria and Prussia, and Freiligrath must have appreciated the way the national spirit was inextricably intertwined with the democratic idea in Whitman's poetry.

Freiligrath's translations are less unconventional than his sensationalist introduction suggests. Of course, *Drum-Taps* contains few poems that would have been shocking (especially in aesthetic terms) for German readers in the first place, and

Freiligrath's choice of poems thus reveals his attempt to avoid criticism on that account (note, for example, the regular stanzaic form and the refrain "I dream, I dream, I dream" in the poem "Old War-Dreams"). But even in these carefully selected poems, we can discern a tendency to "tame" Whitman. While the translation is literal and faithful to the original, it "regularizes" Whitman's rhythm and meters and adds a lyrical tone foreign to Whitman.

Whitman's "Old War-Dreams," for example, renders a horrific war experience literally as a nightmare. Freiligrath, by contrast, produces a painting, thereby substantially modifying Whitman's "landscape of the soul,"[5] as Schaper correctly observes. In Freiligrath's translation of this poem, Whitman's disturbing obsession disappears. The American's "face of anguish" (484) becomes "Gesicht im Kampfe" (a face in the battle). In the second stanza, Whitman's dreamscape is rendered as fairly conventional nature poetry. The "scenes of nature" are turned into "freie Natur" (free, open nature), producing a feeling of relief and liberation; the "unearthly bright moon" is "so geisterhaft leuchtend" (shining ghostlike). Whitman's shocking contradiction between the "unearthly" night and the human carnage becomes, in Freiligrath's version, a harmonious whole.

Stanza 3, finally, totally subjects Whitman to reigning conventionalism. "*Long* have they pass'd" in Whitman's poem does not mean that the whole scene is no longer a vivid psychological experience for the lyrical persona dreaming its nightmarish dream. Freiligrath, though, by repeating "längst" (long ago) four times, poeticizes this passage. The affinity to the sentimental line "Lang, lang ist's her" (long, long ago) in a famous German folksong is obvious and almost completely removes the poem's sharp edges. Finally, the translation of Whitman's "callous composure," showing the strain on the human observer, with "schwieliger Ruh" (tranquillity, even peace) fits this overall picture very well.

Freiligrath was satisfied with the literally, and for the most part politically, understood message of Whitman's poems. In his translations, at least, he had little use for either Whitman's formal experiments or his psychological insight. The political poet seemed to be satisfied with the topicality of Whitman's poetry. Yet the introductory essay shows a much more thorough appreciation of Whitman's formal and aesthetic innovations than his selection and translations themselves suggest:

> [After reading Whitman, our] received forms, our playing with ring and sound, our syllable-counting and measure of quantity, our sonnet-writing and construction of strophes and stanzas, seem to us almost childish. Are we really come to the point, when life, even in poetry, calls imperatively for new forms of expression? Has the age so much and such serious matter to say, that the old

vessels no longer suffice for the new contents? Are we standing before a poetry of the ages to come, just as some years ago a music of the ages to come was announced to us? And is Walt Whitman a greater than Richard Wagner?[6]

Freiligrath was in a difficult bind. He had insight into Whitman's revolutionary poetics but also knew that the time for this poetry was not quite ripe in Germany. His interest in Whitman was really more intense than his translation of only ten poems might suggest. Among his papers located at Weimar, fragments of translations of two longer poems, "Starting from Paumanok" and "Song of the Broad-Axe," have recently been found. He was hoping to publish more poems by "my curious saint," as he called Whitman in his letter to the editor of the Augsburg paper.[7] Although the editor was quite satisfied with the reaction to this introductory selection of Whitman's poetry, stating in a letter to Freiligrath that "by the very fact that you introduced and recommended Whitman, he has become an object of serious interest,"[8] these additional translations were never completed. At that time, Freiligrath had just received permission to return to Germany after his long years of exile and was too preoccupied with other matters to think of Whitman translations.

The Whitman community in the United States was excited over what it considered a great success in Germany. Freiligrath's name had been prominent in the United States for a long time. Emerson had already published some of his poems in the *Dial*, and Freiligrath was known to translate first-rate poets: Burns, Tennyson (whom he knew personally), Byron, and Coleridge. His friendship with Longfellow, whom he had met as early as 1841 and also translated into German, was also well known. After the news of Freiligrath's translation had reached the United States, Whitman boasted in a letter to his Danish friend and supporter Rudolf Schmidt: "Abroad, my book and myself have had a welcome quite dazzling. Tennyson writes me friendly letters. Freiligrath translates and commends me."[9] In an unpublished correspondence "To the Editor of the *Nation*," using the name John Burroughs, he stressed "the splendid euloquiums [*sic*] of Freiligrath in his German translations of the '*Leaves*' " as proof that the magazine's disdain for his work was unjustified.[10]

O'Connor facilitated a translation of Freiligrath's article which was published in several American magazines. At the same time, he attempted to bring the German poet closer to the Whitman circle. In a letter to Whitman, he suggested: "I think a package ought to be made up at once for Ferdinand Freiligrath, and we can send it through Westerman, reimbursing him for the expense of transportation. I suppose it would be best to have it done by my agency, and I suggest that I write F. F. a letter, (to go with the package) explaining things generally, and making him as far as possible master of the situation. What do you think?"[11] The letter, according to Freiligrath, consisted of thirty-two pages.[12] In the letter, O'Connor promises a copy of *Leaves*, his own pamphlet, and "also a little book by Mr. John Burroughs."[13]

The letter itself is a model example of public relations for Whitman. O'Connor severely criticizes Rossetti's edition: "But in whatever you elect to do, I hope you will use the original edition, and not Mr. Rossetti's selection. Mr. Whitman's friends in this country feel greatly indebted to Mr. Rossetti for what he has done; but nevertheless must regard his work as essentially castrated[!], and of little value as enabling one to estimate the Poem in totality."[14]

Whitman and O'Connor were hoping that Freiligrath would undertake the translation of larger portions of *Leaves of Grass*. At the end of his long letter, O'Connor praises Freiligrath for his efforts and places his translation in the context of the German Shakespeare reception: "By no mind so well as by the German, can its [the *Leaves*'] vast and living world of philosophy and poetry be explored and made known. I never forget how Germany excavated Shakespeare, and after two centuries, made England a present of her supreme poet. And I have always said that whenever *Leaves of Grass* came before the immense and all-grasping German intelligence, she would perform a similar office for America. Be it so. Yours, my dear Mr. Freiligrath, the glory of the initiative."[15]

Although Freiligrath wrote to his daughter appreciatively about the letter (calling O'Connor "an enthusiastic admirer of the curious bird" [Whitman]),[16] he was not about to become a professional Whitmanite. He had nevertheless unwittingly become the first German collaborator in the Whitmanites' global propagandistic effort. Much of Freiligrath's construction of Whitman and some of his characterizations of the poetry are indebted to Rossetti's preface and to an article by Moncure D. Conway.[17] Rossetti's introduction was strongly influenced by O'Connor's image of the "Good Gray Poet" and by Whitman himself; Conway had visited Whitman and had been given the red-carpet treatment by the author. Conway's emphasis on Whitman as an ingenious loafer and friend of the people was borrowed by Freiligrath and became part of Whitman's permanent German record. Thus, what Whitman and O'Connor had transmitted to England was propagated by Freiligrath in Germany and then, when retranslated into English with Freiligrath's name tag attached, became an effective public-relations tool in America.

This reception of the reception provides some insight into the ways Whitman attempted (and partly managed) to project a self-created image of his person and his authorship into the world and thereby actively direct his reception abroad. Obviously, the same instincts which were at work domestically (with Whitman's anonymous reviews of his works penned by himself) also influenced his international activities. At times, Whitman's friends engaged in these activities; at times, he tried his own hand.

After the appearance of Freiligrath's translations, the German-speaking countries became one of Whitman's target areas. Not only had he "always wished to know what a real live German—a German born and bred—would make of me,"[18] but he also started to show an active interest in the translation of *Leaves* into German. Freiligrath's translations led him to pursue these efforts with vigor and, at the same time, to retain control of the undertaking.

Freiligrath's return from exile was made possible by a German committee working actively on his behalf. The committee was chaired by Adolf Strodtmann (1829–1879), who was himself a poet, philologist, editor, and translator. Also a revolutionary of 1848, he spent a few years in exile in the United States, where he ran a bookstore and a lending library in Philadelphia before eventually returning to Europe. An early translator of Nathaniel Hawthorne and in Germany a champion of American literature, which he believed to be slandered by British critics, he probably became aware of Whitman through Freiligrath. By 1870, he had translated eight poems, which he included in his *Amerikanische Anthologie.*[19]

The Prussian war against France (1870–1871) had further increased public interest in war poetry; therefore it was only logical that Strodtmann also turned to *Drum-Taps* for his selections from Whitman's poetry. Strodtmann took little interest in Whitman's aesthetics. To him, the importance of Whitman's poems lay in the fact that his "war and battle hymns successfully roused the bravery of the union armies."[20] Slavery to Strodtmann was the "most ruthless and cruel form of exploitation of man by man,"[21] and the reaction against it one of the driving forces in American poetry. Strodtmann, too, addressed the Civil War as a war of liberation and viewed Whitman as its most significant artistic voice. Although his reasons for connecting this war of liberation with the Prussian aggression against France remained obscure, some German readers of Whitman's war poetry at the time must have been able to justify their own war effort through these poems.

While Strodtmann thus praised the Civil War as a national effort to do away with America's number one evil, slavery, he spoke out against the exaggeration "with which his [American] admirers praise the rhymeless long lines of this strange literary bird, whose poetic character oftentimes hinges on wild rhythm, as uncomparable masterworks of genius."[22]

This lack of appreciation for Whitman's poetic revolution is also reflected in the efforts of a third Whitman translator of the period, Ernst Otto Hopp, another returnee from America, otherwise little known. In his anthology entitled *Unter dem Sternenbanner* (Beneath the Star-Spangled Banner, 1877), Hopp included the translation of just one work by Whitman. It was the poem Whitman was "almost sorry [he] ever wrote," "O Captain! My Captain!":

Auf Linkoln's Tod

DER KAPITÄN

Wach' auf, mein guter Kapitän, die Reise ward vollbracht,
Wir trotzten Sturm und Wettersgraus, der Mühen Lohn uns lacht,
Der Port ist da, die Glocke tönt, es jubelt fern und nah,
Bewundernd folgt das Aug' dem Kiel, der Noth und Schrecken sah—
Was klopfst du, Herz,
in tiefstem Schmerz?
Ich seh den Ort,
Am Boden dort
Der wackre Kapitän still liegt,
Von kalter Hand des Tods besiegt.

Steh' auf, mein guter Kapitän, und hör den Jubelsang,
O sieh, man winkt mit Flaggen dir, laut schallt des Hornes Klang,
Dich grüßt der Sträuße bunte Zier, die Tücher wehn im Wind,
Auf dich der Menge Blicke froh voll Stolz gerichtet sind—
O Kapitän,
O hör' mein Flehn,
Es schlingt mein Arm
Um dich sich warm—
Und ist's denn wahr, daß hier er liegt,
Von kalter Hand des Tods besiegt?

Nicht hört mich mehr der Kapitän, so bleich die Lippen still,
Sein Pulsschlag stockt, und nimmermehr er wieder schlagen will;
Vor Anker sicher liegt das Schiff, die Reise ward gethan,
Durch Sturm und Drang erreicht's sein Ziel, zog siegreich seine Bahn,
Jauchz' auf, o Strand,
Hall' wider, Land,
Ihr Glocken, klingt,
Matrosen, singt!—
Doch schweigend steh' ich, wo er liegt,
Von kalter Hand des Tods besiegt.[23]

The translator obviously revels in rhymes and places them even where Whitman did not. The poet wisely left the word "heart" in the first stanza without a partner in rhyme. The German translator, however, using possibly the oldest and certainly the most banal rhyme pair in German literature, rhymes "Herz" with "Schmerz" (pain)—a word which is not in Whitman's text but which certainly underscores the already obtrusive "message." However, it was not just the translator's fault; the German audience was obviously not quite ready for Whitman's innovations, notwithstanding the fact that their own tradition had provided them with various experiments in rhymeless poetry and free rhythm.[24]

CHAPTER TWO

KARL KNORTZ AND THOMAS WILLIAM ROLLESTON

The first generation of Whitman translators—Freiligrath, Strodtmann, and Hopp—were exiles and emigrants acting as intermediaries between American culture and the German-speaking countries. Like this group, the second generation of Whitman translators also had their base of operation outside the German-speaking countries.

After an interval of two decades, the first book-length translation of Whitman was the result of an unusual collaboration between Thomas William Rolleston, an Irish nationalist critic and writer,[1] and Karl Knortz, a German-American educator and cultural historian. Although they shared an enormous enthusiasm for Whitman, their motivation and outlook were very different. These differences, and the discussions resulting therefrom, shed much light on the general problems any translator of Whitman faced.

KARL KNORTZ (1841 – 1918)

Karl Knortz, who had emigrated to the United States in the early 1860s, saw himself as an intermediary between Germany, German-Americans, and the United States. Coming from German philosophical, pedagogical, and cultural traditions, he was an ardent convert to American democracy. He attempted to interpret German cultural and philosophical traditions in the light of the development of democracy in the United States. The popularized results of his efforts were published on both continents.[2] In his important two-volume *Geschichte der Nordamerikanischen Literatur* (1891), Knortz devoted a whole chapter to Whitman. His Whitman translation was part of an educational program for two hemispheres. It would be wrong to assume that the translators focused exclusively on European readers. In a letter to Rolleston, Whitman speculates that the translation "might have quite as much sale here in the United States—as in Germany—perhaps more."[3] The success of other America-related titles written in German and published in the United States proves that German-American readers were indeed a possible market for the German translation of Whitman's poetry, although actual sales have not yet been documented.

In addition to the sales perspective, there was the bicultural political strategy. For Knortz, one of the tasks of German-American literature was to democratize German traditions in order to neutralize "the inheritance of a monarchist upbringing . . . consisting in brutality against inferiors and bootlicking vis-à-vis superiors."[4] Whitman represented a perfect new cultural synthesis of German idealistic traditions and American democracy that could be utilized for this purpose.

In 1886, Knortz gave a lecture on Whitman for a German audience in New York City, which was later published in the United States.[5] In this lecture, as well as in his later publications, Knortz interprets Whitman in the light of his own sociopolitical convictions informed by a rationalist pragmatism. Johannes Schlaf later observed that Knortz lacked the "congenial temperament for penetrating and grasping Whitman's spirit" and that he approached "the Whitman phenomenon more from the point of view of an enlightened and rational democracy."[6]

In Knortz's long lecture, biographical details abound. They obviously originate from the American Whitman community (see KK, 19) and serve not only "to facilitate or at least approximate an understanding of 'Leaves of Grass' " (KK, 20), but also to transfer myths about the poet from the American into the German Whitman discourse. The very first lines are characteristic of the Whitman legend. Knortz summarizes O'Connor's novella "The Carpenter,"[7] likening Whitman to Jesus Christ. This comparison introduces the lecture and mention of Whitman's poem "To Him That Was Crucified" (KK, 40) at its conclusion strengthens the point. Knortz describes Whitman as a good samaritan, always ready to help his fellow human beings; he stresses Whitman's work as a self-sacrificing nurse during the Civil War (KK, 7), claiming the poet was unable to gain riches because he always gave three-quarters of his income to the poor and starving (KK, 9). In so doing, he embodies the spirit of the Gospel according to Matthew, from which Knortz quotes extensively (KK, 41).

It should be noted that Knortz was not at all a man of the church; quite to the contrary, he took strongly antireligious positions. His disdain for the religious conditions "in America, where a stultifying priesthood still exercises too much power,"[8] is a recurrent theme in his works. It is also reflected in his Whitman publications. Borrowing from Ludwig Feuerbach's philosophy of religion, he identifies Whitman with Christ in order to undermine the transcendent function of the Son of God. Triumphantly, Knortz states: "The central questions of religion hardly ever worried him [Whitman]" (KK, 39). "If, at times, he [Whitman] does use the name of 'God,' this refers only to his own moral feeling, with which he invested man and nature. Finally, it proves the old proposition that Gods are inventions of mankind" (KK, 40).[9]

His defense of the *Children of Adam* and the *Calamus* poems must be seen in conjunction with this aim: "Natural modesty has been turned into a laudable virtue by the representatives of Christian religion, for whom the human body, referred to by Luther as a bag full of maggots, is the origin of all sins. But now, there is a poet imbued with the spirit of the Greeks . . ." (KK, 30).[10]

The call for an open-minded attitude toward sexuality and the liberation of the human body is one of the central messages Knortz derives from Whitman: "The essence of modesty and morality will not be found in a robe. Whitman celebrates sexuality in the interest of human progress, in the interest of human physical and moral well-being" (KK, 31).[11] Although the main target here is religious prudishness, such readings would later be taken up by such groups as nudists or early advocates of a liberal attitude toward human sexuality.

Knortz justifies his overly pedagogical approach to Whitman's poetry by pointing out what to him seems the poet's own didactic quality: "As an enthusiastic and decidedly progressive American, Whitman demands that art, poetry, philosophy, and education be permeated with the democratic principle and contribute to shaping the future" (KK, 20). Moreover: "American society lacks this elevating and strengthening moral element and it is the task of literature to infuse society with it" (KK, 21).[12]

Although Whitman does display a certain didacticism, Knortz's interpretation hardly does justice to Whitman's "organic" concept of literature. Knortz's criticism of Whitman's language is absurd, although it makes sense from his peculiar point of view: " . . . the obscurity of Whitman['s language] is inexcusable. The poet or philosopher who wants to give the world the benefit of his new ideas should present them in a language which is comprehensible at least to individuals with an average education" (KK, 19).[13] This reading of Whitman is the result of the commonsensical way of thinking characteristic of a *Gymnasium*-trained German with a rural upbringing. It is the type of reading which allows Knortz to interpret Whitman's multifaceted symbolic "grass" as a "simple, useful, natural product" (KK, 25). Knortz seems to have worried little about the incompatibility of this prosaic Whitman with the Christ-like individual he introduced in the beginning. Rather, the mythic elements serve to strengthen the power of Whitman's "message" the way Knortz understands it.

Knortz also offers his readers a reading of Whitman as a poet of modern life. As a "true American," Whitman admires "technological, industrial, and social progress" (KK, 10). The concept of nature is always connected to his efforts to further civilization (see KK, 10), and the "poet and the man of science should be identical, so that the former no longer has to add his thoughts to fantastic stories, but can say farewell to the supernatural and stand on solid ground. Then he will be able to exert a more extensive and powerful influence on his time" (KK, 23).[14]

In the name of Whitman, Knortz demands that the creative artist adapt to the scientific age: "The American poet must be *modern.* Without ignoring the Good and the Beautiful in the work of his European colleagues, he must stand on his own feet. He must be the yeast with which his nation, and through his nation the world, will be leavened in morals, politics, and literature" (KK, 22; emphasis added).[15] Although Knortz calls for a synthesis between art and science, between the old life and the new, it is finally a synthesis that devalues art. Knortz's construction of Whitman is the product of the mind of a progressive, democratic German-American depicting a Whitman who listens "to the language of the machines in the democratic temple of American industry" (KK, 34). Continuing and expanding on Freiligrath's essay, Knortz interprets *Leaves of Grass* as a guide to American democracy from which Germans should learn. The juxtaposition of mythic biography and *oeuvre* in Knortz's presentation becomes characteristic of the subsequent reception of Whitman in the German-speaking countries.

THOMAS WILLIAM ROLLESTON (1857 – 1920)

T. W. Rolleston's interest in a German translation of *Leaves* developed out of his admiration for Whitman and his love for Germany, but it also has a concrete political background. A stronger Germany and a correspondingly weaker British Empire, Rolleston speculated, would increase the chances of Irish independence. His letters to Whitman show that he truly believed in Germany's future: "These Germans I admire more and more—if they keep their present characteristics, what a nation they will be sometime!"[16] At the same time, he believed that Germans had given up on some of their own very best philosophical traditions only to turn to a destructive positivism. Moreover, since the Germans had no democracy ("none whatever"),[17] he believed Whitman would be of great value to them. His was a much more abstract mind than Knortz's: he believed that a synthesis of German philosophy and American literature could bring about a change in German aesthetic sensibility which would lead to the desired renewal.

In September 1883, Rolleston gave a lecture before the Dresden Literary Society, on which he reported in detail to Whitman.[18] This lecture was printed as a pamphlet and published in Dresden.[19] At the outset, Rolleston expressed his bewilderment over the "scientific conquests of this curious age" and over "modern humanity with its terrible energy, its unparalleled absorption in dialectics, and its boundless courage in word and deed" (TWR, 44f.). For the self-conscious Irishman, the responsibility for this negative development lay with England: "In England, they deal mainly with the laws of appearances, the way they originate and depend on each other, with what is generally referred to as their external effects" (TWR, 46).[20]

The power of this "negative spirit of analysis" (TWR, 45) is criticized vehemently; in the heyday of the generally accepted positivistic and "scientific" world view, Rolleston seems to call for a turnabout. The "purely mechanical view of the universe" had its origin in "the spirit of freedom which has spread through Europe in this and the previous century" (TWR, 50). Rolleston diagnosed a dangerous inclination toward the positivistic method in Germany as well. Repulsed, he wrote to Whitman: "Germany at present is suffering from an unprecedented plague of mediocrity—in all branches of imaginative art. Dry bones everywhere —everything scientific, psychological, faultless, barren—and they are delighted with it all, and firmly believe themselves to be leading an active spiritual existence. Wagner is the only man that is really alive among them."[21] He communicated to the Germans that their own philosophical traditions offered a possibility for such a fundamental reorientation, because they do not proceed "from doing, but from being . . . and from the life of the soul" (TWR, 46). There is yet hope: "German philosophy holds on to the center, to the thinking soul, and does not lose itself in mere observation" (TWR, 47).[21]

Rolleston calls Whitman "the greatest poetic representative of what is usually referred to as the focal point of German philosophy" (TWR, 46), enabling him to "reconcile" a negative "analytic" positivism with "the all-believing spirit of democracy. He incorporates the enormous and confused intellectual efforts of the century and allows them to find their true direction. Through a mysterious and magic strength, he renders that which is scattered and without force powerfully effective" (TWR, 45).[22]

Unlike Knortz, Rolleston did not view *Leaves of Grass* as a direct sociopolitical force. The acquaintance with Whitman's poetry (an "altogether serious business," TWR, 38) would nevertheless have personal consequences for the life of the reader: " . . . the questions about our lives which will arise may be dangerous, whether they are answered or not . . ." (TWR, 38f.).

In his lecture, Rolleston quotes passages designed to convince the reader of Whitman's supposed antiscientific attitude:

> Not you alone proud truths of the world,
> Nor you alone ye facts of modern science,
> But myths and fables of eld, Asia's, Africa's fables . . .
> (*LG*, 412)

In contrast to Knortz, who wanted to do away with old (European) myths and who regarded Whitman as the poet of science, Rolleston wanted to overcome modern positivism with the aid of Whitman's poetry. It is only logical that Rolleston would not quote such Whitman lines as "Hurrah for positive science! long live exact demonstration" (*LG*, 51), for they were hardly compatible with the main thrust of his argument.

It almost seems, in fact, that Rolleston offers Whitman as a way out of the deterministic world of the nineteenth century. He suggests to his readers that they are free to extricate themselves from the deterministic "necessity" ruling their lives. They should turn to Whitman "if knowledge, an understanding of the inner life of things, is *truly more important* to us than the empty acquaintance with names and appearances usually interpreted as true knowledge" (TWR, 54; emphasis added).[23]

But is this really a paradoxical and anachronistic relapse into prepositivistic times? A closer look at Rolleston's line of argument suggests that it is not. Rolleston's demand to see the "reality" of all objects, to return to German idealism and thereby secure "the independence [i.e., priority] of ethical categories" (TWR, 51) cannot be taken literally.[24] Rolleston knew that there could be no return to "formal" Christian religion (TWR, 52), and he quoted Whitman's famous repudiation of religions in *Song of Myself* in order to prove his point:

> Magnifying and applying come I,
> Outbidding at the start the old cautious hucksters,
> Taking myself the exact dimensions of Jehovah,
> Lithographing Kronos, Zeus his son, and Hercules his grandson,
> Buying drafts of Osiris, Isis, Belus, Brahma, Buddha,
> In my portfolio placing Manito loose, Allah on a leaf, the crucifix
> engraved,
> With Odin and the hideous-faced Mexitli and every idol and image,
> Taking them all for what they are worth and not a cent more . . .
> (*LG*, 75)

This passage, which presents religions all over the world as human artifacts, precludes the possibility of reinstating metaphysics through religious belief.

A close reading of Rolleston's lecture reveals that his appeal to the "focal point" of German idealistic philosophy is merely rhetorical and that his version of "metaphysics" points much more to the twentieth century than to Kant or Hegel. Rolleston claims it is necessary that "in some way a new relationship is created between us and the object of our belief so that it is no longer just a name for us, a logical conclusion, a tradition, but a thing, a reality, something that touches the depth of consciousness" (TWR, 52f.).[25]

In this context, Rolleston speaks of a "living spiritual perception," but he no longer refers to the subjective projection of things which assigns to them transcendent station and significance. Quite to the contrary, to "perceive things in our daily life in their reality *is* religion and *produces* ethics" (TWR, 53, emphasis added).[26] Rolleston demands to counteract the "limitations" of the natural sciences by a new irrationalism ("depth of consciousness") stressing the oneness of the perceiver and the perceived objects. Thereby, the latter become "projections, ways of expressing human feeling" (TWR, 51). The "mysterious" quality in Whitman's poetry will be the agent of this process.

Terms such as "morality" and "ethics," which abound in Rolleston's treatise, are misleading. They are formal, purely rhetorical leftovers from the German idealistic tradition which continued to exist in literary and critical discourses but had become empty. This rhetoric also frequently appears in expressionist programs such as the one proposed by Richard Blunck in 1921: "The religion of expressionist man, the relationship he knows to exist between himself and the cosmos, is ethical, is movement, is eternal demand, is dynamic: nothing solid, nothing fixed. The ethos, the law, is nothing external, nothing tied to a being outside the human being: we know that it exists only inside and by virtue of the human being."[27]

An ethic that is not anchored externally can hardly provide the standards which may serve as guidelines for human individuals. Although Rolleston had not yet progressed quite this far by 1883, the direction of his argument is along these same lines. Far from leading us back to a metaphysical world view, Rolleston's interpretation of Whitman anticipates the point at which the world becomes one with its perception, amounting to a "deification" of the "spirit" (i.e., the "I" incorporating the outside world). We will see how German expressionist poets experimented with this idea and implemented it in their poetry.

THE TRANSLATION

The differences in Knortz's and Rolleston's conception of Whitman's poetry and in their political aims resulted in an interesting controversy between the two translators. Rolleston, who had translated the major part of the volume, passed it on to Whitman. Knortz, who received the translation through R. M. Bucke,[28] criticized Rolleston's translation as being "written by a man who thought in English and afterwards tried to write in German."[29] He advocated a thorough revision of the manuscript prior to publication in Germany. In a letter to Bucke, Rolleston retorted:

> But I greatly fear that his [Knortz's] revision would extend beyond the meaning of that term and that he would alter the whole plan of my translation. The latter has been revised by a very competent person, a master for German literature in a school in Dresden. We spent several months over it, weighing every word and line. & much of it was passed afterwards through the hands of another German friend, thoroughly capable of judging such a matter. Both of them said that if W. was to be made acceptable to the German public he must be presented in a different form; but my aim was not to make him acceptable, but simply to make the German translation for a German reader as far as possible what the English original is for an English reader. . . . A German translation of W. which should never startle the "ordinary reader" or seem ridiculous or coarse to him, would not be Whitman at all.[30]

This difference of opinion is very significant. The argument is not, as Knortz wants to make Whitman believe, over Rolleston's lacking knowledge of German. According to the Irishman, Whitman's poetry is calculated to shake up bourgeois aesthetics; his poetry has a special aesthetic effect, as Rolleston explained in his introduction to the finished volume: "Our language and our poetic forms to him have become rigid and lifeless. The latter Whitman rejects totally, and language in his hands assumes a strange new life."[31]

Knortz, solely interested in the political "message," criticizes Whitman for "despising all rules of English grammar" and for "neglecting aesthetic rules" (KR, v)—which, though Knortz leaves the inevitable conclusion unstated, would only obscure Whitman's meaning as the German-American understood it.[32]

Previous commentaries have given mixed evaluations to the translation by Knortz and Rolleston. Harry Law-Robertson calls it precise but rough.[33] In his study of Whitman translations, Edward Allan McCormick leaves out Knortz and Rolleston without giving any substantive explanation. Monika Schaper, however, reaches the conclusion that Knortz and Rolleston managed to translate in a "non-bourgeois way" (i.e., against the poetic conventions of the period). In this way, they strove for "absolute faithfulness" to the author's intention.[34]

By and large, Schaper's estimate is correct. Both translators agreed to transgress the lyrical conventions of their time by preserving the "prose quality" of Whitman's original. However, in the interest of an improved "readability," Knortz was willing to make far more compromises than Rolleston. Only because of Rolleston's continued resistance to changes (the major part of the translation did come from Rolleston, as Knortz himself admitted in the introduction, KR, vi), the translation remained unorthodox and could therefore have its singular effect on German literature.

Rolleston's independence of mind and steadfastness must be admired, especially in view of how difficult it had been to find a German publisher for *Leaves of Grass.* As early as 1884, Rolleston, prior to his contact with Knortz, offered the rough draft of his translation to several German publishers and then reported to Whitman: "I offered it to four publishers before I left Germany, agreeing to pay all expenses myself, and all refused to take it up. . . . I am told there would probably be difficulties with the police, who in Germany exercise a most despotic power."[35] Rolleston's translation included a representative cross-section of Whitman's works suitably characterized by the overall theme of "the poet of democracy." From the controversial "Children of Adam" and "Calamus" cycles, only one poem, "I Sing the Body Electric," was included, but it probably sufficed to justify the fear of "police" intervention.

The Swiss publisher who in 1889 finally did bring out the first book-length edition of Whitman's poetry was the revolutionary democrat Jakob Schabelitz, with whom Knortz was in close contact. This was the very person who, as a young man, had befriended Freiligrath in his London exile. Schabelitz was one of the few radical German-language publishers of his time. Located in Zurich, his *Verlags-Magazin* published many avant-garde authors: Carl Hauptmann, visionary brother of the famous German naturalist Gerhart Hauptmann; Hermann Bahr, innovator, *enfant terrible,* and leader of the Young Vienna group of writers; Karl Henckell, socialist poet and editor; Arno Holz, one of the leading proponents of a German naturalism, also on the political left; and John Henry Mackay, Scottish-born German poet, anarchist, anonymous gay rights author, and the only German member of Horace Traubel's Walt Whitman Fellowship International. The *Verlags-Magazin* was therefore an almost natural literary home for the German *Leaves,* and through this publisher Whitman automatically became associated with the radical, innovative current within German literature.

Grashalme, as Knortz's and Rolleston's edition of *Leaves* was called in German, came as close to an authorized translation as there could be. Both Knortz and Rolleston were personally in touch with Whitman. Knortz probably came into contact with Whitman in 1882 and may well have met with him in person, since he announced such a visit in one of his letters.[36] In a letter to W. S. Kennedy, William O'Connor also wrote of personal contacts with Knortz.[37] Rolleston had known Walt Whitman's work since approximately 1877 and had corresponded frequently with Whitman and his followers.

Whitman's personal contact with the two translators enabled him to influence their translations and other efforts on his behalf, although some of his wishes, such as a bilingual edition, did not materialize. Horst Frenz, editor of the correspondence between Knortz and Rolleston and Whitman, remarks on the latter's interest in the German translation of his works: "Whitman was in the midst of all this; he was deeply interested in the whole project; besides, he had confidence in the two men. According to Horace Traubel, he called Rolleston a 'knight-errant: the real Irish stuff: like William: radiant, forcible and illuminative' and continued: 'I feel that he has always been more than my friend—has sworn his big oath in my interest and battled for me without reservation. . . . I feel as if I was in good hands: as if Rolleston, Knortz, were an efficient team.' "[38]

Whitman looked for absolute devotion in his "knight-errant" translators. Allegiance and loyalty were key values, not only in the domestic Whitman community but also in its international counterpart.

To publicly confirm his interest in the German translation, Whitman had sent Rolleston a dedication to his German readers as early as 1884. It became a part of Rolleston's introduction:

> I approve of your attempt to render some of my poems in the German language. Indeed, as conceited as this statement may seem, I did not only have my own country in mind when composing my work. I wanted to take the first step toward bringing to life a cycle of international poems. The main goal of the United States is the mutual benevolence of all humanity, the solidarity of the world. What is lacking in this respect perhaps may be supplied by the art of poetry, by songs radiating from all countries in the world. To send to all these countries the best wishes in America's name was the purpose of my poems. And I will be glad, very glad, to be accepted by the Germanic peoples. (KR, xii)[39]

Whitman's and his translators' hopes were fulfilled. The first translation secured for Whitman a permanent place in the German-speaking countries. His dedication confirms the author's international orientation. It was also due to this internationalist perspective that Whitman's German reputation survived difficult periods of political tension and war between Germany and the United States.

The immediate reaction of the German public to the new translation seems to have been very positive.[40] Knortz remembered in 1911 that he was at first rather skeptical, but that his expectations were agreeably disappointed: "I was certain that the work would be unmercifully torn to pieces by the newspapers, but to my greatest surprise, I found that the opposite was true. Most of the critics thought it a significant achievement. . . . "[41]

Among these voices were Ernst Ziel and Julius Hillebrand, two important critics of the period, and they reacted in characteristic ways. In the German imagination, America consisted of Cooper's and Charles Sealsfield's prairies and forests, of natural wonders. The Atlantic Ocean one needed to cross in order to get to this magic world was a part of America as well. The first critical discourses dealing with Whitman, therefore, use the language of the American landscape to describe his poetry—often an imagery they derive directly from Whitman: "His rhythms have something wild, untamed, something reminiscent of the roaring of the sea. From America, from giant, free America, all his thoughts emerge; to America, they all return."[42] Similarly, Hillebrand speaks of the purifying force of this "nature" poetry: "But whoever wants to cleanse himself in the Niagara waters of this grandiose poetry . . . whoever prefers to wander through the primeval forest rather than through English and French gardens, whoever, in one word, can still appreciate *original poetry*, should read and study Walt Whitman."[43] Whitman's abandonment of all "rules of metrics and prosody,"[44] his "wild" rhythms, are seen as a reflection of American nature. Whitman himself is constructed along the lines of the German image of America, a "backwoodsman with sinewy arms and a proud chest,"[45] and contrasted with European, especially German-speaking, authors. German writers, according to this account, produce "a literature [which is] pedantic, polished, morbidly lascivious, phony, neurotic-hysterical."[46] This is because European writers "sit too much . . . which results in physical and mental deformation of the spine. . . ."[47]

These reviews show the yearning to escape the stuffy and boring German society of the Wilhelminian era. In a second article in *Die Gegenwart,* Ziel explains this more fully:

> Will these succulent fruits from the free American plains find sympathetic hearts in Bismarck's sabre-rattling country? Who knows? . . . There is an ocean between Walt Whitman and the aging European culture—an ocean also between Walt Whitman's stunning originality and the pale conventionality to

> which we have paid homage in the pulpit and at lectures, in office-suit and in morning-gown since the times of our forefathers: Walt Whitman knows nothing of academic schooling, knows nothing of gentlemanly education, knows nothing of the impudent lies making up our social life and the mindless abandonment of everything that is individual in favor of modern stereotyping and uniformity.[48]

Such mythical characteristics based on relatively sparse biographical information (their accuracy is largely irrelevant) rapidly spread through every review and article on Whitman. This "Whitman propaganda," as Johannes Schlaf would term it later, was obviously very effective as a basis for the further German construction of Walt Whitman. Knortz and Rolleston thus provided the intellectual and material foundation for the development of a German Whitman cult. Their translation allowed Whitman to be received by individuals who had no knowledge of English and no contacts with America, and it served as the textual basis for Whitman's naturalization in the German-speaking world.

CHAPTER THREE

JOHANNES SCHLAF

Johannes Schlaf (1862–1941) is a key figure in the German reception of Whitman. At the same time, he is one of the great, albeit unjustifiably neglected, authors in German literature.

Schlaf was born in the quaint little city of Querfurt near Halle and first made a name for himself as the initiator of a German school of naturalism together with Arno Holz and Gerhart Hauptmann. He worked in the areas of drama, prose, and poetry, translated from several languages, and engaged in extensive metaphysical speculations. An individual with an extraordinarily intense sensibility, he was plagued by constant nervous disorders which occasionally confined him to mental institutions. Much of his later life was spent developing a new version of the geocentric view of the world (denying the central position of the sun on pseudo-scientific grounds) and, concurrently, introducing a "new religion" through amateurish investigations in astronomy, coupled with speculative interpretations of Christian and Judaic theology.

Schlaf's most active discipleship of Whitman lasted from 1892 until approximately 1912. While he has been recognized as an enthusiastic supporter of Whitman, the true extent of his commitment has rarely been understood. Although Schlaf's translation was not published until 1907, its origins go back to the year 1892. Between 1892 and 1919, he wrote a large number of articles and three monographs on his "guter grauer Dichter" (Good Gray Poet). In 1907, he published a German translation of Henry Bryan Binns's Whitman biography and, in the same year, his translation of *Leaves* in the popular Reclam series, which is still in print today. In his own creative works (discussed in chapter 11), Whitman looms large.

Schlaf was Whitman's "hot little prophet" in Germany, the German equivalent of Horace Traubel. He was largely responsible for initiating the German Whitman cult which lasted into the late twenties. The correspondence among the Schlaf papers in Querfurt shows that he played a leading role in the international "Whitman-movement."[1] The closeness between Schlaf and Whitmanites in a number of countries is surprising and confirms both the continuing efforts by U.S. Whitmanites to monitor Whitman's reception abroad and Schlaf's central role in this movement in Europe. Rather than being a marginal figure, as Schlaf has been disparagingly called, he was an internationally recognized member of the community.

The Schlaf papers contain letters from Horace Traubel in which the latter announces his strong support for Schlaf: "You may depend upon me. I will help you all I can. I am sending you a litte book today. You will hear from me again and again. I write now to say only this general thing. For I want you to feel assured . . . that I love and know you for the things you have already said about W. W. and for the things in his behalf that you propose to do."[2] Schlaf's library, which is stored at Querfurt castle, contains Traubel's poetry volume *Optimos*, dedicated to "Johannes Schlaf in Germany from Horace Traubel in America with greetings and admiration and love," as well as books by other members and friends of the Whitman Fellowship such as Edward Carpenter, Karl Knortz, Mildred Bain (author of a book on Traubel), and Ernest Crosby.[3]

Ernest Crosby (1856–1907), who knew German, was obviously charged by Traubel with monitoring Schlaf's Whitman activities.[4] In several letters to Schlaf, Crosby expressed great satisfaction with his findings. The following letter concerns Schlaf's monograph of 1904: "My dear Herr Schlaf: I received your book the day before yesterday and have read it through with the greatest interest. It seems to me the best thing yet written on Whitman. I will suggest to Traubel that he have it translated and published in the Conservator. Mrs. von Ende would doubtless be glad to do the translating."[5] Still, Crosby did not hesitate to "correct" Schlaf's picture of Whitman where he (and Traubel) saw a necessity to do so.

Even twelve years after Whitman's death, the American Whitman community was still attempting to control Whitman's German reception through intensive correspondence, book gifts, and mailings of propagandistic articles. Schlaf's own poems were translated and published in Traubel's *Conservator*, which also officially acknowledged Schlaf's governorship over the Whitman movement in Germany.[6]

The close contacts among European Whitman enthusiasts form another reception context that needs to be considered here. H. B. Binns wrote to his German translator: "I am proud to think that we shall thus become collaborators in the great cause of Liberty and Fellowship."[7] For a time, it seemed as though the

Whitman Fellowship was going to be institutionalized in Europe as well. Schlaf's counterpart in France, Léon Bazalgette, whose letters and cards are part of the Schlaf papers, wrote to Schlaf about his interest in founding a European Whitman Fellowship: "I wonder whether we could not, one day, attempt to found a Whitman society in Europe—like the *Fellowship* of which H. Traubel is secretary—with Binns, yourself, and Dr. K. Federn. Thereby we could bring together all European admirers of the poet and propagate his works. Maybe this idea can be realized one day. We will talk about it."[8] Schlaf's answer must have been encouraging because only nine days later he wrote to Schlaf once more: "I am very glad that you approve of my idea about Whitman in Europe and your moral support alone will be of great help. I will wait until my book on Whitman and my translation have been published, then I will write to Dr. Federn and Mr. H. B. Binns and start doing actual work on the project if it is possible."[9]

Bazalgette, a man with leftist and anarchist leanings, was of course interested in more than just poetic goals. His whole correspondence suggests a political-ideological orientation to which most European Whitmanites adhered. Schlaf's perennial attempts to construct Whitman as a new man, a new human being,[10] also emerge from letters written by French correspondents of Whitman, including Bazalgette (the "Poet-prophet whom humankind, in a few centuries, will count among its gods").[11] The density of contacts between Schlaf and European Whitmanites (including Stefan Zweig and Emile Verhaeren) necessitates that we understand Whitman's German reception in an intercultural context.

In order to appreciate Schlaf's translation of *Leaves*, it is necessary to examine his reading of Whitman. Germany had become quite a different place between Freiligrath's translation in 1868 and the early 1890s, when Schlaf encountered Whitman through the Knortz and Rolleston translation. The German victory in the Franco-Prussian War and the forced unification of the country under Prussian domination had permitted a tremendous accumulation of capital. As a result, sections of Germany, formerly a predominantly rural country, became industrialized with dangerous speed. German capitalists, with the active help of the government and the Kaiser himself, wanted to make up for lost time and join the ranks of the most industrially advanced nations and also, very late, the club of colonial powers. This resulted in an almost uncontrollable process of urbanization. Around 1800, Berlin, essentially a provincial city, had no more than 170,000 inhabitants. By the early 1880s, the population exceeded 1 million; by 1900, the city had 2.7 million inhabitants; by 1910, as many as 3.7 million.

In all countries, this process caused a disruption in the lives of a population that previously was used to rural living; in Germany, however, the shock was tremendous. The intensity of this experience was not only the result of the unnatural speed of this urban development, but also the consequence of a peculiarly German situation, where industrialization took place under the conditions of what was essentially still a feudal social order. Germany and Austria (by now Austria-Hungary, although the Hungarian part did not participate in the process of industrialization) still had experienced very little democratic reform, in spite of the fact that socialist and union movements emerged and rapidly increased in size and importance.

It is to this extreme situation that naturalists like Gerhart Hauptmann, Arno Holz, and Johannes Schlaf reacted. At the beginning of his first, long article on Whitman, an obituary published in 1892, Schlaf inserted the following remarkable passage:

> My work for today is done. It is growing dusky. Tired and deadened from all my writing I lean out of the window and see how the sunlight gradually disappears on the high façades across the street.
>
> And then, after all the reading and all the work, I feel how constricted our lives are, I understand and sense our misery.
>
> The street with the jumble and the noise of traffic stretches far below, loses itself in both directions in smoke and in the confusing bustle of the side-streets. Above, a narrow, scanty piece of heaven, darkened and polluted by rising sultry air, dust, and food vapors. Behind the windows on the other side, all the way down the long street, next to me, above and below me, from all sides, a pressing, shoving, and inhibiting crowdedness and confusion between the gray masses of stone. And, as here, it extends concentrically for hours, far into the countryside.[12]

The third, rather "naturalistic" paragraph depicts a small part of Berlin. It is obvious that this passage was produced by a mind strongly antagonistic to urban life. Schlaf, born in a small, almost rural town, attempts to describe with great precision the part of urban Berlin which he can observe through his window. However, he does not confine himself to a documentation of details, but includes a personal evaluation with words such as "polluted," "crowdedness," and "confusion."

The exhausted speaker of the first paragraph obviously feels very uncomfortable. While he acknowledges his environment, he is highly dissatisfied with it; the naturalistic "knowledge" about the individual's dependence on his surroundings is clearly of little consolation. The feeling of dissatisfaction extends to the realm of human existence: "The countless threads through which our life, our feeling, and our perception are connected to infinite mysteries seem to be cut. We are alone, alone with ourselves, with what our discriminating judgment would call the 'human' realm, alone with ourselves, man with man, in this vibrating restless crowdedness and its nerve-shattering, confusing pell-mell" (*FB*, 979).[13]

Schlaf's long-term nervous disorder had already started when he wrote these lines, and it is hardly surprising that a mind as sensitive as his reacted negatively to the increasingly complex world around him. The new mode of perception he was about to develop with Whitman's assistance was an attempt to find a way out of his dilemma.

At first glance, the solution seems to be the one suggested by Rolleston some years earlier: "And all the refinements of our aged culture cannot hide the great fundamental disease which we have been trying in vain to cure with all kinds of medicines for some time: it is our lack of religion or, if we want, our lack of energy, the atrophy of our perception" (*FB*, 979).[14] "Atrophy of perception" is a criticism one might expect from a naturalist. The quotation as a whole, however, shows that Schlaf is at a point of conversion. The primary object of perception is not external reality but reality as perceived—impressionistic reality: "But how can we help each other, if we have only an understanding of how we are connected with all things near and far but not a *living* perception of them?" (*FB*, 979)[15] "Understanding" refers to the world of causality that governed the perception and the works of realists and naturalists; "living perception" points to the impressionist-to-be. Later, Schlaf was able to explain this much more eloquently. Whitman's poetry, he said, is characterized by "a variety and a sensibility of impression and perception, a subtlety and an intimate ability to differentiate and to ascertain not only external appearances but also spiritual-intellectual reactions and interrelations. This is highly surprising, admirable, and incomparable and suggests a sixth sense for the fundamental realities and the identity of all being."[16] These lines, while expressing Schlaf's enthusiasm for Whitman, stress the integrating, holistic force of "impression" as opposed to the analytic-destructive force of "understanding."

As an explanation for what he meant by "living perception" in Whitman's poetry, Schlaf quotes from "Starting from Paumanok":

Starting from fish-shape Paumanok where I was born,
Well-begotten, and rais'd by a perfect mother,
After roaming many lands, lover of populous pavements

. . . .

Or withdrawn to muse and meditate in some deep recess,
Far from the clank of crowds intervals passing rapt and happy,
Aware of the fresh free giver the flowing Missouri, aware of the mighty
  Niagara,

Aware of the buffalo herds grazing the plains, the hirsute and strong-breasted bull,
Of earth, rocks, Fifth-month flowers experienced, stars, rain, snow, my amaze,
Having studied the mocking-bird's tones and the flight of the mountain-hawk,
And heard at dawn the unrivall'd one, the hermit thrush from the swamp-cedars,
Solitary, singing in the West, I strike up for a New World.

(*FB*, 979f.)[17]

Schlaf's reaction to these lines expresses a feeling of liberation and intense emotion: "How we take heart!—It is as if everything existing miles away in a fabulous distance, everything we feel to be in *contrast* to our life here, which we know, yet do not understand, all of a sudden becomes alive in its fresh beauty" (*FB*, 980).[18]

The Whitman lines quoted are in sharp contrast to Schlaf's urban picture of Berlin. The freshness and openness of the American landscape are pitted against the "nerve-shattering" German metropolis. The optimistic lyrical *persona*, "solitary, singing in the West . . . strik[ing] up for a New World," is in sharp contrast to the persona of Schlaf's essay thinking himself oppressed and constricted in the crowded industrial center of Germany.

A second oppositional pair, less conspicuous at first, is even more important: while Schlaf's speaker *knows* Walt Whitman's world, he fails to *understand* it. As we saw above, "understanding" in the context of this essay is the opposite of "living perception" or "impression." To Schlaf, Whitman's poetry inspires a "jubilant helplessness while a new, infinite wealth of penetrating perceptions" enter the individual (*FB*, 980). With Whitman, Schlaf cries out: "How curious! how real!" (*FB*, 980).[19]

What has changed? Why was the speaker's consciousness previously unable to process his impressions in such a positive way? Earlier, the self was *determined* by an environment perceived through the agency of *understanding*. In the new "reality," however, the self is "free." That it is "free" largely because it has disappeared does not matter. That the strange fascination with Whitman's "solitary" individual is at best a reminiscence, a fantasy of autonomous individuality, is also of little importance. The "I" has surrendered itself to "jubilant helplessness," to an "infinite wealth of penetrating perceptions" paralleling a "blessed, vigorous turmoil of living growth inside" (*FB*, 980).[20]

Far from any conceptualization and intellectual reasoning, the individual's mind has once more found harmony, this time on the level of an impressionistic consciousness: "[Reading Whitman] we have overcome the isolation and separation which has confused us and made us afraid. Misery and happiness, poverty and wealth, all the incomprehensible oppositions which tortured us in our constriction: they can no longer harm us or obscure the connectedness of all things. . . . Although: everything is there: but everything in its place, ordered and redeemed from all conflict through the powerful rhythm of the eternal cycle of all occurrences and appearances" (*FB*, 981).[21] This new "order" which transcends all conflicts is purely "physical"—in the sense that it is based on the human nervous system. Isolation and separation have been overcome by simply disregarding the social, even conceptual, categories from which they sprang. The order of external reality is replaced by the "rhythmical" order of Whitman's poetry.

Schlaf initiated Whitman's construction as healer addressing the ills of modern existence, a "wound-dresser" taking care of the disruptions caused by modern civilization. Schlaf has confirmed this in terms of his own biography. He felt like a "prisoner" of his mechanistic world view and suffered greatly until he encountered Whitman: "But then, at a point in time when my innermost loneliness threatened to become most unbearable, I became acquainted with the poet of *Leaves of Grass*."[22] Schlaf repeatedly emphasized this therapeutic effect of Whitman's poetry. In his article for a socialist monthly, Schlaf, formerly on the left himself, praised his hero: "It is wonderful to feel the sympathetic forces passing from his songs into one's person. They have a spiritual healing power which, a few books of the Bible and Goethe's *Poetry and Truth* excepted, I myself get only from Walt Whitman's poetry. . . ."[23]

The same article also featured the well-known motif of Whitman as Christ reborn and stressed the "*gentle hand* [*linde Hand*] of the man."[24] In 1899, Schlaf followed Bucke, Traubel, and others by referring to Whitman as prophet of a new religion: "I am not exaggerating when I call him venerable like one of the early prophets of religion and when I say: here he is, tall, full of blessings and life like the first poet-prophet of a third gospel. . . ."[25] This boundless enthusiasm should not mislead us about the true significance Whitman had for the German naturalist. Schlaf is calling for a "religious" version of naturalism which would relate to the "new, modern mode of human existence."[26] Like Rolleston, he does not advocate the return to traditional forms of religion. Rather, it is a religious *rhetoric* which has become a permanent part of Whitman's reception in the German-speaking countries and which may serve different functions. Rolleston called for a return to a "living spiritual perception," and later we will see how Franz Werfel adapts Whitman's love rhetoric in his pseudometaphysical poetry. Whitman's poetry obviously functions in lieu of religion; for many readers, his poetry replaces religion in an increasingly secularized age. To Schlaf, the religious feeling associated with Whitman meant the liberating effect on the human mind caused by the final dissolution of an oppressive external reality. Whitman led Schlaf to an epistemology resting exclusively on the human nervous system—replacing external "reality" by a series of dreamlike "impressions."

Through his many articles, Schlaf's cultish images and rhetoric started to dominate the German Whitman discourse. Schlaf constructed Whitman using many of the same features O'Connor had emphasized, but he added some messianic elements of his own which became vital for the expressionist generation of poets. Naturally, this also fundamentally influenced the nature of his translation.

THE TRANSLATION

Schlaf's translation has been criticized in various ways. His enemies charged him with plagiarism, and his former colleague and co-worker Arno Holz even accused him of ignorance and of completely lacking knowledge of English. Yet Schlaf never maintained that his was an entirely original achievement. He never denied that his translation was based on Knortz and Rolleston, and his friendly relationship with Knortz shows that his use of the earlier translation was accepted.[27]

Schlaf's translation has repeatedly been criticized on philological grounds for dilettantism. Several critics including Harry Law-Robertson and Edward Allan McCormick have demonstrated such "mistakes."[28] As an overall estimate of Schlaf's achievements, these criticisms are wrong—especially in view of the fact that Schlaf translated large parts of *Leaves of Grass* which Knortz and Rolleston had not included in their edition. The Schlaf edition contained—for the first time—a representative cross-section of Whitman's poetry.

Regarding the charge of translation "errors," there is another, more general misunderstanding. Schlaf did not see himself as a philologist but as an enthusiastic mediator. Monika Schaper's contention that "for Schlaf, the translation of *Leaves of Grass* was a medium to express his own personality [*Selbstdarstellung*]" is only *one* aspect of his translation.[29] It does not explain the tremendous response to Schlaf's translation on the part of German readers. For Schlaf, the essence of Whitman's poetry was to be found in the power of its impressionistic visions. These visions he expressed in a rhetoric and with a *Pathos* that superseded even Whitman himself. Schlaf added his own unmistakable touch to the book. While Rolleston translated Whitman as literally and as closely to the original as possible, Schlaf added the messianic fervor characteristic of the expressionists.

Schlaf's additional dose of *Pathos* can be demonstrated in many of the sections in which he differs from his predecessors. In the famous section 24 of "Song of Myself" Whitman wrote:

If I worship one thing more than another it shall be the spread of my own
body, or any part of it,
Translucent mould of me it shall be you!
(*LG*, 53)

In Schlaf's translation, these lines read:

Wenn ich ein Ding mehr verehre als ein andres, so soll es mein Körper sein
von oben bis unten, oder irgendein Teil von ihm.
Lichte Gestalt, du sollst es sein!
(*LG*, 59; emphasis added)

Knortz and Rolleston simply ignore "*the spread of* my own body" (see KR, 47) while Schlaf attempts to transfer the physical quality of this line into the German by translating it into "von oben bis unten" (from head to toe). Schlaf's masterpiece in this section, however, is his translation of "translucent mould." Indeed, Knortz and Rolleston's "durchsichtig" (transparent, KR, 47) is closer to the English original. However, Schlaf's "lichte Gestalt" (light, luminous figure) gives direct and immediate expression to his messianic understanding of Whitman, which was understood and shared by so many readers of his translation.

In order to achieve a special effect, Schlaf abandons faithfulness to the original. The last line of "For You O Democracy": "For you, for you I am trilling these songs" was translated by Knortz and Rolleston: "Für dich, für dich trillere ich diese Lieder" (KR, 93). While "trillern" does maintain the acoustic character of the text, the German reader is reminded of a warbling bird. Schlaf's "jauchzen" (*LG*, 129), by contrast, has a religious connotation (jubilate, rejoice) and expresses the boundless enthusiasm of Schlaf, the naturalist reborn.

"The Mystic Trumpeter" is another poem included in both Knortz and Rolleston's and Schlaf's collections. Its final section 8 similarly shows Schlaf's different emphasis, although much of the wording is the same. At the "close" (*LG*, 471), the poem's speaker asks the trumpeter: "Give me for once its [the future's] prophecy and joy." Knortz and Rolleston, possibly confused about which prophecy Whitman was referring to, simply translated: "Zeig' mir die Zukunft und Freude" (Show me the future and joy, KR, 159). Schlaf, to the contrary, with characteristic intensity, translated this: "Gib mir mit Vorahnung zugleich Wonne der Erfüllung" (With premonition, give me also blissful fulfillment, *LG*, 214). In the next line, Whitman's speaker cries out: "O glad, exulting, culminating song!" Knortz and Rolleston, a bit low-key, render this: "O frohes, erhebendes Lied des Schlusses" (O glad, uplifting song of the conclusion! KR, 159). Schlaf in turn: "Oh frohes, jauchzendes Lied der letzten Höhe!" (O joyful, jubilating song of the ultimate altitude! *LG*, 214)

One of Whitman's most *Pathos*-laden poems is "A Song of Joys"—a poem not included by Knortz and Rolleston. In the important middle part of the poem, Whitman describes the soul "receiving identity / through materials and loving them, observing characters / and absorbing them . . . ." (*LG*, 181). In Schlaf's translation, "identity" changes into "das wahre Sein" (true existence, *LG*, 159), and "materials" into "Materie" (matter): Schlaf turns Whitman's speculations into a new theology.

The critical as well as the popular reaction shows that the audience fully appreciated Schlaf's efforts. Johannes Urzidil, a junior member of the expressionist movement, reminisced about the effect of Whitman and Schlaf's Whitman translation on his generation. In his afterword to the 1968 Reclam edition of Schlaf's translation, he states: "He [Schlaf] believed that he recognized most of all a decided monistic feeling in *Leaves of Grass.* The basic triads of comradeship, love, and democracy, Whitman's yearning for the equality of the sexes, and a kind of sensibility which remotely resembled Friedrich Nietzsche were the dynamic forces in Schlaf's translations. He speaks of Whitman's 'New *Pathos*,' and in this phrase we already hear the signal of literary expressionism on the rise."[30]

Schlaf's translation is indeed an early document of German expressionism. Franz Werfel and Johannes R. Becher became acquainted with Whitman through this translation. Even Franz Kafka, despite his doubts about the accuracy of the translation, may have used this edition and, according to Gustav Janouch, he believed Whitman had "brought together contemplation of nature and civilization . . . in one single intoxicating impression of life."[31] This judgment corresponded very closely to the intentions of Schlaf's translation.

By this time, it had become quite obvious that the German medium lent itself readily to Whitman's poetry. The Germanic stock of both languages rendered them quite similar, and the fact that some of Whitman's long lines became even longer in German really did not matter. Ernest Crosby generously praised Schlaf's translation: "It is wonderful how well Whitman translates into German. It hardly loses anything in the process. I am not sure that sometimes it does not gain."[32]

Schlaf's translation appeared as a part of the Reclam series—a precursor of mass-market editions. Just a bit larger than an audiotape cassette, it fit into everybody's pocket, could be carried everywhere, and could be used on a variety of possible and impossible occasions. It was cheap, sold not only by bookstores but also by stationery stores and therefore truly available to the mass readership. The publication of *Leaves* in this well-established series that included the whole of

German and much of world literature clearly was a major breakthrough for Whitman's works in the German-speaking countries. At the same time, the edition did not have anything of the "definitive" classicism of the later edition with its gold-lettered spine.

One of the most characteristic and most fascinating documents relating to Schlaf's translation exemplifies the unorthodox ways the little booklet was used. A communication from an Austrian prisoner of war in a Russian camp during World War I was found among Schlaf's papers in Querfurt:

> From: POW Austrian Officer
> Rudolf Wacker[33]
> *Tomsk* (Siberia)
> Prison camp
>
> Tomsk, POW camp
> 11 February 1918
>
> Dear Mr. Schlaf!
>
> I have to communicate to you that there is somebody who feels eternally grateful!—Last summer, your translation of "Leaves of Grass" fell into my hands. What Walt Whitman has since come to mean for me, what good fortune it is for me that he entered my life at just that point, is impossible to say in a few words. He immediately became so close and so dear to me, it was as if I had just waited for this man. To me, too, he is the most extensive "confirmation," and will remain my leader for my whole life (in this way, I am just following life itself!)—I have also pointed him out to my friends in Germany and am reading him to my soldier comrades.—I feel an urge to tell you that his community grows and that we are thankful to you, who has opened the doors to the new kingdom for us! . . .[34]

CHAPTER FOUR

KARL FEDERN AND WILHELM SCHÖLERMANN

By the turn of the century, Whitman's name had become well known to the German literary and artistic establishment. A large number of articles in literary, philosophical, artistic, and other journals introduced Whitman and his "message" to the public. These contributions included excerpts from poems and repeated in stereotypical ways biographical elements of William O'Connor's "Good Gray Poet" as they had entered Germany through Freiligrath, Knortz, Schlaf, and others. Many articles openly canvassed for Whitman's "cause" and attempted to recruit new members for the German Whitman community.

The nature of the interaction between American and European Whitmanites changed, but the transatlantic influence remained significant. The person through whom the Whitman Fellowship influenced the German literary world in a most direct way was Amalie von Ende (1856–1932), one of the most remarkable personalities ever to work as a mediator between Central Europe and the United States. Although she was not herself a translator of Whitman, she involved herself in the translation efforts of the first decade of the twentieth century and contributed significantly to the construction of Walt Whitman's image in Germany.

Von Ende was a French-German-Polish immigrant to the United States, born in Warsaw. Together with her husband, Henrich von Ende, a radical journalist, she first engaged herself in journalism and education. She wrote on German literature in American magazines and on American literature in German journals. She also worked as a translator and is credited with the first German translations of poems by Emily Dickinson. Moreover, she was a pianist, a music teacher, a composer, and an activist in the women's and peace movements around the turn of the century.[1] As a contributor to the influential literary bimonthly *Das literarische Echo*, von Ende was a highly effective agent for American literature in Germany. Her "Letter from America," which appeared regularly in that journal, contained penetrating accounts of American literary and intellectual life. Her critical European intellect combined with an understanding and appreciation of the United States rarely found among (European) leftist intellectuals. Above all, she abhorred any form of nationalism, which she believed to be on the increase in Germany since the Franco-Prussian War.

Since 1898, Amalie von Ende had used her columns in the *Literarische Echo* and other journals for frequent reports on Whitman. Her first article which prominently mentioned Whitman attempted to answer the question of whether America had developed a national literature of its own. Von Ende claimed that "classic" American writings by Cooper, Hawthorne, Longfellow, and others only developed after the British "yoke had been shaken off."[2] The "post-classical" Whitman then initiated the true literary emancipation from England: "[This amounted to] an intellectual regeneration . . . and this regeneration helped to overcome the rigidity and pedantry of puritanism and to assimilate everything new and extraordinary growing in the new environment. It is a Herculean task; but the most recent America has recognized that it will not be able to draw forever on colonial traditions. It will measure up to its mission in the twentieth century."[3] Whitman became the "intellectual leader literary America stood in need of; from his example they [American writers and thinkers] took heart."[4]

Von Ende, an anticlerical freethinker, was always favorably inclined toward Whitman. Although at first slightly critical of the cult staged by the Whitman Fellowship, she soon joined its inner circle and used her influence in the German media to spread Traubel's message. From 1907 until 1918, she was a member of the fellowship's board of directors. Through her communications in the *Literarische Echo*, the American Whitman community managed once more to exert control over German Whitman reception. With the advent of World War I, however, this situation changed radically.

Von Ende's writings on Whitman are important for an understanding of the character and the success of the various Whitman translations. She claimed that Freiligrath's translation was doomed to failure owing to the "revival of a military and imperial patriotism, from the contagion of which even Freiligrath did not escape. As the great democratic ideals of 1848 were forgotten, so was the temporary interest in the American poet of democracy, which Freiligrath had awakened."[5] The German naturalist movement, "the new school headed by Bleibtreu, Conrad, Mackay, Henckell, Heinrich and Julius Hart and others,"[6] fostered a renewed interest in Whitman.

Von Ende awarded great praise to Johannes Schlaf, "one of the most gifted writers of the young generation." In her view, Schlaf's essay of 1892 should be "accorded a place of honor in Whitman literature."[7] Karl Federn, however, made a special impression on her: "[He is] a man who has pared the core [of truth] from a tangled mass of erroneous ideas about American circumstances which continue to exist in Germany in spite of the [submarine] cable and screw steamer. He attempts to draw an unclouded picture of our cultural life, free from prejudice."[8] Elsewhere she stated that Federn "has grasped the meaning of American life and understands the character of Americans, repeatedly emphasizing their health and strength as compared to the decadent hyper-culture of Europe."[9]

KARL FEDERN (1868 – 1943)

Karl Federn was responsible for one of the two book-length Whitman translations published in 1904. A Viennese critic, writer, and translator, he had written on Dante and translated Emerson, Melville, Benedetto Croce, and several others. Amalie von Ende's biases—her belief in the opposition between American vigor and European decadence, both in the arts and in social conditions—amount to cultural clichés which describe Federn's translation.

In a review of the translation, Theodor Achelis confirmed the impression that Whitman "is a representative of the most vigorous love of life in the midst of neoromantic effeminacy and preciousness. . . ."[10] In a second article, Achelis emphasized Whitman's supposed "realistic conception of life," which he contrasted with the "stale pseudo-wisdom of an emaciated aestheticism . . . spreading through our modern life in such a repulsive way."[11]

This antiaestheticist orientation, however, did not mean "formlessness." In fact, Federn turned against the "prose" translation of Knortz and Rolleston: "One should avoid speaking of formlessness. Walt Whitman's poetry is indeed rhythmical and often full of music. The attempt to render his poetry in prose form the way Knortz and Rolleston have done would be like the attempt to convey the experience of an opera through its libretto."[12] Rather, as his opera example suggests, Federn strove for a congruity between form and content. He turned against the aestheticism of the *décadents*, but also against the antiartistic "naturalism" of Knortz and Rolleston's translation.

Both points can be demonstrated by comparing two versions of Whitman's first "Inscription," "One's Self I Sing":

One's-Self I sing, a simple, separate person,
Yet utter the word Democratic, the word En-Masse.

Of physiology from top to toe I sing,
Not physiognomy alone nor brain alone is worthy for the Muse, I say the
Form complete is worthier far,
The Female equally with the Male I sing.

Of Life immense in passion, pulse, and power,
Cheerful, for freest action form'd under the laws divine,
The Modern Man I sing.

(*LG*, 1)

Knortz and Rolleston's version:

Ein "Ich" singe ich—
Ein "Ich" singe ich—eine einfache, abgesonderte Person,
Doch sprech' ich das demokratische Wort aus, das Wort "En masse."

Die Physiologie vom Kopfe bis zum Fuß singe ich,
Nicht die Physiognomie allein, das Antlitz allein ist der Muse
würdig—ich sage, die vollständige Gestalt sei bei weitem würdiger,
Das Weib, gleich wie den Mann, singe ich.

Das Leben, unermeßlich an Leidenschaft, Herzschlag, Kraft,
Fröhlich, zur freiesten Thätigkeit unter göttlichen Gesetzen gestaltet,
Den neuen Menschen singe ich.

(KR, 2)

Finally, Federn's translation:

Das Ich sing' ich

Das Ich sing' ich, das einzelne, getrennte,
Doch brauch' ich das Wort Demokratisch, das Wort En-Masse.

Das ganze Leben vom Scheitel zur Zehe sing' ich!
Nicht das Gesicht allein, noch das Hirn allein ist der Muse
wert: ich sage, die vollkommene Form ist würdiger weit,
Vom Weiblichen wie vom Männlichen sing' ich.

Vom unendlichen Leben in Leidenschaften, Pulsen und Kraft,
Vom fröhlichen Leben, der freiesten Tat, geformt unter hohen
Gesetzen . . .
Den Modernen Menschen sing' ich![13]

The very first lines demonstrate how Federn's translation is much closer to Whitman's melody. While Knortz and Rolleston attempt to find a perfect, dictionary-based equivalent for every single word, thereby totally destroying the rhythm of the line "Ein 'Ich' singe ich—eine einfache, abgesonderte Person," Federn shortens the line by omitting "person" and by relating the whole line to the "self." "Utter" in German is, Knortz and Rolleston are correct, "aussprechen," but this German verb separates into two parts: "Doch sprech' ich . . . aus," thereby once more destroying the flow of Whitman's line. Federn's term for "utter" is "brauchen" (use), which allows him to keep Whitman's rhythm.

Federn's subsequent translation choices are characteristic of his antiaesthetic orientation, although they are more problematic from the standpoint of textual adequacy. His avoidance of terms such as "physiology" and "physiognomy" might have to do with an aversion toward German intellectualist academic terminology, a problem Whitman of course did not face. But why would he replace "physiology" with "das ganze Leben" (life as a whole)? This is where his (and the general turn-of-the-century) appreciation of Whitman as a poet emerging from "life," strongly in contrast with the "antilife" aestheticist currents, comes in. In this way, "Life immense in passion" can emerge as "Vom unendlichen Leben" (of infinite life). "Cheerful" in the next line is rendered as "Vom fröhlichen Leben" (of joyous life). And, whereas Knortz and Rolleston had still translated "Modern Man" with "neuen Menschen" (new man) because "modern" had not yet become a catchword, Federn, fully aware of the artistic development of his time, can put "Den Modernen Menschen" (with "Modernen" capitalized against German orthographic rules).

Federn's antiaestheticist translation sold Whitman to the German-speaking readers as an antidote to effeminacy, degeneration, and neoromanticism. Such an attitude, however, had dangerous implications: all too easily, this cult of "nature," "health," and vitality could become connected to a repulsive German nationalism, as evidenced only too clearly in the Whitman translation by Schölermann also published in 1904.

WILHELM SCHÖLERMANN (1865 – 1923)

By the time Wilhelm Schölermann came out with his Whitman translation, he had already made a name for himself as a xenophobic nationalist cultural "critic." His belief in the "racial" superiority of the "Germanic peoples" anticipates the confused racist rhetoric of the National Socialists. Thus, Whitman fascinates him not as a writer from a foreign culture but as a fellow Germanic poet and bard. Schölermann calls Whitman a "Vollmensch" (complete, fully developed human being) and a "Kraftbehälter" (energy container, powerhouse).[14] This logic, however, leads to the point where Whitman is constructed as an idealized representative of a master race, a member of a class of superhumans ("Klasse der Überlebensgroßen").[15] This personality, according to Schölermann, will "heal" what he considers his sick, degenerate age, characterized by "apoplectic socialism."[16]

Even worse: Schölermann's approach to Whitman was essentially racist and protofascist. He noted that in Whitman the general "Anglo-Saxon character," typified by the (negative) separation of religious and professional life, is happily dominated by his "lower German [i.e., Dutch] blood," calling for harmony between work and belief.[17] According to this theory, Whitman represented "faithful work" ("gläubige Arbeit")[18]—life and work as a nonalienated totality. It is not surprising, then, that Schölermann's favorite poem was "Pioneers! O Pioneers!" which to him represented a "parade march in a shower of bullets to a band" and which he put at the beginning of his selection.[19]

One may, as I do, consider "Pioneers" a weak poem, in line with "O Captain! My Captain!" Still, the original poem definitely lacks the outright militaristic character it assumes in Schölermann's translation. A few examples can easily demonstrate this. Line 1, "*Come* my tan-faced children," becomes "*Tretet an*, gebräunte Kinder" (Fall in, bronzed children)—the innocuous, almost biblical "come . . . children" is replaced by a military formula.[20] Stanza 3, line 1, "*O* you youths," gives Schölermann a chance to use the classic "Germanic" salutation "*Heil*! Ihr Jungen aus dem Westen"—the very word that would later reappear in the ubiquitous Nazi salute "Heil Hitler!" In stanza 13, line 1, "On and on the compact ranks," is further militarized by the commandeering line "Vorwärts! vorwärts! Marschkolonnen" (Onward! onward! marching columns).[21]

Schölermann believed that Americans should have set *this* poem to music and selected it as their national anthem rather than the "inane Yankee Doodle."[22] That "Yankee Doodle" was at no time the American national anthem seems to have bothered Schölermann little. Whitman's works, Schölermann claimed without offering support, show that if the "genius of fulfillment of the twentieth century" should be European, "it will have to be born on Germanic cultural soil."[23]

Although the two translators' ideological and aesthetic orientations were fairly different, their construction of Whitman was remarkably similar. The strong antidecadent, antiaestheticist thrust was very revealing because it reacted against modernist artistic developments that both translators found difficult to accept. Whitman was portrayed as a force reinstating a natural and holistic lifestyle and an equally natural and holistic art. Again, however, these Whitmanites did not understand Whitman's own essential modernity, did not understand that with Whitman, they were catapulted further into the very twentieth century that they so deeply mistrusted and that seemed so alien to their sensibility.

The two translations appeared in attractive cloth-bound volumes as well as in paperback; Schölermann's from the German-nationalist publisher Eugen Diederichs (with a *Jugendstil*-type tendril and snail illustration on the cover obviously designed to reinforce the natural and holistic message of the translation). They added quite a few poems to the repertoire already translated, although, as the history of the republication of translations shows, they were not nearly as influential as either Knortz's previous or Schlaf's subsequent edition. This may have been for reasons of distribution, but certainly also because their translations "blocked" Whitman. In an anachronistic and—to us—ironic manner, they used Whitman to battle against a movement of literary and artistic modernism of which Whitman himself was a not insignificant part.

CHAPTER FIVE

FRANZ BLEI

In spite of the fact that there were by now four book-length translations, including a mass-market edition, more German translators became willing to try their hand at Whitman's poetry and more publishers became interested in bringing out their own Whitman edition. In fact, it seems as though every German publishing house had to have its own Whitman.

The renowned Insel Publishers wanted to include his poetry in their popular series of German and World Literature. The small book that appeared in 1914 contained selections and translations by Franz Blei (1871–1942), an Austrian-born, Berlin-based *littérateur* specializing in erotic literature, sophisticated aphorisms, and witty literary criticism, frequently in essay form. Franz Blei states in a short note that his selection owed its existence to no overriding concern but was solely the result of his private, subjective "taste," and it does reflect the aesthetic biases of the translator. The Whitman we encounter in Franz Blei's *Hymnen für die Erde* (Hymns for the Earth) is not the messianic prophet that the title promises,[1] but a representative of the very aestheticism that Schölermann and Federn attempted to escape.

Monika Schaper has demonstrated this using the famous first section of "Starting from Paumanok."[2] The line "Or rude in my home in Dakota's woods, my diet meat, my drink from the spring" (*LG*, 15) obviously describes the existence of a backwoodsman; "rude" therefore refers to the "rough" living conditions, which may also have had an effect on the personality of the lonely dweller. Schlaf attributes "rude" to "forests" ("in Dakotas unwirtlichen Wäldern," inhospitable forests, 17). Blei, by contrast, the well-mannered urban poet, puts a characteristic value judgment on such a mode of existence: "rude" is translated as "ungesittet" (uncultured, uncivilized, unmannered, 4), a word used to refer to a kid behaving badly at the dinner table. In the last line of this section, "Solitary, singing in the West, I strike up for a New World," Blei translates "striking up" with "aufspielen" (4)—the way a band would play at a village wedding.

In "Song of Myself," Blei's attitude of refinement (influenced strongly by his admiration for rococo art) jars with Whitman's pose of the simple loafer in an almost comical way. "I loafe and invite my soul" (*LG*, 28) is translated "Ich vergeude und lade meine Seele zu Gast"; the word "vergeuden" is usually associated with squandering money. In the next line, "I lean and loafe at my ease" becomes "Ich liege und lungere, raste und liege" (I lie and hang out, rest and lie). "Lungern," like "vergeuden," has a much more negative connotation in German than "loafe" does in English. In order to offset this negative ring of the line, however, Blei introduces two extra words with a more neutral character ("rest and lie") which are not in the English original.

Blei's ambivalent attitude toward Whitman results not only from his personal aesthetic preferences. It shows that the heyday of the aestheticist movement was over. An original representative of the movement would have looked at Whitman's reflection of grass leaves with great interest—although many other sections might have found less favor. Blei's aestheticism is full of sophisticated irony and commercialism. His construction of Whitman ("the great Pan who never died because he is immortal, he alone among Gods, although often hidden for long periods of time in the deepest grottoes of the earth,") is ironical—anti-*Pathos*—at a time when expressionist authors and artists were taking Whitman very, very seriously.[3] The book itself is a collage of small sections of Whitman with a decidedly commercial appeal and with little regard for the integrity of individual poems or sections.

CHAPTER SIX

GUSTAV LANDAUER

When Kurt Wolff (1887–1963), patron saint and publisher of young expressionist poets and writers such as Franz Werfel, Georg Trakl, and Franz Kafka, decided to publish a Whitman edition, he turned to Gustav Landauer (1870–1919). Landauer is one of the most remarkable personalities in the history of the German left as well as in the German history of letters at large. The variety of his occupations and vocations rivals that of Whitman: critic, translator, journalist, writer, and, for a brief time, politician through his membership in the short-lived revolutionary Bavarian government after the breakdown of the German Empire in 1918. He was a Jewish anarchist, a visionary mystic, a self-management socialist—and a Whitmanite.

When Wolff turned to Landauer for a translation of Whitman's works in 1916 because he believed him to be "fairly well informed about Whitman,"[1] Landauer replied immediately: "Concerning your inquiry about a German edition of Whitman I am hardly able to answer you—so keenly am I interested in this poet and so strong is my wish to publish him in German."[2] In this letter, Landauer also mentioned his acquaintance with German editions of Whitman: "I know many translations: by Strodtmann, Knortz, Bertz, Schölermann, Federn, Schlaf, Blei."[3] However, he declared his dissatisfaction with his predecessors "because they do not know the secret of Whitman's prosody or at least the way in which he needs to be recreated in German." And he added: "I freely admit that, so far, only one person has managed to render Whitman's poetry in German as strong and beautiful poems with Whitmanesque effects. Myself. . . ."[4]

Landauer had indeed long been acquainted with Whitman's works. In 1907 he had written a lengthy and frequently reprinted essay which is essential for an understanding of his translations.[5] In 1921, when Landauer's Whitman translation was finally published by Kurt Wolff, this essay was used as an introduction.[6]

Landauer was a special sort of leftist. He did not share Marx's materialist analysis of society; his ideas were rooted in the mystical tradition ranging from the German medieval mystics to Walt Whitman.[7] What was important to him in Whitman was the fact "that human beings carry the whole world in their Self, in their *spirituality*, that the world is but an infinite wealth of microcosms . . ." (GL, 91; emphasis added).[8] Landauer's main objective was the liberation of this "Self"—and it was spirituality which he considered Whitman's most important contribution toward a transformation of society.

The term "spirituality" ("Geistigkeit") is not quite as empty as it may seem at first. Landauer does not want to replace Marxist analysis with "a vague, general love for humanity; rather, like the love that founded the family, there should be a spirit of exclusiveness which connects certain people, males with males, females with females and, of course, also males with females, making up new social groups" (GL, 88).[9] For Landauer, such "spirituality" would manifest itself in the establishment of new human collectives because the older communities had degenerated and the "nonspiritual" state with its repressive institutions had increasingly filled the resulting power vacuum. (This, incidentally, is much the same type of analysis Whitman pursues in *Democratic Vistas.*) In this process, voluntary participation in social affairs was replaced by a tyrannical bureaucracy, "spirit"-filled human activities by a materialism devoid of any spirit.

Like Whitman, Landauer also considered the development of American society a "threat" to its people ("excess of prosperity, 'business,' 'worldliness,' materialism," GL, 89). However, the new world was special because it represented "an empire of the future, of a *Volksgemeinschaft* [community of the people] which is still growing together and not yet finished" (GL, 86). Eventually, Landauer believed, America would develop in the right way. Whitman is "an early precursor of an American-Periclean age" (GL, 87).[10] The federal organization of the United States with its limited central power was a model for "all peoples of the earth" (GL, 87).

Volksgemeinschaft later was prominently employed by the Nazis and has Nazi connotations for the modern speaker of German. However, Landauer's use of the term denotes a voluntary association of individuals as opposed to repressive coercion (in whatever form) by the state. The ideal society emerging from Whitman's "democracy" is a home to "a free people made up of active individuals who have left behind all obstructions caused by a caste-spirit, who have broken through all phantoms of the past; each on his land or in his trade, at his machine, each man for himself" (GL, 87).[11] Criticism of class society, recognized mainly as the result of a "wrong" way of thinking, goes hand in hand with a utopian conception of self-sufficient farmers and tradespeople.

In Whitman's works, Landauer thought he had found a confirmation for his own thesis that a new society could only be built on the basis of an autonomous, self-managing community. The capitalist order would be replaced by nonprofit "exchange banks," the alienation of the worker/producer counteracted through a lifestyle which combined manual and intellectual labor. Little wonder that Whitman's biography with its variety of different jobs and the mix of intellectual and manual labor appealed to Landauer (see GL, 90). This version of socialism is far removed from orthodox Marxist programs and rather resembles present-day conceptions of alternative lifestyles; it is also very close to Whitman's ideal vision of an artisan community.

The sense of community, then, is one of the most important characteristics of the socialist-anarchist society Landauer dreamed of. He considered it the noblest task of poetry to develop a "spirit" which would lead to this goal. "Poetry," not a transformation of the material basis, became the prerequisite for a new society. "Only a great people," Landauer summarized Whitman, "can have great poets; but before that, it must be poetry which shapes a great people, lends it 'artistic character, spirituality, and dignity' " (GL, 89).[12]

Using Whitman as his foremost example, Landauer developed his theses concerning the tasks of the poet: "As a poet Walt Whitman wants to be a priest, prophet, and creator. It is certain that he has exerted extraordinary power over his people and over the spirit of his people—as well as over those who, among foreign peoples, belong to his people as individuals. And it is certain that he continues to do so" (GL, 89).[13] Whitman's people (as well as Landauer's) are obviously just in the process of emerging ("still growing together," GL, 86). Membership is not determined by accidental birth but by a shared belief in standards defining a new humanity. Among "foreign" peoples there are also individuals belonging to "Whitman's people," an idea strongly expressed in the translation. Landauer quotes what for him is a line central to Whitman's work: "Here is adhesiveness, it is not previously fashion'd" (*LG*, 153). To Landauer, "previously fashioned" means an artificial organization of society through the state; the German translation reads: "Hier ist Zusammenhalt, künstlich gedrechselter nicht" (Here is cohesion, not artificially lathed).[14]

Although it was Landauer's vision of a self-managed socialist society that brought him to Whitman, his choice of Whitman selections to translate was strongly influenced by his war experience. The war was Landauer's first concern;

unlike his Social Democratic colleagues, he did not believe that war would eventually bring about socialism—quite to the contrary, it would prevent it.[15]

In 1911, when war already seemed a strong possibility, he explained the relationship between his utopian society and war: "The war drum should be a call to unity for all those whose consciousness has gone beyond the state, beyond the realm of the antagonisms between states. They should make clear to themselves and also to others: these means [i.e. war] are dead for our spirit: they no longer have a hold on our innermost self; we have long since found other possibilities of relationships between individuals and the people [as a whole] and among peoples."[16] Predictably, all of Landauer's creative activities, including his translations, were dominated by the war and the problems arising from it.

Nineteen out of the twenty-six poems contained in the Wolff edition had already been published in 1915 and 1916 in such pacifist journals as *Die weissen Blätter, Neue Jugend,* and *Aufbruch.* The clear-cut pacifist strategy of Landauer's translation can also be shown in the way he frequently highlights individual sections of poems. From "The Return of Heroes," he translated only section 6—a rather explosive appeal to put down arms. In this way, the poem ends with the following lines:

> Melt, melt away ye armies—disperse ye blue-clad soldiers,
> Resolve ye back again, give up for good your deadly arms,
> Other the arms the fields henceforth for you, or South or North,
> With saner wars, sweet wars, life-giving wars.
> (*LG*, 362)

It was this pacifist understanding which was responsible for Whitman's omnipresence on the battlefields of World War I.

Landauer's pacifist commitment during World War I and his political activities as a member of the Bavarian Soviet government immediately after the war prevented his translation from growing beyond forty pages.[17] The edition did not appear until 1921, two years after Landauer was murdered in prison; it is a slender, very beautiful volume whose carton cover is made of stylized grass leaves.

His translation was not one of the most popular, but it was certainly known and used in specific situations. "Turn O Libertad," for example, was printed in Landauer's translation on the very first page of *Plan*, the first literary journal that appeared in liberated Austria after World War II. In a very real way, Whitman stands at the beginning of a new, free, and democratic Austria and Austrian literature:

Turn O Libertad, for the war is over,
From it and all henceforth expanding, doubting no more, resolute,
 sweeping the world, . . .
Then turn, and be not alarm'd O Libertad—turn your undying face,
To where the future, greater than all the past,
Is swiftly, surely preparing for you.

(*LG*, 326)[18]

CHAPTER SEVEN

MAX HAYEK

In 1919 and in 1920, two volumes with translations of Whitman's poetry by Max Hayek were published by two Viennese publishing houses.[1] The first contained a cross-section from *Leaves*, the second "Song of Myself." Although these translations were appearing for the first time as collections, many of the individual poems and sections had been published during the war in *Sozialistische Monatshefte*, an influential theoretical-political monthly owned by the German Social Democrats. Other socialist and leftist journals and papers also published translations of Whitman poems between 1914 and 1918. What was the reason for this sudden wartime interest in Whitman on the part of the Social Democratic Party?

In 1915, the Stuttgart-based Social Democratic paper *Neue Zeit* wrote: "In these war months, the German workers' press has repeatedly published verses from Walt Whitman's 'Leaves of Grass.' Only a few lines, but very effective. At present, Whitman is indeed the poet whose voice may command special attention."[2] The article indicates that aspects not related to traditional socialist concerns must have been involved in the response to Whitman and that the war, specifically, was related to this reception. But why was Whitman "very effective" just at that time and why especially for the Social Democrats?

Traditionally, the socialist movement throughout Europe and North America took strong pacifist positions. According to one of Marx's most tragically erroneous theses, nationalism was supposed to be (merely) a mystification designed to confuse the international working class as to its true interests. In a war, workers are sent out to fight each other in the name of their nation, while capitalists on an international scale reap the profits of the military buildup—the workers as cannon-fodder of their exploiters. According to Marxist theory, workers have to learn that their true interests lie with international proletarian solidarity and that they need to counteract any attempts by international capital to fuel nationalist feelings.

The theory proved to be a blunder in view of the fact that nationalism, whatever its foundations or functions, is far too much a part of individual and collective (sub)consciousness to be eradicated by a simple call to internationalist solidarity. In the course of the increasing tensions and the military armament just prior to World War I, the international workers' movement became deeply split along national lines. Shortly before the actual outbreak of the war, most socialist leaders (except those on the radical left who would later become Communists) agreed with their national governments as to the necessity of a "salvation" of their homeland.

In Germany and Austria, this meant no strikes and protests, but, rather, parliamentary support for loans which would finance the war machinery. With great satisfaction, the German emperor could say after this act of national solidarity on the part of the left: "I do not know any [political] parties any longer, I just know Germans."

Many socialists to the left of these positions likened Social Democratic support of the war effort to the Fall in paradise. Communists in particular have repeatedly criticized the Social Democrats for what they considered an act of treason. The Social Democrats themselves felt very divided. On the one hand, they wanted to maintain their basic pacifist orientation; on the other, they had in effect endorsed the war and were still sharing in the war effort. If they wanted to live and survive with that contradiction, they had to find a theoretical ideological justification for their political decision. Whitman played an interesting role in this endeavor.

In 1915, Franz Diederich, socialist critic and editor of an anthology of poetry for workers,[3] wrote an essay on Whitman entitled "An Example of War Poetry." This essay is a good illustration of the ideological strategy developed to come to terms with the ambiguity of Social Democratic war policies. In the very first lines we read: "The bloody horrific world leaped suddenly from the phantom empire of peacetime visions into the naked glare of reality and forced the world to answer the fatal question of how to maintain a defiant upright posture. The best answer is that veiling one's head and turning away avails nothing. The point is to face the worst boldly."[4] The adjectives, seemingly critical of the war, should not mislead us into believing that the author is presenting a compromise: the point is to find a "defiant" way to "maintain an upright posture," to retain (national?) pride. The basic antagonism to war (the pacifist claim of socialists) emerges from these lines, but also the desperate attempt to justify, indeed, to promote it. That "turning away" (from war) "avails nothing" is a defeatist assertion that furthers the war effort.

Added to this is the speculation that, in analogy to peacetime class struggle, war might function as a socially creative force which could favor the emergence of a new social order. This is the Social Democratic version of the fatal conservative thesis of the purifying power of war, which was widespread in the period preceding its outbreak. Diederich adds imploringly to his readers: "We should never forget the elementary truth of our movement: we are not here just to negate. Out of our negation, we want to push yet more strongly for affirmation."[5] In the war context, this "affirmation" assumes a ghostly, macabre dimension.

The lines just quoted and analyzed introduce an article that employed the poetry and person of Walt Whitman to keep alive the Social Democratic vision of a peaceful society in spite of the increasingly loud roar of the cannons. In his essay, Diederich masters this complex ideological task in a rather original way. He calls Whitman's poetry from and about the Civil War an example of war poetry which stresses human ability to maintain integrity in the face of the war. Whitman's war poems "show how he comes to terms with a dreadful reality by squarely facing it."[6] He then goes on to show—and emphasize—how Whitman entered the Civil War as a *volunteer* and a *nurse.*

The image of Whitman as nurse and wound-dresser who, through his mere presence, helped wounded soldiers assumes central importance for Diederich, but also for the Social Democrats in general. As a nurse, while participating in the war, Whitman was able to express his abhorrence of bloodshed, destruction, and mutilation: "He did not reach for the murderous weapon—as a wound-dresser, he entered the ranks of the soldiers."[7] Structurally speaking, the position of the wound-dresser was analogous to the ambivalent Social Democratic position toward war. Whitman could naturally serve as a model for identification. When Social Democratic commentators frequently stressed that Whitman himself did not take up weapons, they expressed their fantasies of an innocent, even productive participation in the war (as a kind of wound-dresser of the people).

MAX HAYEK (1882–?)

Max Hayek, the most important of the Social Democratic Whitman translators, had fewer misgivings about the involvement in the war than thoughtful Franz Diederich. In spite of the fact that he described himself as a "philosophical" author and worked as a journalist and translator (in addition to Whitman, he introduced Prentice Mulford to the German reading public),[8] he was rather naive politically. He comprehended neither the reasons for nor the meaning of fascism's rise in Germany and Austria; eventually, the Jewish-Catholic Hayek managed to escape Austria, possibly to the United States. His essay on Whitman as a "poet of war" reflects more his uncritical view of his own service as an officer in the Austrian army during World War I than a genuine vision of a socialist society eventually emerging from the battlefields. His essay attempts to prove that Whitman was quite willing even to promote war in exchange for a vague vision of a socialist future: "There has never lived a man with a more powerful belief in mankind and humanity than this great American. And the blood-soaked soil has not darkened the light of his soul, this divine inextinguishable light, always filled with new hope."[9] Far from protesting the "blood-soaked soil," Hayek advocated an acceptance of the war in the interest of a vague "belief in humanity."

Some Social Democratic voices went even further than Hayek. The only excuse for their warmongering attitude is that they operated as part of furious propagandistic campaigns on both sides. Still, they might have asked themselves whether they, as Social Democrats, did not have a special moral obligation to rise above the general level of nationalist propaganda. An anonymous contributor to the official Social Democratic daily *Vorwärts*, for example, in reaction to the American entry into the war, makes use of Whitman in what amounts to a characteristic strategy of anti-Americanism. First, an alienation between the ideals of the artist and the (political) practice of his (since degenerated) homeland is hypothesized: "25 years ago, on 27 March 1892, one of the noblest American spirits closed his eyes. We may safely assume that he would have objected in the strongest terms to the present-day policies of the United States [i.e., the U.S. entry into the war against Germany]. . . . this perfidy, ambiguity, and insincerity of recent American policy would have been deeply repugnant to him."[10] The author then claims that Americans had always failed to understand one of their greatest spirits anyway: "'Leaves of Grass' were and have remained a failure, and the understanding for this original poet grew only very slowly. Even today, he does not, and probably never will, count among the favorites of American readers."[11] Whitman, now characterized as a German ally repudiated by his fellow Americans—this is indeed a demagogical masterpiece.[12]

Max Hayek's choice of Whitman poems for the *Sozialistische Monatshefte* during the war years roughly corresponds to this analysis of their specific wartime context. The majority of these poems were not taken from *Drum-Taps*, which had fascinated Freiligrath and Strodtmann. Rather, they were poems such as "The Mystic Trumpeter" which permitted an integration of the (subjectively) negative experience of war into an (overall) positive framework.

To Social Democratic critics, a systematic analysis of the causes and effects seemed less important than a "truth" grasped intuitively: "He [Whitman] is real truth, not some knowledge derived from observation, but an understanding of things from inside. Therefore, external categories must vanish."[13] This evaluation of Hayek's full-length translation of *Song of Myself* can explain both the selection and the translation of many of the individual Whitman poems that appeared during the war years. The war in "Mystic Trumpeter," for example, is interpreted as an "unreal" experience and becomes a private vision:

Blow again trumpeter—conjure war's alarums.

Swift to thy spell a shuddering hum like distant thunder rolls,
Lo, where the arm'd men hasten—lo, mid the clouds of dust the glint of bayonets,
I see the grime-faced cannoneers, I mark the rosy flash amid the smoke, I hear the cracking of the guns . . .
(*LG*, 470)

This same sound of the trumpet can provide a positive, deceptively reassuring inner vision, harmonizing the experience as a whole. It makes the war threat less real and "spiritualizes," even ennobles, the militaristic effort:

Now trumpeter for thy close,
Vouchsafe a higher strain than any yet,
Sing to my soul, renew its languishing faith and hope,
Rouse up my slow belief, give me some vision of the future,
Give me for once its prophecy and joy.
(*LG*, 471)

Finally, these lines lead into the Beethoven-like triumphant finale, which, to the Social Democratic reader, could only mean that—in the way of a prophetic promise—the end of the war would bring the socialist revolution: "A reborn race appears—a perfect world, all joy!" (*LG*, 471)

A similar situation is presented in "Proud Music of the Storm," also translated by Hayek and published in 1915. At the beginning of section 2, the lyrical *persona* instructs its soul: "Come forward O my soul, and let the rest retire, / Listen, lose not, it is toward thee they tend" (*LG*, 403). What follows, including the war scenes, is therefore not "real" but a vision:

Now loud approaching drums,
Victoria! see'st thou in powder-smoke the banners torn but flying? the rout of the baffled?
Hearest those shouts of a conquering army?
(*LG*, 404)

At the same time, there is the pacifist, critical dimension, a kind of lip service to and secret yearning for pacifist positions:

(Ah soul, the sobs of women, the wounded groaning in agony,
The hiss and crackle of flames, the blacken'd ruins, the embers of cities,
The dirge and desolation of mankind.)
(*LG*, 404)

This horrific vision finally dissolves in an image of a harmonious world replete with music. The lyrical persona, awakening from its dreamy state, says to "my silent curious soul out of the bed of the slumber-chamber":

Come, for I have found the clew I sought so long,
Let us go forth refresh'd amid the day,
Cheerfully tallying life, walking the world, the real,
Nourish'd henceforth by our celestial dream.
(*LG*, 410)

This structure is characteristic of quite a few of the poems selected, translated, and published in Social Democratic papers during the war. They fit the prevalent interpretation of Whitman as an apologist for the war. We may not, of course, agree with such an interpretation of these and other poems; but it is important to realize that specific interpreters with certain political interests found such uses of Whitman expedient.

After the end of the war, Hayek and other translators continued translating and publishing Whitman poems in the Social Democratic press until the 1930s, almost until the Nazi takeover. The various leftist constructions of Whitman are discussed in chapter 15, but in general the translations have much of the quasi-religious flavor of impassionate proletarian writing. In this way, Whitman became a poet of the left, alongside such American prose writers as Jack London and Upton Sinclair.

While the two important editions of 1919 and 1920 (the latter republished in 1926) are reflections of the German and Austrian Social Democratic nightmare, their participation in the war they hated, they are also documents of a working-class culture that has long since disappeared. Hard- and soft-cover editions of these two translations with a variety of different, often very beautiful, jackets can to this day be found in many libraries of German and Austrian trade unions and Social Democratic Party organizations.

CHAPTER EIGHT

HANS REISIGER

In 1919, just a few months after the close of the war and in time for Whitman's centenary, one of Germany's most important publishers, S. Fischer, brought out an edition which eventually became the standard among the many German translations of Whitman. The translator, Hans Reisiger (1884–1968), a close friend of Thomas Mann and an important writer in his own right, was one of the most significant translators of the twentieth century. He had "come to Whitman" as early as 1909 and translated Whitman's poetry since 1912.[1] Individual poems were published in the leftist journal *Das Forum* and other magazines. In his preface to the (one-volume) edition of 1919, he views Whitman as a source of renewed hope for a depressed country and nation:

> At Germany's borders, there are mountains of hatred and revenge casting their shadows on the country. Like moraines from glaciers, the hollow materialism of wanton enemies pushes into the country. They are out for land and material goods. The fluid layers of the country's own population surge destructively against one another. The deep yearning for global happiness and justice merely throws up mud, hardly reflecting one shimmer of the dawn of a nobler future. The world, which has been shaking in bloody spasms from the very beginning, has always had a gate through which it looked pure, serene, spiritualized, and divine! This gate, the gate of the individual soul, is blocked a thousandfold. The stones blocking it a thousandfold are pity, exhaustion, lack of faith, hatred, hunger, fear. . . .
>
> In this gloomy moment, I dare again to invoke Walt Whitman with the sounds of German, although to many of us he is already as familiar as light and air.

> Forever and eternally, the aim of all earthly striving will be the creation of a new humanity. And where else is the paradise of this new, higher human being than, again, in one's own self? True sympathy can only flow from the power of creation in oneself. "Be a man to yourself and a comrade to your fellow human beings" is Whitman's belief about the human community. He wants to plant fiery, disinterested, selfless, and yet, in the noblest sense, selfish companionship, yearning for souls, wants to plant them as "thick as trees along all the rivers of America." It is such a proud democracy of self-confident spirits and magnetic bodies that we yearn for out of all the agony and fever of Germany.[2]

Reisiger was not alone in his view that Whitman could help with the reestablishment of a new, democratic Germany and that his poetry and his ideas could actually assume community-building character. His friend Gerhart Hauptmann, for example, envisioned a very specific and constructive place for Whitman in the young German Republic. The new state was to be founded in Weimar, the city of Goethe and Schiller, far away from Berlin, which had connotations of militarism and imperialism, to demonstrate to the world that a new, democratic Germany, taking up the ideals of classical German literature, was in the making. Hauptmann suggested that two poems by Whitman, "For You, O Democracy" and excerpts from "Song of the Broad-Axe," be published in Weimar newspapers on the occasion of the foundation of the new republic.[3]

Similarly, Thomas Mann, Reisiger's close friend, foresaw a special place for Whitman in the Weimar Republic. On the occasion of Reisiger's two-volume Whitman edition eventually published in 1922, he wrote an open letter to Germany's most influential daily, the *Frankfurter Zeitung*, which was printed on the title page of the edition of 16 April 1922:

> Dear Mr. Reisiger!
>
> I am delighted to have your Whitman book and cannot thank you enough for this great, important, indeed holy gift; for that matter, the German public, it seems to me, can not be grateful enough either. Since I have received the two volumes, I have opened them again and again, reading here and there. I have read the biographical introduction from beginning to end and consider it a little masterpiece of love. Indeed, dear Mr. Reisiger, it is really a great achievement on your part that after years of devotion and enthusiastic labor, you have brought close to us this powerful spirit, this exuberant, profound new personification of humanity. We Germans, who are old and immature at the same time, can benefit from contact with this personality, symbol of the future of *humanity*, if we are willing to accept him. To me personally, who has been

striving for so many years, in my own laborious way, after the idea of humanity, convinced that no task is more urgent for Germany than to give a new meaning to this idea—which has become a mere empty shell, a mere school phrase—to me this work of yours is a real gift from God, for I see that what Walt Whitman calls "*Democracy*" is essentially nothing else than what we, in a more old-fashioned way, call "Humanity." I see, too, that awakening the feelings of the new humanity will not be accomplished by Goethe alone, but that a dose of Whitman is needed: all the more so because these two have a good deal in common, these two ancestors of ours, especially as regards sensuality, "Calamus," the sympathy with the organic . . . In short, your deed—this word is neither too large nor too strong—can have an incalculable effect and I, for my part, though a bit late, want to be among those who, with a knowing heart, have *congratulated* you on your work!

Accept the very best regards from your
Thomas Mann[4]

Mann's letter is extraordinarily enthusiastic. He associates Whitman's work with his favorite concept, "Humanität," and claims there is "no task more urgent for Germany" than to renew its humanistic tradition through Whitman, with "incalculable" effects! Mann, the formerly conservative author, seems to have switched to the side of democracy.

Whitman, together with Goethe, at the beginning of a new Germany? Had Whitman finally assumed a decisive role in the German cultural-political discussion? And, if so, did Reisiger's edition meet the requirements for such an enormous task?

One tendency in the edition of 1919 is fairly obvious: with the exception of individual longer poems such as "Crossing Brooklyn Ferry" and "Salut au Monde!" the selection is made up of poems with predominantly erotic and particularly homoerotic character as well as war poems. Especially in the first part of the volume, the erotic tendency predominates. As did Schlaf's edition, Reisiger's two-volume edition of 1922 contains "Song of Myself" in full. In addition, emphasis is placed on the "Children of Adam" and "Calamus" cycles. The translation includes all of the former and the major part of the latter. The impression gained from a mere glance at the table of contents that the selection focuses on erotic poetry is confirmed by the preface, some ninety pages in length.

Reisiger's biographical introduction takes up a few of Whitman's myths popularized in Germany by Schlaf (e.g., his "perfect" parents and ancestors). At the same time, the homoerotic dimension is emphasized. In a key passage of the introduction, he states:

> And this desire is not only directed to the receptive female "Thou," to whom you are drawn by all magnetic flashes of your body, but also to the "Thou" of the male, the comrade, the friend in "the Garden the World." To him, too, the magnet is drawn, with him, too, you like to walk hand in hand or with the arm on the shoulder or around the hip, with profound desire, with your pure, well-shaped, spiritual friend. Only more "ethereal," "as though bodiless," although always a physical delight; in a way experiencing the miracle of one's own manhood again in the Adamic brother, a creation identical to oneself. Males exchanging the "token of manhood," embodied in the keen phallic symbol of the calamus-root plucked in the forest shade next to a swamp, exchanging it in the frenzy of the all-powerful love in animated nature, in glowing-smiling camaraderie of those communally walking together here on earth and sharing each other's feelings. Deeper yet than the female delirium in conception, the erotic daydream stirs in the loving comrade. . . . To deny the eros in these poems [Calamus], as busy moles have attempted to do, would mean to sin against them. Eros vibrates through them just as through the quiet air of the afternoon before the gates of Athens, when Socrates talked with Phaidros under the plane tree next to the brook.[5]

Reisiger's openness is surprising. There is not even an attempt at justification, apology, or coverup. Passages such as these construct the homoerotic Whitman in Germany.

> Only at this point can we feel the true demonic power of these ardently whispered Calamus songs, when we realize that in them the singer wants to get something out of the stillness of the Pan-like forest destined to become the nerve of the community life of the future and of all countries and cities, the heartbeat of true democracy, electrically playing between all those men forming a true community, freeing each individual from stifling egotism, prejudice, maliciousness, and dullness. . . . (HR1, lxxi f.)[6]

Reisiger derives the idea of a democratic community born out of homoeroticism from Whitman, whom he quotes at length:

> Intense and loving comradeship, the personal and passionate attachment of man to man—which, hard to define, underlies the lessons and ideals of the profound saviours of every land and age, and which seems to promise, when thoroughly develop'd, cultivated and recognized in manners and literature, the most substantial hope and safety of the future of these States, will then be fully express'd. It is to the development, identification, and general prevalence of that fervid comradeship, (the adhesive love, at least rivaling the amative love

hitherto possessing imaginative literature, if not going beyond it,) that I look for to the counterbalance and offset of our materialistic and vulgar American democracy, and for the spiritualization thereof. (HR1, lxxii)

Similarly, Thomas Mann, on the occasion of Gerhart Hauptmann's sixtieth birthday in 1922, gave a speech in which Whitman and Whitman's homoeroticism figure prominently. With Whitman he addresses "Eros as statesman, as creator of a state" to bring about a "unity of state and culture."[7]

This programmatic eroticism calls for a maximum degree of explicitness with regard to the presentation of sexuality and sexual imagery in the translation. In section 24 of "Song of Myself," we find an unparalleled concentration of sexual imagery. Already Knortz and Rolleston and Schlaf had been very open in their translations of this passage. The following two examples, however, show Reisiger's special qualities in this respect.

"Copulation is no more rank to me than death is." For "rank," both Knortz and Rolleston (KR, 46) and Schlaf (*LG*, 59) use "anstößig" (offensive, indecent). Reisiger, however, uses "geil" (HR2, 45, horny). Several lines below, "fibre of manly wheat" is rendered as "Faser kräftigen Weizens" in the earlier translations (strong fiber of wheat), "manly" obviously interpreted as "strong." Reisiger, with a homoerotic insight that is more explicit than even Whitman's original, has "Samen des männlichen Weizens" (semen of male wheat).

Although the (homo)erotic context and character of Reisiger's translation is obvious, contemporary criticism hardly reacted to it. The critic of *Der Kunstwart* believed that Reisiger "solved Whitman's riddle": "Walt Whitman has been discovered! A German poet has discovered him. Many have felt him, suspected, praised, in their way 'translated' him. But only Reisiger has discovered and conquered him."[8] Characteristically, the anonymous critic did not reveal *what* had been discovered; rather, he offered the usual mixture of messianic fervor and American clichés.

Instead, critics emphasized that the translation had a certain timeless quality. The comparison with Goethe in Mann's letter already suggested that nexus. Indeed, gold-lettered spines of the two-volume set (in Gothic script) almost automatically placed Whitman into the "classical" canon and certainly ensured him a prominent place on readers' bookshelves. Although Reisiger (as we have seen) did have an agenda of his own—which Schaper, correctly though insufficiently, describes as his greater psychological insight[9]—he drew on his extensive knowledge of German styles and registers to achieve greater "lucidity" and balance, greater "objectivity," lacking some of the missionary fervor of Schlaf's or Hayek's translations. Unfortunately, the "classical" character of this translation can be postulated but not demonstrated here. Such a demonstration would require not only a comparison with the diction of "classical" German literature (Goethe, Schiller), but also with such modern poets as Rilke.

With Reisiger's edition, Whitman was finally a generally known and accepted author in the German-speaking countries and an indispensable part of (the German canon of) world literature. Reisiger's two-volume translation was republished four times before 1933 and several times after the war. In 1956, a revised and slightly modernized edition was published by Rowohlt in the Federal Republic and by Aufbau in the GDR. Some of the most optimistic passages from the biography, however, were modified or omitted altogether.

The optimism and hope Whitman had inspired in his translator had disappeared in the course of the Nazi era. Reisiger had at first attempted to escape Hitler by moving to Austria; after the *Anschluß*, he was jailed for a short time for standing by his friend Thomas Mann. Mann's attempts to get Reisiger a professorship in the United States failed because of the latter's refusal to leave Germany. During the war, he became a recluse, growing increasingly bitter. After 1945, Whitman was supposed to lift Germany once more out of a postwar depression, but the outcome was uncertain. "Sometimes," Reisiger wrote in a letter to Mann expressing his hope that Whitman might have an educational effect on Germany's post–World War II youth, "sometimes one would like to despair of the ability of Germans to learn or to convert—and not only of young people."[10]

CHAPTER NINE

. . . .

TRANSLATIONS AFTER WORLD WAR II

One might have expected that Reisiger's "definitive" edition would bring the long series of Whitman translations to an end. However, after twelve years of Nazi rule, Whitman again received great attention, although the level of interest, for reasons discussed below, never again reached that of the prewar period. Some of the older translations (Schlaf, Blei, Reisiger) were republished, and new translations appeared. Four smaller editions came from Switzerland, Austria, and West Germany, while two lengthy translations appeared in West and East Germany.

All of the postwar Whitman translations had to struggle with Whitman's *Pathos* and messianic rhetoric—both Whitman's own and the intensified versions of his earlier German translators. The Nazis used their ubiquitous *Blut und Boden* (blood and earth) rhetoric in songs as well as in propagandistic speeches, and this diction in some ways resembled Whitman's. Through no fault of the poet, the characteristic Whitmanesque *Pathos* was spoiled for speakers of German; while Whitman's democratic message was quite suitable for the building of the two postwar German states, his rhetoric had to be tuned down. This compromise, however, produced translations which are much less appealing to readers than the earlier ones and less significant in the history of the German reception of Whitman in general. This is the characteristic tendency of two editions, one published in West Germany and one in the German Democratic Republic.

ELISABETH SERELMANN-KÜCHLER AND WALTHER KÜCHLER

The bulky West German Whitman translation by Elisabeth Serelmann-Küchler and Walther Küchler, a daughter and father team, appeared in 1947 on poor-quality postwar paper and was soon out of print.[1] It is a faithful translation, a diligent, but not an inspired work, characterized by the soberness of the immediate postwar era. Both translators had suffered professionally during the Nazi regime and their attempt to avoid any abuse of the German language the way the Nazis practiced it forms the linguistic background of the translation. By consciously avoiding passion and emotional involvement, however, they also lost much of the energy and moving spirit of Whitman's poetry.

ERICH ARENDT

Erich Arendt's translation, published in the GDR in 1966, predictably emphasized some of Whitman's more social-minded and "revolutionary" poetry and prose.[2] This was an aspect which many other translations, including the Social Democratic ones, had neglected or chosen to ignore. Whitman's "A Song for Occupations," though part of the first edition of *Leaves*, remained untranslated until Arendt, as was the highly political "Europe, The 72d and 73d Years of These States," the earliest of the twelve poems contained in the 1855 edition. In this way, Arendt's edition added many new poems and prose pieces, especially from *Democratic Vistas*, to the translated canon.

Erich Arendt (1903–1984) was one of the GDR's best-known poets.[3] He started out as an expressionist, but did not really become acquainted with Whitman until his middle years. Forced into exile to Latin America, Arendt was introduced to Whitman by some of his Latin American friends, especially Pablo Neruda (whose works Arendt translated into German in a prize-winning translation). With this "Latin" Whitman as a foundation, Arendt's poetic instincts and care made for a very readable translation, with only a few infusions of the rhetoric of "socialist realism" or of the expressionist rhetorical traditions from earlier German Whitman translations.

More than any other translator, Arendt employs contemporary, colloquial German, taking particular care to avoid archaisms. The line from section 24 of "Song of Myself," which was earlier used in a comparison, is once more very instructive: "*Translucent mould* of me it shall be you!" In Knortz and Rolleston, this is rendered by "durchsichtige Gestalt" (transparent shape) and in Schlaf by the highly suggestive "lichte Gestalt" (light/luminous shape, *LG*, 59), while Reisiger translates it as "durchsichtige Form" (transparent form, HR2, 45) and Arendt as "klare Gestalt" (clear shape).[4] "Transparent" is not equivalent to "translucent," and "luminous" is one of Schlaf's great translations which appealed to the *Pathos* of the expressionists but was hardly appropriate to the soberness which characterized post–World War II German language. Arendt's "clear," however, is simple and still suggestive.

The GDR translation appeared in a fine volume and the poetry section was later reprinted in a mass-market edition. The East Germans kept up their interest in Whitman. In 1985, Eva Manske, an Americanist at the University of Leipzig who initiated pioneering editions of many American writers in her country, edited the first complete edition of *Specimen Days* in a translation by Götz Burghardt with an interesting and inspiring commentary,[5] different from the usual critical discourse in the GDR and foreshadowing the ideological changes in the country that were to develop four years later.

GEORG GOYERT

Given the scarcity of material resources in 1948, Georg Goyert's smaller Whitman edition is surprising, in terms of both the fancy paper used and the care given to printing. It is one of the most beautiful books that appeared on the German book market in the depression of the immediate postwar period. In 1947, Goyert had translated Henry Seidel Canby's biography of Whitman.[6] In spite of this close acquaintance with the American poet, there is relatively little congeniality between Whitman and his translator.

Monika Schaper states that "his *Leaves of Grass* are extremely subjective, in diction, selection, and format."[7] Goyert's edition has a much stronger "artistic" character than that of Serelmann-Küchler, but is relatively far removed from Whitman. The arbitrary collages of passages taken out of context are strongly reminiscent of the weak edition by Franz Blei.

MAX GEILINGER

The small edition translated by the Swiss poet Max Geilinger combines selections from Whitman and Vachel Lindsay. It was published in Zurich in 1947.[8] In the preface, Geilinger deals with questions of Whitman's form. Himself a poet, he "defends" Whitman against charges of formlessness; in his own translation, however, he moves away from Whitman by refining and aestheticizing the poetry and giving it a curiously "classical touch."

ELSE AND HANS BESTIAN

Ein Kosmos was published as a part of the bilingual Schwiftinger Lyrikreihe series,[9] which places Whitman in the context of authors such as Rubén Darío, Giorgios Seferis, and the Austrian writer Elfriede Jelinek. It appeals to a leftist readership, feminists, and veterans of the sixties with a sentimental tendency toward Latin cultures and red wine. For the first time, a German edition carries Whitman's famous photograph of the 1855 edition on the cover. Inside, there are nine photographs and photocollages expressing, even more than the Whitman selections, images of America held by many European leftists, such as the electric chair on which miniature figures of Sacco and Vanzetti are seated or a police action against blacks.

The bilingual text of the edition, introduced by a short characterization of the author on the inside cover as a singer of equality, evokes very mixed feelings. On the one hand, the volume contains some of the very best German translations of Whitman to date. Especially in the case of the homoerotic passages, the translations are very precise. More even than in Arendt's translation, the translators Else and Hans Bestian attempt to use a colloquial, idiomatic, contemporary German. The volume shows that there *are* ways to transfer the power of Whitman's poetry into German in a time that is antagonistic to *Pathos*. The way individual poems are abbreviated and pasted together, however, is very disappointing for those who are acquainted with the original texts or other translations. "Song of Myself"—cleverly translated with "Ich singe von mir selbst" (I Sing of Myself), thereby avoiding the awkward German "Gesang," which has more specific musical connotations than the English "Song"—is compressed into three pages, a collage of well-known passages that give the impression of a literary satire. Blei's method of "concentrating" Whitman reaches its absurd peak in this edition.

SUSANNE SCHAUP

The translator of the most recent edition, published in 1987 by a religious publisher, is an Austrian, Susanne Schaup. The choice of poems and the translation are what one would expect given the publisher's ideological background. In Schaup's introduction, there is not one word about Whitman's cultural criticism and nothing on homosexuality or homoeroticism or the problematical personality of Whitman himself. Not burdened with the knowledge of any Whitman criticism, Schaup repeats the old clichés about the American author.

The translation does not live up to the claim made in the introduction that it wants to modernize the diction of Whitman's translations;[10] rather, it reproduces the linguistic conventions and the imagery of the Bible. The word "really" in the line "These are really the thoughts of all men in all ages and lands, they are not original with me" (*LG*, 45) is translated as "wahrlich,"[11] a characteristic biblical term whose English equivalent is "verily." "I Sing the Body Electric" becomes "Ich singe den Leib, den entflammten" (I sing the enflamed body),[12] another example of German biblical rhetoric. A weak, allegorical and didactic, pseudo-"visionary" text from the "Sun-Down Papers" of 1840 is included in the small selection because "it reflects the basic religious convictions of the poet, who had just turned twenty."[13]

In this way, Schaup's edition falls behind Whitman's own level of religious criticism. It forms part of Whitman's reception by special-interest and subcultural groups using Whitman's polysemic texts in naive ways for their own purposes. It also demonstrates that such naive forms of reception—and translation—are possible even after an author's works have become the object of intense intellectual scrutiny.

Whether a united Germany will bring forth new Whitman translations remains to be seen. After the establishment of two German states, many publishers such as Reclam and Insel split off into an eastern and a western section, in effect becoming independent companies in the process. With the emergence of a unified, post–Cold War Germany, literary strategies and publishing policies will have to be rethought and reformulated. Whitman was one of the few American poets to be published and read in both Germanies. However, the *Pathos*-laden German translations of Whitman have become pathetic to the ears of the very nation that has created them. It may well be that future Whitman translations will have to be less "serious" and heavy in tone, more ironical and playful in order to appeal to the contemporary German audience.

CREATIVE RECEPTION

. . . .

CHAPTER TEN

. . . .

WHITMAN IN GERMAN LITERATURE

Since its first introduction to the German-speaking world, *Leaves of Grass* has repeatedly challenged poetic and literary conventions and prompted artists to redefine their artistic conceptions. Freiligrath asked himself, after having encountered Whitman, whether his age had so many and such serious things to say that all aesthetic rules needed to be abandoned. However, his questioning remained purely speculative and had no consequences for his own work or even for his Whitman translation.

Many authors reacted similarly. They acknowledged that Whitman's poetry presented an extraordinary turning point in literary history and became deeply immersed in his work, but their encounter with Whitman produced no noticeable changes in their own writing practice. Other writers, however, found that they *had* to react to Whitman in their own poetry. When the famous German satirist Kurt Tucholsky received a poetry manuscript from Walter Bauer,[1] then a young poet, he replied: "I am much more interested in your intellectual parents than in your professional aspirations. Just so there are no misunderstandings: this does not change anything, not in the least, about the value of your poems. Their rhymelessness is almost a matter of course . . . and one just cannot avoid Whitman."[2]

One could not avoid Whitman. Oskar Loerke, poet and reader for the Fischer publishing house, wrote in 1919, after having read Whitman in Reisiger's translation: "After we have heard whole choirs of poets technically and intellectually dependent on Whitman in recent times, we are shocked over the truth [of his poetry] when reconfronted with the original. It is obvious that the mere appearance and presence of this sun had to turn generations of quiet singers of private nature and sentimental devotion into epigones."[3] In writing such a passage,

Loerke, a careful observer of the German literary marketplace, was not exactly complimentary to his fellow writers. The ironical observation that traditional German poetry suddenly attempted to reform itself through a wholesale adoption of Whitman is bitter; yet Loerke did not close his eyes on the important role Whitman played in German literature: "[In speaking of Whitman, we have to take into consideration] the enormous extent of his literary influence, both creative and destructive. Only an apathetic mind could be left unmoved by the discovery of such a daringly unconventional kind of poetry as Whitman's."[4] Loerke mainly referred to the expressionist poets of his time, but he also stated that "generations" of poets were impressed by Whitman's poetry. Not only the intensity of the Whitman experience was remarkable, but also its duration. For several generations, the acquaintance with Whitman offered German authors a possibility to define or redefine their own poetic standards. Whitman's poetry contained multiple layers that were to be discovered, one after the other.

The following chapters are concerned with the literary reception of Whitman's works, especially with the "creative reception": Whitman's presence in German literature itself. The discussion focuses on the two most important "generations" of creative readers of Whitman: the naturalists, born mostly in the 1860s, who emerged as important writers in the 1880s and early 1890s, and the expressionists, whose representatives were born around 1890 and started publishing sometime after 1910. In focusing on these two groups and on selected authors within these groups, I can best judge the ways in which German-speaking authors creatively reworked Whitman in their own *oeuvre* and the contributions Whitman made to the modernization of German poetry and literature at large. A comparison between the American model and his European followers contributes to an understanding of the specific significance Whitman had for writers in German-speaking countries.

Apart from this focus, cases of creative Whitman reception between and after these two periods are also treated. Whitman's significance for several nationalist poets prominent in the Nazi period are discussed in the section on politics (chapter 17), since his impact on them is more ideological than artistic-creative. For reasons already touched upon above and elaborated in the chapters on politics, Whitman lost his massive creative appeal for German poets after World War II. His personal example and his themes still managed to inspire poets, especially in the GDR, but the pervasive influence we find in the German-speaking countries prior to the Nazi takeover in 1933 had vanished.

CHAPTER ELEVEN

NATURALISM

Prior to the publication of Knortz and Rolleston's translation in 1889, the textual base of translated Whitman poetry was too narrow for Whitman to become a significant inspiration for German-speaking poets. Freiligrath and Strodtmann largely ignored Whitman in their own creative work; it was not until the late 1880s and early 1890s that Whitman could act as catalyst in the first modern (i.e., naturalist) revolution of German literature.

The fact that naturalist writers were so intensely interested in Whitman's poetry may seem rather surprising, especially in view of the messianic and mystical traits of *Leaves.* There are, of course, "mainstream" naturalist features such as urban settings, social problems, and sexually explicit material in Whitman's poetry which could interest these writers. However, in order to understand the naturalist affinity to Whitman, the special character of German naturalism must be taken into account. German naturalism was strongly affected by the subjectivist orientation which had dominated German philosophy and literature since Kant and the German Romantics. As a stable movement focusing on objective external reality, naturalism would not exist for long—subjectivist tendencies would soon modify it significantly.

Together with Gerhart Hauptmann, German literary history credits Johannes Schlaf and Arno Holz with the introduction of "naturalist" literary principles into German literature. Following Emile Zola's definition of a work of art, Holz developed his famous formula: "Art = nature − *x*," *x* being artistic variables such as the artist's ability and the limitations imposed on the artist by "material" such as language or color. In this formula, the role of artists is a negative one: depending on their ability, they can at best hope to *approximate* "nature," but never completely succeed in depicting it. As far as possible, the formula seems to imply, the artistic, subjective temperament must be eliminated.

However, German naturalists—unlike their French counterparts—never took this recipe very seriously. Holz himself soon began to modify it in order to allow room for a more positive definition of artistic creativity. In his polemic against Zola's *roman expérimental*, published in the first volume of the German naturalist journal *Freie Bühne* (later *Neue Rundschau*), he stresses the impossibility of naturalism in its pure form: "An experiment which takes place merely in the experimenter's mind is not an experiment, even if it is written up ten times. At best, it can be the recollection of an actual experiment, but nothing more."[1] From the very start, German naturalism was an ambiguous phenomenon. While the reaction against traditional (neo)classicist forms which precluded an "objective" artistic presentation of reality was strong, the actual flirtation with a nonsubjective art was very short-lived.

The attempt at *total* exclusion of subjectivity always implied the opposite possibility of the elimination of "reality" altogether. The self-inflicted elimination of the perceiving subject, its surrender to the external world, enabled the other extreme—a radical, boundless subjectivism. The naturalistic self, meticulously registering external reality second by second, underwent a process of disassociation and disintegration. It changed into the monistic self of impressionism, which was contained in all the things that were formerly the objects of perception. This is a further step in the "reduction" of "layers" of human consciousness (*Bewußtseinslagen*) which had started with the individual's emergence from the hierarchical medieval order and led to the secularized and materialistic modes of perception in the nineteenth century.[2]

To the naturalist writers themselves, this process appeared to be a consistent, albeit sometimes painful and mystifying development. Even long after he had long lost himself in his Whitmanesque and anything but naturalistic *Phantasus* epic, Holz still continued to refer to himself as a naturalist. As late as 1912, Schlaf celebrated the "neo-religious completion of the naturalist principle" with "Whitman and Emile Verhaeren as signposts."[3]

Whitman played an interesting role in this development, as the naturalists took a great interest in his poetry. In 1885, even before Knortz and Rolleston's translation, an early naturalist's anthology of English and American literature included selected Whitman poems in Freiligrath's and Hopp's translations.[4] After Whitman became prominent, there was a heated debate over the question of who had initially "discovered" him. This debate, though fairly ridiculous in itself, is proof of the American poet's importance for the whole movement.

Schlaf's attempt to set himself up as the supreme Whitman apostle in Germany was challenged by Arno Holz, formerly his friend and his collaborator. He claimed that Schlaf's "Whitman bally-hoo had not even grown in his own backyard but came, just like most everything else about which he is now bragging, from me. To me he owes not only his *enthusiasm* for Whitman . . . but also his . . . *entire 'knowledge'* about him!"[5]

Holz's assertion that he himself "discovered" Whitman for the naturalists was in turn contradicted by Gerhart Hauptmann, who claimed this achievement for himself.[6] In his autobiography, published in 1937, he describes Whitman's influence on a host of naturalist emigrés assembled in Zurich in the late 1880s. In addition to Gerhart and his brother Carl, this group included Peter Hille, Karl Henckell, John Henry Mackay, Wilhelm Bölsche, and Frank Wedekind, all of whom were acquainted with Whitman and considered him one of their own. Gerhart Hauptmann wrote retrospectively: "Walt Whitman was the author of another poetic work which had made an immense impression on us. In German, it carried the title *Grashalme.* Our enthusiasm has contributed significantly to the success of the book. Through a magnificent translation it has become an essential part of our literature."[7] In spite of Hauptmann's life-long interest in Whitman, his increasing preoccupation with drama distracted him from a continued creative commitment to the American poet. In Schlaf's and Holz's works, however, Whitman retained a strong presence, despite the latter's disavowal of any such influence.

JOHANNES SCHLAF (1862 – 1941)

Johannes Schlaf is one of the central figures in the German reception of Whitman. In the first section of this study, I have discussed his significant translation of Whitman's poetry. In this section, I am concerned with his creative reception of Whitman, which in turn explains the messianic fervor of his translation. Although Johannes Schlaf is well known to literary historians and students taking survey courses of German literature, most German readers today are no longer acquainted with his creative works. His significance in German literary history is recognized, but he is no longer present on the German book market. His reception was blocked for a number of reasons, most importantly because of his ignorant support for the Nazis late in his life. His by then confused mind hardly understood the nature of Hitler and the Nazis and, in spite of his unfortunate signature under an authors' declaration of loyalty for Hitler, his works did not receive any support during the Third Reich because they hardly fit Nazi ideological requirements. Schlaf is really much more than a pioneer among naturalists—and his significance to a large extent is based on his acquaintance with Whitman's works.[8]

In 1900, Amalie von Ende wrote about Schlaf in the American journal the *Critic*:

> . . . Johannes Schlaf is the master of free rhythm and of the prose poem, forms that lend themselves gracefully to his philosophical fancies; for however beautiful may be his little impressionistic *Stimmung*-pictures of nature, his delicately spiritual love-songs, he is most original when he sings the mysterious attraction of atoms, the growth of the cell, the chaotic fermentation that sets cosmic nebulae awhirl, all the forces of mind and matter that rule the motion of the orbs and control the impulses of the brain and quicken the beat of the heart; or when, like a true poet of the universe, he proclaims the eternal unity of man and nature, seeing in the principle of evolution the salvation of mankind.[9]

To von Ende, Schlaf's affinity to Whitman is obvious:

> There is something Whitmanesque in spirit and form about the dithyrambic effusions of the German poet-scholar, who found a brother-soul in the self-taught American poet-seer.[10] For, even without knowing that he has written one of the best essays about Whitman that the Whitman-cult in Germany has produced,[11] one readily recognizes, in his latest volume of verse, that he has caught the ring and the swing of the lines that echoed through the brain of the "good gray poet," as he tramped through the streets of his beloved Mannahatta. Johannes Schlaf represents a most artistic fusion of the Teutonic Faust-spirit with that incarnation of American activity, energy, and health typified in Whitman.[12]

Von Ende, we can tell from these passages, belongs to the cult herself, but many of her claims are indeed borne out by an analytic comparison between the two poets.

Schlaf's departure from naturalism, already discussed in connection with his translation, is documented not only in his letters and statements but also in the development of his creative works, which was significantly influenced by his discovery of Whitman. The skeptical first-person narrator of the prose collection *In Dingsda* (1892) is a man who, after a prolonged absence, returns to his small hometown that has preserved its earlier rural quality and there experiences a mystical awakening in nature:

> And my eyes widen and my nostrils expand and breathe in the air, and I feel as though I want to take all of this into me with every fiber of my being, all of this light, singing, wide, magnificent world!
>
> And I stammer strange, insane-blissful words that I do not hear. It is as though something flows out of my soul, overflowing life and energy. And everything is far below me, far below in the sun. . . . And I lie there as though in a daze, and stare into the short grass, not daring to look left or right. . . . [13]

In Dingsda appeared in the same year as Schlaf's obituary for Whitman; he probably wrote these lines with a knowledge of Whitman even though they were not yet "Whitmanesque" in "the ring and the swing" as von Ende put it. What is important is that these lines were programmatic for his new, postnaturalist poetics: "No intelligent, cold observation: give up yourself, dissolve with your feelings in life, rather, become life itself. . . . To be fully yourself and yet be rid of your own self, this is the *Pathos* with which the world shakes us up and soothes us as though with a religious shudder." [14] Clearly, we can see here the naturalist turning subjective, "impressionist," and yet more: there is an attempt at the preservation of the "self" in the very process of its dissolution. This is a productive contradiction fueling the development toward a modernization of the self in the poetry around the turn of the century, reflecting the general crisis of the self that would become one of the key *topoi* of twentieth-century literature.

What was announced in *In Dingsda* continued in one of Schlaf's most significant works, *Frühling* (Spring). First published in 1894, it received much critical attention and praise in its time. The influential literary historian Albert Soergel called it "unspeakably blissful poetry" and one of the "most beautiful works of art of our present time." [15] Elsewhere, it was called "one of the most delicious fruits which our lyrical prose has given us." [16]

Frühling is a miniature version of *Leaves* in which the longest piece, also entitled "Frühling," corresponds to "Song of Myself." A second longer piece, "Zwielicht" (Twilight), and twelve shorter pieces which take up many of the themes in "Frühling" complete this seventy-page volume.

The parallels between "Frühling" and "Song of Myself" are striking. In the course of one long afternoon, the lyrical persona (whose sex is not clearly identified but who is probably male) investigates the relationship between self, soul, and universe. Just as in "Song of Myself," a number of metamorphoses of identity occur, leading to a union of self and world. Moreover, there are characteristic and, for interpretive purposes, relevant differences.

The point of departure is once more the self in open nature. Grass functions as a central symbol and, in the whole work, almost as *leitmotif*: "And then I lie in the high grass, in the bright sun, hands under my neck, whistling, and I reflect the blue sky and the milk-white spring clouds."[17] A bit later, the persona is already "totally immersed . . . in young, fragrant green" (*F*, 4).[18] This mystical immersion is also expressed in the position of the body: "Deeper the head into the grass" (*F*, 6).[19] Schlaf's persona now is ready for his voyage: "Here I lie, stretching myself, a loafer and malingerer of the worst kind" (*F*, 29).[20] The parallels to Whitman's "Song of Myself" are obvious.

Like Whitman in the famous section 5 of "Song of Myself ("I believe in you my soul . . ."), Schlaf's persona starts addressing his soul as if it were his lover:

> My head lies on your chest.
>
> And you, golden, light, young, are leaning over me.
>
> With a gentle hand you are trickling heliotrope on my forehead. I breathe its sweet fragrance and your breath, which is sweeter yet.
>
> My face feels your heartbeat, your quiet, quiet heartbeat.
>
> And eye in eye, ever deeper, ever more immersed.
>
> Quiet, quietly, you bend quietly down to me and quiet, quietly, I come upward to you. You smile, leaning your head backward, and your hands press weakly against my chest with roguish urge.
>
> And now: lips to lips. For a long time . . . between half-closed eyelids your look darkens. And nothing but your splendor and a sweet warmth from you to me.
>
> Peace. And from it, energy, ideas, resolutions, brighter, ever brighter, keener and keener, and recognitions. . . . (*F*, 23)[21]

In spite of Schlaf's greater loquaciousness, he creates a picture very similar to that in Whitman's section 5 of "Song of Myself." Technically, the passage also shows how Schlaf gets closer to Whitman's long lines.

Schlaf's lyrical persona is erotically tied to his soul and, through his soul, to the world around him:

> With every beat of the pulse, with every trembling of my body, with every movement, I caress the wide and happy world. And I am caressed by the beetles, the flowers and trees with humming and blossoms and leaves, with colors and odors and a hundred gentle touches. The quiet wind through leaves and branches caresses me. . . . Cool, surging, clinging caresses. (*F*, 4)[22]

The physiological presentation of the "beat" of the pulse and of the "trembling" body, its direct and immediate physical representation, goes far beyond the conventions of traditional German nature poetry. This revolution, inspired by Whitman, radically reverses a traditional illustrative topos. Eros no longer dissolves in nature imagery; rather, nature is decoded in erotic metaphors. There are dozens of passages in *Leaves of Grass* where Schlaf could have found examples for such erotic relationships with nature. One characteristic example, although far more explicit, in "Song of Myself" is: "Winds whose soft-tickling genitals rub against me it shall be you!" (*LG*, 53). The difference is that while sexuality remains a metaphorical vehicle for Schlaf, Whitman directly refers to the body itself: "If I worship one thing more than another it shall be the spread of my own body, or any part of it . . ." (*LG*, 53). The American is serious about the deification not just of his soul, but also of his body.

Settled down in the midst of nature in a mystical pose, Schlaf's persona now starts a very Whitmanesque activity: to assume the identity of other creatures. First he becomes "Braak-Klaas," an old man and a characteristic north German local-color figure, then a child, finally an insect. Every time, the persona actually seems to become that creature, as, for example, in the case of the animal:

> Now through my desirous divining senses I become smaller and still smaller, and now I am miniscule, very, very small. I have a golden-green little skirt on a round, firm, flexible little body, I trot with six little legs and have two small eyes like red rubies. . . . (*F*, 6f.)[23]

Just as in Whitman's "Song of Myself," Schlaf's persona manages to project itself into other creatures, thus proving and experiencing the identity of self and world. The difference is quantitative: what takes many pages in Whitman's catalogues is only a few lines long in Schlaf's *Frühling*.

The mutations—old man, child, and animal—represent different stages and qualities of life. Subsequently, Schlaf's persona attempts to break down the "thin, thin wall between us and a newly expanded world of new miracles" (*F*, 18), thereby becoming increasingly universal. Finally, he wants to identify with all human sufferings and joys throughout history, coming extremely close to Whitman's diction and tone:

> I share in all vices and virtues. I have suffered with Christ, the Lord, through his night of suffering in Gethsemane, and have recognized the innermost secret of the world with Buddha. I am sexless, am man and woman. I am innocent and naive like the purest of children, and experienced like the most blasé roué! I am emperor and hero and the lowest of slaves, the most nimble, most dangerous, and most foolish, simple-minded lover. I am and I have what I want. (*F*, 29f.)[24]

This passage concentrates many dimensions (and lines) of Whitman in one paragraph, especially the incorporation, and thereby dissolution, of good and evil in one person. In "Song of Myself," Whitman's persona proudly proclaims:

> I am not the poet of goodness only, I do not decline to be the poet of
>   wickedness also.
>
> What blurt is this about virtue and about vice?
>
> (*LG*, 50)

The theme of sharing other persons' suffering is very prominent in Whitman's poetry, most notably in section 33 of "Song of Myself":

> I am the man, I suffer'd, I was there. . . .
>
> I am the hounded slave, I wince at the bite of the dogs. . . .
>
> I do not ask the wounded person how he feels, I myself become the
>   wounded person . . .
>
> (*LG*, 66f.)

Schlaf's passage quoted above also modifies the significance of religion in Whitmanesque ways. If the persona has indeed been with Christ and Buddha, he is on the same level with them and does not have to recognize them as authorities. There are several poems in *Leaves* and several sections in "Song" expressing limitations of the validity of traditional religious teachings.

The presentation of parallels necessitates an analysis of the differences between the two writers. One of the most obvious intertextual similarities, almost certainly a controlled allusion, is a good starting point:

> Afar, red, warm little lights glow narrowly between broad black treetops.
>
> And under this wide golden splendor I wander with quick feet through the white fog to the lights, to the poor, glowing, secret lights.
>
> To you, ma Dame! To you! . . . (*F*, 31)[25]

Those acquainted with *Leaves* immediately recall passages in Whitman's works where "Democracy" is personified as "ma femme." For example in section 12 of "Starting from Paumanok":

> Democracy! near at hand to you a throat is now inflating itself and joyfully
>   singing.
>
> Ma femme! for the brood beyond us and of us . . .
>
> (*LG*, 22)

The poem "For You O Democracy" refers to the "love of comrades":

> For you these from me, O Democracy, to serve you ma femme!
> For you, for you I am trilling these songs.
> (*LG*, 117)

The first obvious difference is that between "femme" and "Dame." Whitman refers to the woman in her sexual role, Schlaf to a person with social status and rank. Moreover, Schlaf's personification does not refer to a specific principle such as Whitman's "Democracy," but remains indefinite. The comparison of the two works in their entirety shows that sociopolitical themes are not very important for Schlaf, as they are for Whitman.[26] There is only one passage in *Frühling* where the social sphere is specifically addressed. In section 15, the persona finds herself in "another [imaginary] world":

> The sun here shines brighter and the shadows are more hidden. . . . Tall, beautiful people have come together here, like brothers and sisters, each of them a king, in freedom and in a state of blissful happiness far removed from the world. (*F*, 20f.)[27]

Even this utopian passage hardly represents a hymn to the democratic principle as we find it in Whitman. Rather, the visionary egalitarian society lives "in a state of blissful happiness *far removed* from the world"—denying, therefore, the possibility of actual social emancipation. Schlaf's cosmos does not reach out to society but limits itself to nature, which is confronted with the subjective yearnings of his self.

Whitman's *Leaves* emphasize the social aspect of human life much more strongly and do not exclude the political dimension. By "political" I do not mean party politics but a universal yet political egalitarianism characterizing both the poetry itself and its function. In its uniformity, Whitman's grass symbolizes egalitarian American society. When Whitman concentrates on one individual leaf, he does so in order to suggest its exemplary simplicity. Schlaf's persona contemplates not grass but reed, where "one leaf is folded around another and one hull around the other and so on into eternity" (*F*, 9).[28] Here it is the structure of the leaf that matters; it functions as a hierarchical rather than an egalitarian symbol.

Whitman's *Leaves* projects a social utopia pressing for radical equalization of society. This egalitarian process is facilitated not so much by rational thought as by the senses, especially the tactile sense. The erotic relationship between observer and environment permits a union between subject and object not on an intellectual but on a very "low," sensual level. Schlaf, however, hardly as naive as sometimes suspected, reads Whitman from the position of philosophical monism. Monistic thinking does not recognize a difference between individuals, and the self is only an expression of a pan-material and pan-psychical world. According to Schlaf's judgment, Whitman represents a philosophy and a new way of feeling based on an ethical-religious foundation.[29] In Schlaf, then, Whitman's democratizing impetus is missing. And Schlaf's sexual-physical dimension is hardly as strong and pervasive as Whitman's. The German's "new man," his "new being," is furnished with a new epistemology but does not exist in a politically and socially changed society. Schlaf has a program for a "new man," but not for a new society.

This becomes even more obvious in Schlaf's equally forgotten but most noteworthy novels that appeared at the turn of the century. Dr. Liesegang, for example, the protagonist of the novel *Das dritte Reich*, speculates that "new developments in the human nervous system" will lead to a new "physis" and therefore to "new citizens in an emerging new secret empire."[30] He asks himself the significant question:

> Is Whitman correct with his jubilant verses:
>
> 'Nature and Man shall be disjoin'd and diffused no more,
> The true son of God shall absolutely fuse them.
> Year at whose wide-flung door I sing!
> Year of the purpose accomplish'd!'[31]

And he recognizes, completely overwhelmed by a view of modern Berlin, "as in an inner vision . . . the completed power of the human spirit over the entire globe."[32] "The millennium was here!"[33]

The role Whitman plays in the construction of Schlaf's novels is illuminating. The most important and most innovative feature of these novels is that they combine naturalist literary *topoi* such as urbanization, technologization, and loss of individuality in modern mass society with the development of "modern" consciousness. Long before the theoretical speculations of cultural psychologists and literary critics, Schlaf treats this nexus in a novelistic context.

Somewhat in the tradition of the *Bildungsroman*, these novels present the development of young men who, usually after a socialist phase, attempt to interpret their lives and environment with Darwin, Nietzsche, and especially Whitman. The novels link the intellectual learning process of his protagonists with their personal and emotional development. This often manifests itself in tedious philosophical discussions that might have been responsible for some of the negative reactions on the part of the critics.

Yet, though the wordiness in parts of these novels may be tiring, the protagonists are extraordinarily interesting. In his preface to *Peter Boies Freite* (Peter Boie's

Courtship, 1903), which forms a trilogy with *Das dritte Reich* (The Third Kingdom, 1900) and *Die Suchenden* (The Seekers, 1902), Schlaf states that he wants to present a "psychology of our generation."[34] He wants to demonstrate the "cultural transition" to a new type of human being: " . . . an emerging type of new being, attempting to liberate himself from the atavistic influences in early youth and from the skeptical materialism of his later development, to reach a new, modern holistic world view" (*PB*, 9).[35]

In his preface, the author identifies himself closely with his protagonist, Peter Boie: "Possibly it is one of its [the trilogy's] merits, and probably not the least of them, that it traces the emergence and development of the type of human being produced by this new generation and that it follows this development up to a positive result which is perhaps not unpleasant" (*PB*, 11).[36] What exactly does this "not unpleasant" result (i.e., the "new being") look like? First of all, its psyche and its nervous system are highly unstable. When reading these novels, it first seems as though Schlaf is totally unable to draw coherent human characters. His protagonists swing back and forth between different moods, lovers, and places. It eventually becomes clear that this is not a weakness of characterization, however, but a specific quality of this "new being."

Peter Boie, himself an example of this "positive" result of the process of modernization, is a very disagreeable character, even by our standards some ninety years later. This judgment, however, is a result of our underlying traditional, humanistic concept of personality. Peter Boie, a highly nervous individual not unlike characters in the novels of the French *décadence*, for example by J. K. Huysmans,[37] follows the traditional model of the *Bildungsroman* only superficially. Actually, Boie is continuously seeking new impressions, new sensations, aimlessly traveling around the continent.

Only by taking into account the theme of the nervous system, which plays such an important role in the book, are we able to understand and appreciate Boie's erratic character. At several points in the novel, the protagonist believes he has had a basic insight, has understood one of the fundamental laws of his world, or has met a person decisive for his future life. The reader is led to believe in the possibility of a coherent end to the story, but soon a new surprising turn changes the situation completely and disrupts the reader's expectation of the harmonious development of the protagonist's personality.

After a seemingly positive sexual experience with his girlfriend, Peter's state of mind is described with Whitman's words, "The universe is duly in order, every thing is in its place" (*PB*, 288; *LG*, 432). The very next morning, he already feels quite differently: "Again, his emotion for her [his girlfriend] was in that moment completely dead" (*PB*, 292).[38] Boie reacts with the flightiness and instability of

Jean Des Esseintes in Huysmans's *A rebours*.[39] Boie, too, lives in "moods," with associative (logically inconclusive) "connections of ideas . . . not in any way controlled by consciousness" (*PB*, 223).

The programmatic formula for this new humanity is defined at the end of the book. It sounds like a summary of the essence of Schlaf's trilogy: "Ah, what now? We are all lonely. Each of us represents a world of our own. Everything else, how one meets and is repelled by one another, all of these touches and 'holy bonds,' 'faithfulness,' love, etc. etc.: chaos, accidents finally, chaos, chaos! . . ." (*PB*, 332f.).[40] All of this is not said with regret, but is designed to express a human "ethos" adapted to modern existence. Schlaf describes Peter Boie in his preface: "He is modern, without scruples and doubts. He is a thinking person, philosophizing and reflecting at times like a true German: but he is not worried about things any longer. He fits into the world as it is today" (*PB*, 14).[41]

Peter is no longer worried about traditional philosophical categories of morality. A philosophy of life according to which a "new feeling," the increased activity and sensitivity of the nervous system, is everything and where the traditional ideal of the "harmonious personality" effectively dissolves fits the awkward character of Schlaf's protagonists. Relationships are reduced to magnetic processes of attraction and repulsion and take place on the tactile level, the most important level of human communication for both Schlaf and Whitman.[42]

What is remarkable in Schlaf's novels is the way he "deconstructs" traditional relational ethics and rules of human communication. In *Die Suchenden*, the triangular relationship of Falke (a physician), Falke's wife, and Falke's lover is based, according to Schlaf's own words in the preface, on "complete mutual openness and mutual trust" (*PB*, 13). Schlaf defends his "experiment" against philistine attacks by critics: " . . . incidentally, one can never know what new and useful consequences such unusual *ethical experiments* [emphasis added] may have, also in other situations! Humans of tomorrow will no longer be those of today; the ethics of the society of tomorrow will no longer be the ethics of the society of today" (*PB*, 13f.).[43]

In 1902, such radical openness and insight is surprising in a German author with a relatively traditional background. A new look at his works and his biography shows that he frequently attempted to break literary ground for a "modernity" that was elsewhere condemned as "decadent." It is Schlaf's achievement to have recognized the modern quality of decadent literature, its potential as a testing ground for an expanded consciousness. Schlaf followed up Whitman's song of the "modern man" with novelistic models of such new humans. In these creations, characteristics of the *décadent* are reinterpreted as "progressive" and modern in human development. Schlaf thus develops in his remarkable prose some of Whitman's most important motifs.[44]

Whitman also appears *explicitly* in a number of Schlaf's novels, primarily through quotations from *Leaves*, through Schlaf's Whitmanesque female characters, and through his image of America. According to several protagonists in Schlaf's novels, a new human race is emerging in the New World.[45] Indeed, truly "modern" life first manifests itself in the society of the United States in large part because of its advanced technological-commercial development and the international mix of its people. (One can see why Schlaf's novels were not particularly inspiring to or useful for the Nazis.) Whitman's emphasis that he is "One of the Nation of many nations" (*LG*, 44) fell on fertile ground in Schlaf's novels.

Whitman quotations are an integral part of Schlaf's turn-of-the-century novels. They serve to demonstrate the validity of the modern world view Schlaf's protagonists are developing. Boie is described as an individual who at times enjoys "a comprehensive synthetic overview," a "vista over humankind almost like Christ or Buddha had in former times or like Whitman in our modern time" (*PB*, 94). Such a vista is characterized by "a lack of respect and prejudice which resulted in the liberal openmindedness of our modern time, in modern tolerance and human brotherhood. The lack of love for one's own country alongside with the desire to roam through all countries, continents, [to visit] all peoples and nations, [all of this] has become so productive culturally . . ." (*PB*, 98). This kind of "modern" personality must become the "normal type in the modern civil culture" (*PB*, 98).[46]

To characterize this modern man, Schlaf has Boie read and comment on Whitman. Boie is frequently seen using a Whitman passage as a starting point for reflections on his own life. In the middle of the novel, he quotes from "Song of Myself" (still in Knortz's translation):

> "I think I could turn and live with animals. . . .
> Not one is respectable or unhappy over the whole earth." . . .
> Peter Boie read Walt Whitman's "Song of Myself." . . . Peter liked what he read about the animals. (*PB*, 159f.)

When Boie embraces these words from "Song of Myself," their explosive force becomes truly apparent. For Boie, Whitman's lines do not simply advocate a retreat to a pastoral rural existence; the point is to live *with* the animals and *among* them, to be *like* them, because they do not worry about moral considerations or metaphysical speculations.

In spite of this modernist tendency toward regression, Boie does not become a Whitman-type democrat. One of Boie's favorite poems by Whitman is "I Hear It Was Charged against Me":

> 'I hear it was charged against me that I sought to destroy institutions,
> But really I am neither for nor against institutions,
> (What indeed have I in common with them? or what with the destruction of them?)
> Only I will establish in the Mannahatta and in every city of these States inland and seaboard,
> And in the fields and woods, and above every keel little or large that dents the water,
> Without edifices or rules or trustees or any argument,
> The institution of the dear love of comrades.'
>
> The institution of the new elite!—The institution of power and peace, with the simplest, all-natural perception!—The new empire, the new home of the emerging elite! (*PB*, 248f.)[47]

Whitman criticism has variously interpreted the "dear love of comrades" as homosexuality (especially in the context of the "Calamus" poetry) or as ideal democracy (in more conventional criticism). Boie's interpretation of this "institution" as the "new elite" is unusual and reminiscent of Nietzsche. It completely contradicts Whitman's democratic spirit. The reader is encouraged not to take Boie's mood too seriously because it can change at any moment (and does). But as a momentary glimpse of a modern character, the strange perspective on this poem is revealing: the Whitman of Schlaf's novels, as this example shows once more, is not the democratic Whitman with all his *Pathos* (the way the expressionists would read him later on); it is a Whitman for ultranervous, elitist "new human beings."

Schlaf's Whitmanesque women also demonstrate the affinity of the two poets. Female emancipation was a favorite topic of discussion in German bourgeois circles in the 1880s and 1890s and the topic takes up much space in Schlaf's works in general. The texts by this confirmed bachelor contain remarkably emancipated and self-confident women. They are independent and refuse to fulfill the expectations of their male-dominated families and friends.

The emancipatory tendency of Schlaf's women alone, however, would not establish a Whitmanesque influence; it is their specific literary presentation that creates a nexus. The emancipation of Whitman's women occurs mainly on the sexual and physical level:

> A woman waits for me, she contains all, nothing is lacking,
>
> . . . .
>
> Without shame the man I like knows and avows the deliciousness of his sex,
> Without shame the woman I like knows and avows hers.
>
> . . . .
>
> They are not one jot less than I am,
> They are tann'd in the face by shining suns and blowing winds,
> Their flesh has the old divine suppleness and strength,
> They know how to swim, row, ride, wrestle, shoot, run, strike, retreat, advance, resist, defend themselves,
> They are ultimate in their own right—they are calm, clear, well-possess'd of themselves.
> (*LG*, 102f.)

Such passages are the literary origin of Peter Boie's girlfriend Geesche, a self-confident, athletic child of nature, who feels equal to Peter and who tells him so. In a bathing scene, she reminds us distinctly of Whitman's women:

> She was slender and white like ivory. Strong and round was her shining neck, its whiteness still more shining because of the darkness of the loose hair. Her healthy chest was strongly curved and fleshy. Slender yet strong, the deliciously rounded flanks and the slender legs came down from the hips with beautifully shaped thighs and strong, bold calves. (*PB*, 271)[48]

Her physical character, referred to as the "blessings of a whole new gospel" (*PB*, 275), is described in detail in ways clearly reminiscent of "I Sing the Body Electric":

> From her breasts down to the flanks, over the white stomach and hips and thighs, small pearls of water ran down in zigzag lines in short, rocking thrusts.—On the white, fleshy chest. . . . From the dark red-blonde flood of hair. . . . And ever clearer and whiter the delicious white skin emerged, with its pure healthy shimmer not clouded by the least spot or the smallest impurity. (*PB*, 275f.)[49]

Although there is no exact textual correspondence, the sensual catalogue clearly derives from Whitman, especially since this section of the novel contains quite a few Whitman quotations. The physical qualities of Schlaf's women allude to passages in "I Sing the Body Electric":

> Poise on the hips, leaping, reclining, embracing, arm-curving and
>   tightening,
> The continual changes of the flex of the mouth, and around the eyes,
> The skin, the sunburnt shade, freckles, hair,
> The curious sympathy one feels when feeling with the hand the naked
>   meat of the body,
> The circling rivers the breath, and breathing it in and out,
> The beauty of the waist, and thence of the hips, and thence downward
>   toward the knees,
> The thin red jellies within you or within me, the bones and the marrow in
>   the bones . . .
>
> (*LG*, 101)

Whereas Schlaf responded only hesitantly to Whitman's sexual imagery in *Frühling,* he became much more "physical" in his novels, especially in the trilogy of 1900–1903. As a sexual partner, the woman is emancipated. In her naked state, she is at last equal. Human beings are identical with their physical nature. As the quotation from the preface of *Peter Boie* shows, Schlaf was ready to experiment with sexuality as an "ethics of the society of tomorrow." True and genuine human interaction takes place only on the level of sexual contact. This was a very Whitmanesque strategy; in his presentation of Peter Boie, Schlaf probably approached Whitman more closely than in any of his other works.

Schlaf's novels are remarkable because of their unconditional acceptance of the "modernity" of human existence, even though this modern state was characterized by a lack of communication and the reduction of all human interaction to sexuality. The disintegration of the self is not viewed negatively, as a crisis of the individual, but suggests positive and exciting future developments for the human race. This is a rare attitude in German literature, with its strong orientation toward traditional humanism, and the fact that it was inspired by Whitman underscores the importance of his creative example. At the same time, Schlaf's novels express strong hostility toward modern *society.* Unlike Whitman, Schlaf rejects the emergence of a mass society. Although individual characters can become very enthusiastic about the panorama of a city presenting itself as a "large collective body," Schlaf's novels mostly contain a negative message regarding the "modern" organization of society. In his works, the vision of a "modern being" parallels Whitman's, but there is no equivalent to Whitman's vision of a modern society.

ARNO HOLZ (1863 – 1929)

The second important naturalist author writing in the Whitman tradition was Arno Holz. His example is different because he denied having anything to do with Whitman's poetry; in fact, in later years, he denied ever even having been very interested in Whitman. Reception documents, however, suggest otherwise. In 1890, one year after the publication of Knortz and Rolleston's translation, Holz wrote to his friend Emil Richter after negatively critiquing a series of newly published German books: "But you have to buy Walt Withmann's [*sic*] 'Leaves of Grass' (Schabelitz, 2 Mk.), that is a book!!!"[50] Three exclamation marks, no less. In fact, Holz was so interested in Whitman that he went to the trouble of procuring four additional items relating to the American poet: a French article by Thérèse Bentzon from 1872,[51] Freiligrath's essay, the printed version of Rolleston's Dresden lecture, and Knortz's article on Whitman in the German-language *New Yorker Staatszeitung* of December 1882.[52] Yet later he claimed that Whitman interested him only as a human being, not as an artist.[53]

One of the reasons for such an obstinate denial was his infuriation with critics who constantly compared his work to Whitman's. Throughout his life, Holz battled bitterly against what he considered a conspiracy against his person, and the "charge" that his work was related to Whitman's played an important role in these fights. However, critics in our time, even without mentioning Whitman, still characterize his work in Whitmanesque terms. Gerhard Schulz, author of an interesting monograph on Holz, describes his life's work, the *Phantasus*, which "has swelled up over almost forty years from a modest cycle of poems in *Buch der Zeit* to a three-volume *oeuvre*, in which a world is designed which only turns around the axis of the author's self."[54] This description could easily serve to describe *Leaves*, and Holz had to be aware of these similarities.

Like Whitman, Holz attempted to create a highly subjective world in a large, ever-growing book. The early naturalists Julius and Heinrich Hart already wrote "global" poetry, and Julius Hart's "global self" ("Welt-Ich," literally, World-I) in *Der neue Gott* (The New God) is reminiscent of Whitman's persona. The Hart brothers knew Whitman's work; this nexus is interesting and relevant even though the globalization of economy, technology, and politics (not least in importance Germany's development as a colonial power) may have suggested such global themes to any author writing at that time. In Holz's work, however, the parallels are so detailed that we can postulate Whitman's direct involvement, even though they may not be controlled allusions. The growth patterns expressed in the evolution of Holz's work itself and in the many biological metaphors pervading it are characteristically Whitmanesque.

The history of Holz's life's work, *Phantasus*, can be traced back to 1886. As far as his connections to Whitman are concerned, the editions of 1898–1899, containing some one hundred poems, and an oversized edition of 1916, which expanded the 1898 edition in characteristic ways, are relevant.[55] Thematically, later editions did not change much, except for an increasing concern with the physical properties of language.

Phantasus had a special significance in Holz's artistic theory because he wanted to create a work of art "which dispenses with any word-transmitted music existing for its own sake. Formally speaking, it is to be solely carried by a rhythm which lives merely by what it expresses."[56] For Holz, this meant the abolition of "unnatural" poetic means such as rhyme, stanzas, or regular meters by realizing an idealized identity of a word ("what it expresses") with its "form." Holz believed that he was the only poet who managed to carry out this program. Even poets like Whitman did not completely manage to tear themselves away from the "street-organ" character of traditional poetry: "The hidden street-organ which, I maintain, anybody who listens closely can hear in all of our poetry up to the present also rings through the so-called 'free rhythms.' They may claim to be 'free' of whatever they well please, but they are not free of the false *Pathos* emptying words of their original values."[57] True enough: Whitman's *Pathos* had no place in Holz's poetry, especially because the latter injected heavy doses of irony into his work. But Holz also suffered delusions about his own achievement. That a particular word has some sort of idealized "original value" which the poet, or rather Arno Holz alone, could realize in his poetry was the tragic error of his life which led to his almost permanent frustration.

As an example of Whitmanesque lines which repelled him and which supposedly revealed the wide gap between his own work and Whitman's, Holz quoted the American's famous physiological-anatomical passage from "I Sing the Body Electric":

> Head, neck, hair, ears, drop and tympan of the ears,
> Eyes, eye-fringes, iris of the eye, eyebrows, and the waking or sleeping of
> the lids,
> Mouth, tongue, lips, teeth, roof of the mouth, jaws, and the jaw-hinges,
> Nose, nostrils of the nose, and the partition . . .[58]

By quoting this passage and referring to it as characteristic of Whitman, Holz ignored the organic character of large parts of Whitman's poetry, which is of course very much characterized by a congruency of form and content.

Holz's attempts to demonstrate the differences between his own poetry and

Whitman's only prove the cultural differences between the two poets—they do not support Holz's loud claims to independence. Indeed, the differences in form between Holz and Whitman are significant as far as they manifest themselves in printing technique. Holz arranged his lines around an imaginary central axis and concentrated words and word groups in the individual lines. This creates a balanced visual page that is centrally occupied by language instead of Whitman's blank page on which words are cast like filaments, reaching out into space.

Holz claimed that his form could be identical with what it expresses:

Sieben Septillionen Jahre
zählte ich die Meilensteine am Rande der Milchstrasse.

Sie endeten nicht.

Myriaden Aeonen
versank ich in die Wunder eines einzigen Thautröpfchens.

Es erschlossen sich immer neue.

Mein Herz erzitterte!

Selig ins Moos
streckte ich mich und wurde Erde.

Jetzt ranken Brombeeren
über mir,
auf einem sich wiegenden Schlehdornzweig
zwitschert ein Rotkehlchen.

Aus meiner Brust
springt fröhlich ein Quell,
aus meinem Schädel
wachsen Blumen.
(*Ph*, 98)

It is, of course, impossible to prove scientifically the "necessity" of this printing arrangement and the selection of each word and word group, although Holz spent much of his later life trying to develop a mathematical system corresponding to his poetry. If we disregard the difference in printing technique, however, there are striking similarities between the two authors. Holz's lines can easily be converted into Whitmanesque lines, as the following translation of the above text, arranged in Whitman's rather than Holz's manner, proves:

For seven septillion years I counted the milestones bordering the
milky way.
There was no end to them, myriads, aeons.
I sank into the miracles of one single drop of dew.
Ever new ones opened up to me; my heart trembled.
Blissfully I lay down in the moss and became earth.
Now raspberries grow above me,
On a rocking twig of a sloebush a robin chirps.
From my chest, water springs happily forth,
From my skull flowers grow.

This not only sounds very Whitmanesque, but it looks that way, as the following parallel passages from "Song of Myself" prove:

And as to you Corpse I think you are good manure, but that does not
offend me,
I smell the white roses sweet-scented and growing,
I reach to the leafy lips, I reach to the polish'd breasts of melons.

And as to you Life I reckon you are the leavings of many deaths,
(No doubt I have died myself ten thousand times before.) (*LG*, 87)

I bequeath myself to the dirt to grow from the grass I love,
If you want me again look for me under your boot-soles.
(*LG*, 89)

This juxtaposition of passages demonstrates that the similarities between Whitman and Holz are not limited to aspects of form. Holz's theses may have been derived from the monistic philosopher Ernst Haeckel, and there may also be parallels to Nietzsche as critics have discovered, but the poetic processing in this particular form undeniably points in Whitman's direction.

This can also be demonstrated by the characteristically strong, indeed egotistical, self-confidence both authors display in these passages. In Holz's 1916 edition, the identifications of the lyrical persona with historical figures and prehistorical life forms assume the character of a catalogue strongly reminiscent of Whitman. The following passage summarizes the "atmosphere" of the edition of 1916:

Ich werde niemals
untergehn!

Ich kehre fortwährend, bis in alle Ewigkeit, myrionengestal-
tig mich verändernd
immer wieder!

Ich bin schon stets,
und von allem allerersten Uranfang an,
gewesen!

Durch alle Kulturen,
in Glück und Unglück, in Schuld und Sühne,
durch alle Jahrhunderte,
durch alle Länder, durch alle Erdteile,
aus Höhen in Tiefen,
aus Leid in Lust, aus Lust in Leid,
von allen Begierden durchwühlt, von allen Empfindungen durch-
schauert, von allen Leidenschaften durchzittert
als Mann, als Weib, als Kind, als Greis,
immer wieder sterbend, immer wieder geboren werdend,
trieb,
riß und wirbelte mich
mein Fatum![59]

The 1898–1899 edition already contained the following poem:

Sieben Billionen Jahre vor meiner Geburt
war ich eine Schwertlilie.

Meine Wurzeln
saugten sich
in einen Stern.

Auf seinem dunklen Wasser
schwamm
meine blaue Riesenblüte.
(*Ph*, 59)[60]

In a letter dated 25 June 1900, Holz wrote to one of his disciples: "The final secret of the . . . *Phantasus*-composition consists basically in the fact that I constantly split into the most heterogeneous objects and shapes. Just as I have gone through the whole *physical* evolution of my species *prior* to my birth, at least in its main stages, I have gone through its *psychic* development *since* my birth. I was 'everything' and its numerous relicts are colorfully stored inside me."[61] Gerhard Schulz emphasizes that in writing *Phantasus* Holz actually wanted to create a religious book:

> . . . Holz . . . had attempted to demonstrate throughout his *Phantasus* . . . that the self that is changing into everything, that is changing everything into itself,

> is the actual center of the world, from which, when all walls between self and non-self are broken down, a new conception of God may emerge—"God becomes"—a conception difficult to grasp with traditional terms such as "pantheism." Rather, we could call it a kind of "deification of the self," because Holz's Phantasus-self lacks . . . basically any real experience of transcendence. . . .[62]

Splitting the self into the most heterogeneous objects and figures, the creation of a new universe, a new religion, the deification of the self, the lack of transcendence—all of this is reminiscent of Whitman, whose *Leaves* also set out to create a cosmos mediated through the self of the persona created by the author. The identification of the lyrical persona with its real author is also a characteristic moment of the self-centered personalities of both authors.

These are just some of the textual, atmospheric, and philosophical parallels guiding Holz toward his grandiose plan to create a lyrical universe. But the implementation of this plan makes the differences between the European and the American poet very obvious.

The main difference between the two authors lies in their attitudes toward their texts. A newspaper critic offered a very appropriate judgment:

> Namely, it was the Bible that influenced him [Whitman] strongly, and the tone of the psalms rings clearly and unmistakably through his verses. Arno Holz and all the moderns attempting to follow Whitman almost always overlook this important point, which is why they can never fully comprehend this poetry born out of the depth of the spirit.[63]

Holz was unable to adopt Whitman's *Pathos*; his irony immediately subverted and disrupted it so that its "religious" quality became highly unbelievable. The development of Holz's poetry documents the increasing amount of irony entering his *Pathos*. The small fleur-de-lis section of 1899 metastasizes into a monstrous structure, essentially untranslatable, in the "deathbed" edition:

Sieben Billionen . . . Jahre . . . vor meiner Geburt
war ich
eine Schwertlilie.

Meine suchenden Wurzeln
saugten
sich
um einen Stern.

Aus
seinen sich wölbenden
Wassern,
blumenblätternarbig, goldpfeilfädenstäubig,
traumblau,
in
neue,
wallende, werdende, wogende,
brauende, brodelnde,
kreisende
Weltenringe
wuchs,
stieg, stieß,
steilte, teilte, speilte,
verglühte, zerströmte, versprühte
sich,
geheimnisträchtigst, geheimnismächtigst,
geheimnishehrst
sich selbst begattend, sich selbst befruchtend, sich selbst beschattend, sich selbst
zerzeugend,
Flammenkugelmeteore,
Kometenkaskaden, Planetenbuntkränze
verschwenderisch
um sich regnend, verspenderisch um sich segnend,
vergeuderisch
um sich
schwingschleudernd,
meine
dunkel-metallische, halkyonisch-phallische, klingend-kristallische
Riesenblüten-Szepterkrone!

Noch
in mein
schweres Frühauferjachen, in mein Wiedermenschwerden, in mein wieder volles Erwachen
sturzlachte,
sturzjubelte, sturzleuchtete
ihre

Kraftstolzfreude,
ihre Schöpfermutanfeuerung, ihre
Zuversicht![64]

No matter how much the graphic representation of the poem may remind us of a flower, this sort of poetry hardly supports Holz's claim to an "organic" art. The poem is so obsessed with wordplay, language commenting on itself, that any discernible "meaning" disappears.

At the same time, there is a sense of resignation as a result of the author's strong discomfort with his "reality." When reminiscing about his youth, for example, the persona ends with the following sigh:

> O to be young once more! To see the world with new eyes!
> O to be able to do that!
> (*Ph*, 92)[65]

It is hard to imagine such lines in Whitman's poetry. Cosmic poetry? In ways all too superficial and obvious, Holz's poetry treats the experience of alienation thematically rather than sublimating it like Whitman.

There is also a telling difference with regard to the two authors' treatment of sexuality. In Whitman, the whole (lyrical) cosmos is erotically charged, from his human beings to the American landscape and beyond. In Holz's work, by contrast, a certain lecherous quality is obvious. Whitman's omnipresent sexuality is reduced in Holz to male genital desires leading to aggressiveness with unfulfilled frustrations in the background.

Holz, originally a naturalist, had come a long way and, just as in Schlaf's case, Whitman accompanied him for part of it. Schlaf was able to adopt Whitman in his development of an interesting version of impressionism in which human beings with extraordinary sensibilities and nervous systems made their peace with the modern world. Holz, by contrast, attempted a Whitmanesque work integrating all ages and the whole cosmos, but he was obviously too skeptical to carry out his own endeavor successfully. As the comparison with Whitman makes clear, he lacked the sincere *Pathos* necessary for the creation of such a literary cosmos.

All in all, still too much a European skeptic, strongly influenced by the rationalism and scientism of his naturalist beginnings, Holz found it impossible to take his own "Elephantasus," as critics soon called it, seriously. This lack of seriousness is echoed in the lyrical presentation of Whitman in Holz's second important work, *Die Blechschmiede*: "Walt Whitman, Yankee and 'reformer,' / [comes] on a whirling fan."[66] In matters of form, Holz clearly responded to Whitman, although with significant differences, and what eventually became of his *Phantasus*, with all its linguistic, rhythmical, onomatopoetic, and typographical experiments, innovations, and nuances, is remarkable. In this way, Whitman's example proved very productive. Holz's own intention to create a cosmos—as Whitman had wanted to do and had done—had to fail, if only because of the German's temperament. The German expressionist writer Alfred Döblin later noted in Holz, in comparison with Whitman, a lack of American optimism and democratic temperament. In this, the expressionist poets, with much, much more *Pathos* at their disposal, proved to be more successful.

The naturalist movement represented the first revolution in modern German literature. Revolting against the traditional pseudo-classical, neoclassical, late-romantic, and sleepy Biedermeier drawing room forms which had degraded the status of poetry to an elegant occupation of otherwise idle minds, naturalists wanted to reconnect poetry with the "real world." Given the necessity to overthrow traditional and stifling poetic conventions, Whitman, as the most important formal revolutionary of the period, became an obvious model for them. At the very onset of the naturalist period, Whitman also stood at the beginning of German writers' new experimentation with form.

As we have seen in these two paradigmatic case studies, Whitman sped up the development of German literature in several directions. Neither of the two writers discussed here stayed a "pure" naturalist for very long. Whitman's multifaceted lyrical personae suggested to them lyrical possibilities for dealing with the increasing disintegration of the self. Schlaf achieved this through his lyrical prose and through the emotionally unstable, ultranervous characters of his novels; Holz through the linguistic and poetic experiments at the beginning of a modern tradition anticipating later twentieth century poetry.

The findings suggest that German writers looked toward Whitman for help in the definition of problems they had already recognized and that he offered models to implement necessary changes in their writings. That characteristic differences between the American and European authors continued to exist and, after a point of near convergence, widened again is not surprising and points to the continuing differences between European and American literary and intellectual traditions.

CHAPTER TWELVE

BETWEEN NATURALISM AND EXPRESSIONISM

In his novels, Johannes Schlaf indicated the ways Whitman could have inspired those antinaturalist groups representing German equivalents to the French *décadents* and aestheticists as well as authors belonging to other groups or "periods" such as *Jugendstil*, the German version of *art nouveau*, symbolism, or neoromanticism. The aestheticist dimension in Whitman's poetry (which, after all, made possible the appreciation of his work by a Pre-Raphaelite such as William M. Rossetti) has traditionally been disregarded, mostly because of the messianic ideology coming out of Camden and other Whitmanite quarters.

However, his own experimentation with *décadent* elements notwithstanding, Schlaf so insistently proclaimed Whitman as the representative of a healthy, natural, non-"degenerate" literature and art and he himself was so closely tied to the naturalist movement in the view of the German public that the American was almost automatically seen in *opposition* to the various short-lived but highly significant antinaturalist literary movements at the end of the century. Moreover, as we have seen in the discussion of the translations by Federn and Schölermann, critics constructed Whitman as the original "manly" genius against the "effeminate" literature of their day. It is therefore not surprising that many turn-of-the-century authors were not particularly prone to "learn" from Whitman.

Neither Rainer Maria Rilke nor Stefan George, the most important representatives of German symbolism, even mentioned Whitman's name. George, with his own very secretive homoerotic literary circle in Germany, had excellent reasons to avoid Whitman's loud homoeroticism, which he probably also considered vulgar in the extreme. From Stefan George's circle, only one dissident representative,

Max Dauthendey (1867–1918), can be linked to Whitman. The "global" orientation of his poetry, especially *Die geflügelte Erde* (The Winged Earth, 1910) with its conspicuous long lines and its catalogue-type representation of the world, reminded critics strongly of Whitman.

Although one of the most important Austrian writers of the period, Hugo von Hofmannsthal (1874–1929), mentioned Whitman frequently and enthusiastically in his correspondence with his friend Ottonie Degenfeld, Whitman's importance seems to have operated mostly on a personal level: "A few months ago the book by W. Whitman sometimes meant more to me than one might think a book could mean to a person."[1] There are few Whitman traces in his creative work, even though Hofmannsthal himself pointed, somewhat unclearly, to Whitman connections in his drama *Das Salzburger große Welttheater.*[2]

There are other authors, for the main part precursors of expressionism, in whom the significance Whitman would eventually assume for expressionist poetry can already be discerned. The cosmogonic lyrical works by Alfred Mombert (1872–1942) are clearly indebted to Whitman, as is the "global" poetry by the Frankfurt poet Alfons Paquet (1881–1944), who found it easiest to apply Whitmanesque techniques in the literary processing of his world travels.

HERMANN BAHR (1863 – 1934)

These were just experiments, however. The only preexpressionist writer who could see through Whitman's messianic rhetoric and who appreciated Whitman as forerunner of the very literary movements that seemed antithetical to him was Hermann Bahr, an influential Viennese dramatist and cultural critic. Bahr showed a greater willingness to accept Whitman's modernity than most of his colleagues. He started out as a naturalist, but soon "overcame" this phase and emerged as one of the literary leaders of "Young Vienna," a group of antinaturalist Viennese modernists. Always ready to turn a new page in German/Austrian literary history, he was also one of the first critics to welcome the advent of expressionism.[3]

In a review of books by G. B. Shaw and J. V. Jensen, a Danish Whitmanite, in the *Neue Rundschau* in 1908, Bahr ends up focusing on Whitman. The article, entitled "Barbaren" (Barbarians), reflects the important changes in attitude that occurred between Bahr's earlier years and the beginning of the expressionist period. Art seems to have turned away from an emphasis on "culture" and "civilization" and is apparently moving in a refreshingly retrograde direction: "It almost seems as though we are on the way to becoming barbarians. These words have a different meaning for us. The intellectual and moral properties which our parents called culture or civilization have become questionable for us."[4]

With Whitman, Bahr welcomes this cultural revolution. While society and technology develop with great speed and consistency, human consciousness lags sadly behind; "the human hand is faster than the head and heart."[5] According to Bahr, Whitman attempts to establish a new harmony between "hand" and "head"—not, however, through the negation of the world of machines but through the unconditional acceptance of technology. Bahr thus praises Whitman as the poet of the machine age: "If Leonardo, Goethe, were to live in our period, what would they say about the telephone, about being in an automobile or in the air? But if Goethe wanted to become acquainted with the works of the poets in order to examine their expression of these new human conditions, whose names could we mention? Just one: Walt Whitman."[6] By calling for an accommodation of human consciousness to the technological conditions of life, Bahr goes much further than most of his colleagues, authors, or critics:

> Between these [machines], however, and the inner life of human beings there is something artificial which separates them. There is a tangled mass of thoughts and feelings, alive neither in inner nor in outer life, neither in our souls nor in our machines. Our souls are yearning for our machines, which are identical to them, and this yearning is what we suffer from. This obstacle must be removed. It is not the external world by which humans are harassed—it [the external world] is like them. But something artificial separating humans from the external world, a wall of thoughts and feelings, denies the inner as well as the outer life of humans.[7]

Cultural tradition, an obstacle to modern life, must therefore be removed. The "modern human being is already among us, but they [modern human beings] are still invisible and he [man] does not know it yet himself. How strange that humans have not recognized themselves yet!"[8] This modern human, the barbarian, again lives in paradise, in modern innocence: "In their naive innocence, [modern humans] really have something barbarian about them. . . . The apple from the tree of knowledge has been digested and humans can no longer tell the good from the bad, everything is acceptable, they are once more walking in paradise."[9]

The digestion of the biblical fruit is an almost postmodern continuation of the Old Testament myth. A new age of innocence has begun—but it is the innocence of an age which has dispensed with the category of sin. These barbarians are technological, programmable, and morally indifferent. In accordance with technological development, moral judgment has been replaced by sensual perception. A modern poet such as Jensen or Whitman "is not just all eyes, he is all ears, all nose, all tongue, all skin, this whole human being seems to consist exclusively of the senses. Young Maupassant was similar but then his brain wanted to follow suit and that disturbed him."[10] The villain is obvious: the intellect.

It comes as no surprise that Bahr celebrates Whitman's sexualized poetry as entirely in keeping with the modern perception of the world: "Walt's perception always starts as a sensual experience, he thinks with his eyes and his ears, he is one of the sensual, extrasensual suitors who philosophize with the phallus. His Eros precedes Caritas. . . ."[11]

Bahr's road to Whitman was different from Schlaf's. Schlaf, repulsed by the urban industrial world, broke down an unpleasant reality. Bahr, by contrast, willing to take on the challenges of modern life, went in search of the poet of modernity. Whitman's work seemed to offer a suitable poetic answer to the technological challenge.

Some ten years later, Bahr, too, found himself on a back-to-nature platform and reshaped his reading of Whitman accordingly.[12] However, this does not diminish his original achievement. By going beyond the antimodernist interpretation of Whitman, he paved the way for the productive reception of Whitman by the expressionists, even though in his own writings (dozens of plays and novels) there are hardly any traces of Whitman.

CHAPTER THIRTEEN

EXPRESSIONISM

Expressionism is one of the most interesting, productive, and innovative periods in modern German literature. Yet most Germanists, although they agree that "expressionism" is a useful term, have difficulties in formulating a workable definition. Even if the terminology is not clear, however, what *is* clear is Whitman's looming presence among the figures that have shaped that period. Together with Nietzsche, the French symbolists, the Italian futurists, and the "Russians," Whitman is frequently mentioned as a significant "influence"—but usually without any indication of how this influence was felt. An analysis of Whitman's reception can contribute to our understanding of this highly complex and controversial period.

German expressionism may be viewed as the artistic consequence of a profound crisis in the life and thinking of turn-of-the-century Germans and Austrians. It was a direct reaction to the political and social effects of the rapid industrialization and urbanization that I have already described in connection with naturalism. By the second decade of the twentieth century, however, this development had not only accelerated dramatically but also had culminated in a profound crisis in human sensibility. The individual experienced great difficulties in attempting to locate his/her identity in this new, ever-shifting context, and it was the ensuing (primarily psychological) disruption that laid the groundwork for expressionist literature.

Most studies of German expressionist literature identify two main currents. One (some claim the more sophisticated and interesting of the two) tends more toward the abstract, the opaque. It thematizes the crisis, the "dissociation" and disintegration of the self, and reacts to an increasingly incomprehensible reality with "private," abstract art. Writers often included in this group are Georg Trakl, Georg Heym, Gottfried Benn, and, most importantly, Franz Kafka.

The other group, instead of retreating to the abstract, saw a solution to the crisis in the call for a "new man," a rhetoric that coincided, of course, with the *Pathos* of Schlaf's Whitman translation. These "messianic" expressionists emphasized the solidarity of humankind and the establishment of a new world order (which essentially reflected old, premodernist values). The visionary quality among these writers is frequently said to be "loud," emotional, and pseudometaphysical. "O Mensch!" (O Man!) they would cry out in their poetry; this apostrophe is responsible for their second label: "O Mensch-Expressionisten." Generally, this expressionism is considered a more optimistic counterpart to the first variant because of its underlying hope for a better world, a hope the more skeptical abstract expressionists did not share. Names frequently associated with this second group include Ludwig Rubiner, Ernst Stadler, Ernst Toller, Johannes R. Becher, and Franz Werfel.

In terms of Whitman's creative reception by German-speaking authors, it is the second, messianic group that we need to focus on, especially Franz Werfel, internationally the most famous of the messianic expressionist poets. In order to understand Whitman's expressionist reception, however, we must first look at the cultural context of German expressionism as well as Whitman's role in it. In so doing, we will also document Whitman's widespread significance in this period.

THE CULTURAL CONTEXT

In 1919, the expressionist critic Max Picard gave a lecture in which he attempted to view the expressionist interest in Whitman as a historical phenomenon:

> In the expressionist era, everything is supposed to be different. From the chaos in which things hardly have names with which they can be called by all and to all, from this *nameless* chaos, the new Expressionist calls the thing out to him, calls things by their *name*: You Forest, he says, and you City, so that forest and city can be separated from chaos.
>
> You Mississippi, Walt Whitman sings. The Impressionists have only heard the all-uniting *You*, and Lublinski, in his book *The Close of the Modern Age*, calls Whitman a natural Impressionist.[1]
>
> You Mississippi, sings Walt Whitman. The Expressionists hear only the isolating name of the Mississippi and Whitman to them is a prophet of expressionism.

> But Walt Whitman neither moved the Mississippi closer to things, as the Impressionist half sees, nor did he call the Mississippi out of things, as the Expressionist half hears. You Mississippi is not a call but a song.
>
> It is characteristic of expressionism not that Walt Whitman is being propagated, but what in Whitman is being propagated.
>
> The Expressionist loves Whitman because he believes Whitman saves things from chaos by naming them. He uses the same words as Walt Whitman, but louder than he, because his desire to be heard by chaos is greater than Walt Whitman's. Therefore, the Expressionist's calls are loud and full of *Pathos*, not out of *some sense of vital consciousness* but out of necessity.[2]

Apart from the many other points Picard makes, this passage suggests that the "expressionist decade" (1910–1918 or 1920) was possibly the most significant period in the history of Whitman reception in the German-speaking countries; and in fact, in terms of the intensity of this reception and the originality of Whitman's contribution to an emerging new literary movement, it was the most important period. It is no exaggeration to say that the American poet during these years became a truly significant force in the literary and cultural development of the German-speaking countries. His influence was felt in the realm of cultural expression as well as that of politics (discussed in subsequent chapters).[3] The efforts and battles of the early Whitmanites finally paid off: lightheartedly and carelessly, the new generation took up the legends and the prophecy.

The image of the "Good Gray Poet" which had been constructed by the Whitmanites coincided with the puerile desires and yearnings of many expressionists. The naive demands made by "intellectual activists" among expressionist poets could easily be interpreted into or out of Whitman's work and biography: the "new religion," the "new ethos," or the "rule of the spirit" ("Herrschaft des Geistes"). The prophecy of a new humanity strongly appealed to the authors of the expressionist period, during which Whitmanesque poetry became a mass phenomenon.

A strange phenomenon, indeed. For, although the "abstract" expressionists focused on the effective epistemological criticism of a "world of illusionary values, of materialism and the idolatry of power,"[4] and withdrew into abstract "new forms,"[5] the messianic group felt intensely attracted by the Whitmanesque myth, regardless of its obvious fictionality: Whitman as mystic healer, Whitman as Christ figure, Whitman as a "whole" human being not affected by the processes of human fragmentation and alienation. To these hymnic-messianic-activist expressionists, Whitman was *the* answer to the hopelessness and "transcendental homelessness" of modern existence—a specific expression of an attitude which earned this group a reputation for naiveté and inconsistency.[6]

It may very well be true that this version of expressionism with its "naive fervor [has something] awkward and, at the same time, breathtaking" for us.[7] For similar reasons, Whitman, too, was frequently attacked by critics. But these texts are not as naive as they may seem. They would indeed be simplistic if they would merely attempt to reestablish older systems of human values and social norms. But frequently they do so only on the surface, while actually suggesting radically "modern" solutions to modern conditions. They can be read as responses to the uneasiness and restlessness of the age. The seeming naiveté of this messianism must be questioned if we desire an understanding of the regressive solutions behind the rhetoric. What is required is not just an understanding of the dialectics between radical criticism and utopian goals, but an investigation of the critical potential of the messianic element in expressionism.

In the context of German Whitman reception, this means an investigation into what made Whitman an expressionist model and cult figure and in what way his critical as well as his creative reception is a reaction to deep-seated feelings of dissatisfaction. Furthermore, if we accept the thesis that Whitman's poetry itself is an early result of the alienation between "self" and "world," we should ask ourselves to what extent elements and structures characteristic of this alienation were imported into German poetry by way of Whitman's *oeuvre.*

Since Schlaf's beginnings in 1892, German Whitman enthusiasts were continuously constructing the American bard as "wound-dresser" for the ills caused by the conditions of modern life. As the definition of what constituted "reality" constantly changed, the various epistemological layers making up this reality were increasingly broken down. Schlaf sought a way out of the naturalist dilemma and discovered it in Whitman's "impressionistic" dimension, which dissolved naturalist "reality" (as a function of milieu or family origin). Around the turn of the century, Whitman figured as a counterpart to aestheticizing impressionism and decadent artificiality. Expressionism, finally, with its radical negation of tangible "reality," fully explored the possibilities offered by Whitman's poems. The world created by the expressionists became a function of the fragmented consciousness of the artist.

Literary histories have failed to demonstrate and analyze Whitman's significance for the messianic version of German expressionism. They have traditionally emphasized Whitman's role as an innovator of form (free rhythms, long lines) and his democratic impulse. While this analysis is not incorrect, it is incomplete and misses the complexity of the phenomenon. Although there are frequent references in German literary histories to Whitman as lyrical "pioneer," his significance for the expressionist movement has seldom been given adequate treatment. Many important studies of German expressionism even remain silent on the topic of Whitman. The scattered observations and speculations in various kinds of secondary literature are in no way commensurable with the wealth of material documenting the breadth and intensity of the Whitman experience.[8]

In 1918, Arthur Eloesser reported: "Walt Whitman's western prairie with its continual surging of broad verses has reached Prague. . . ."[9] Retrospectively, Johannes Urzidil, one of the youngest expressionists, remembered "Whitman's demonic omnipresence" in that center of expressionist writing with Werfel, Kafka, Brod, and many others.[10] Walter Mehring included Whitman with the "canonized geniuses," who were read and discussed by the *bohème* in the Berlin Café des Westens as well as "in all the metropoles of Europe" at "conspiratorial coffee tables."[11] Stefan Zweig, who read and memorized Whitman at a very early age, called him, in reference to the expressionists, "the driving force of modern poetry."[12] Declarations such as these abound in autobiographies, reminiscences, and diaries.

The generation of writers born around 1890, such as Ludwig Rubiner, Karl Otten, Armin T. Wegner, Franz Werfel, and Ivan and Claire Goll, came to know Whitman mostly through Schlaf's edition, often during secondary school. Characteristic anecdotes highlight this encounter. Armin T. Wegner supposedly concluded the graduation speech for his class with the line "Resist much—Obey little!" from Whitman's poem "To the States."[13] The Bavarian poet Oskar Maria Graf, who had won a copy of Schlaf's *Leaves* edition as a prize in a school competition, claims that he learned Whitman's verses by heart while he was delivering bread.[14]

Whitman is frequently mentioned in reviews of expressionist authors' works, thus documenting critics' awareness of the American's popularity and influence. A typical example (from dozens which could be cited) is in a review of a work by the poet Ernst Lissauer: "The strongest impulses for new subjects and new forms which German poetry has received in the last two decades came from abroad: from Walt Whitman in America and Verhaeren in Belgium. The American was the first to grasp the facts of modern life with the force of his expansive soul. His unwieldy rhythms seem to be trimmed with an axe which he, the farmer, knew so well how to use."[15] Similar claims abound in reviews and prove once more how Whitman and various Whitman legends (the farmer and his axe!) were part of the daily literary discourse in the German-speaking countries.

Other documents more indirectly demonstrate Whitman's standing. His presence was felt so strongly that some authors confronted the Whitman phenomenon with sarcastic criticism and irony. Already in 1918, Carl Sternheim ridiculed the "educated bourgeois crowd" who imported the supplies for their "intellectual wants" "mainly from Walt Whitman and Co., New York, which sold uninhibited Christianity like hotcakes. It is a brand of Christianity which, unlike Tolstoy's, does not require continual spiritual and cerebral purification from its adherents but which merely celebrates itself and the whole world."[16] Similarly ironical commentaries which point to the massive dissemination of Whitman's works can be found in plays by Bertolt Brecht and by Ernst Toller, writer and revolutionary activist in the Bavarian Soviet Republic.[17]

This small sample of documents suggests Whitman's ubiquity during the period, but the central question remains: *How* did expressionists read Whitman and what did they see in him? A good place to begin this analysis is the first issue of the expressionist journal *Das neue Pathos,* referred to in the introduction. The title of the magazine derives from an article by Stefan Zweig in the *Literarische Echo,* originally published in 1909. Excerpts from this article make up the programmatic manifesto introducing the first issue of the new journal.

Zweig recalls the poetry of primitive times, the "archetypal poem" ("Urgedicht") which was "nothing but a modulated cry, as yet hardly language":[18] "This [archetypal] poem and its delivery was not something finished, presented for examination, not a tool or an ornament already hammered and whole. It was something in the process of becoming, developing in the very moment [of its presentation], a battle with the audience, a struggle for their passion."[19] What followed was the Fall—to paper: "Since the beginning of writing, poets have lost this close, ardent contact with the masses."[20]

In recent times, however, owing to the new conditions determining human existence, and especially compact urban living, new possibilities have opened up for this original form of poetry:

> Just at present, there seems to be a return to this original close contact between author and audience, a new *Pathos.* . . . The time of the poet's separation from the masses, once conditioned by the great distances of the nations, seems today to be overcome by a new closeness, by the industrialization of the cities. Today, poets again deliver their own poetry, read in assembly rooms, in the popular universities of America. Even the churches resound with Walt Whitman's verses, with an American consciousness. What was formerly produced only by hot, politically revolutionary days . . . is now on the agenda almost every day.[21]

The reference to Whitman in this quotation is important. Whitman is a model because of his passionate address to the audience, not merely because of his personality or the formal characteristics of his poetry. Whitman's supposedly intimate contact with the reader, to whom so many of his poems reach out, becomes exemplary for a new expressionist poetry appealing to humankind. Just as in Whitman, expressionist poetry combines extreme subjectivist eccentricity with a *Pathos*-laden appeal to the masses, to *the* human being. By necessity, this calls for a destruction of traditional forms: "Whoever wants to appeal to the masses must contain the rhythm of their new and restless life, who speaks to them must be inspired by a new *Pathos*."[22]

Obviously, expressionists easily detected the rhythm of the "masses" in Whitman's long rhymeless lines as well as the masses themselves in his catalogues, and the American could therefore become the model for a poet filled with "new *Pathos*."

A second demand Zweig makes of expressionist poetry also leads directly to Whitman: "*The new Pathos must contain the will to action, not emotional vibration or aesthetic sensation*" (emphasis in original).[23] Art should not be limited to aestheticization, but should "break forth" into "life." It must have an "effect." The artist needs to leave the ivory tower and become an "activist" (a term with which these authors are often described). Which Whitman reader would not be reminded of the American's attempts to get in touch with life and with the "reader" through his poetry, to get onto the "Open Road,"[24] to work for the progress of humankind?

> Americanos! conquerors! marches humanitarian!
> Foremost! century marches! Libertad! masses!
> For you a programme of chants.
>
> . . . .
>
> Take my leaves America, take them South and take them North . . .
>
> (*LG*, 17)

How seemingly paradoxical—and yet how revealing—that these activist fantasies were uttered by authors as caught up in themselves as Whitman and the expressionists were!

In a yet purer form, this activist impulse emerges from a second programmatic text, a prospectus announcing the expressionist series *Der jüngste Tag* (The Day of Judgment), published by Kurt Wolff:

> The new poet will be unconditional, he will start afresh. There are no reminiscences because he, like no one else, will feel that literary retrospection is without substance, that pleasure in sounds is unnecessary. He will know that a poem is not a sentence in a book but a part of life, a weak, unspeakably fine drop of his large, all-merciful, dedicated life intervening everywhere and any-

> where. It is a stroke of lightning coming from his heart in which alone the trembling earth can find herself. It is his duty to rise, eternally, to be the expansive preacher of coexistence and death common to all of us. . . .
>
> O, may the [unenlightened] scribblers feel how contemptible they are! How their intellectuality is treason and falsehood.
>
> May they turn away from this enormous profession with which they cannot cope. May they suspect which steps lead to the truth! May they feel that this earth has borne Isaiah and Tolstoy. That Whitman was crying when he took care of injured brothers in a military hospital at sundown. . . . [25]

This prospectus, written by Franz Werfel, defines the task of the poet in a way similar to Zweig, but with more *Pathos*: the poet is asked to intervene in real life. The nursing myth has been carried to its greatest extreme: at sundown Whitman was crying(!) when he cared for his wounded brothers. The connection between *Pathos* and activism becomes explicit. It is not so much the deed itself that counts, but the violent outbursts of emotion that accompany it. Whitman is *crying* as he cares for the wounded soldiers.

Such an emotional activism also emerges in a Whitman commentary by a nonmessianic expressionist, Franz Kafka. Kafka's knowledge of Whitman may have been much more intense than we are aware of.[26] According to his friend Gustav Janouch, he commented at length on Whitman:

> Doctor Kafka presented me with a little Reclam booklet, a centimeter thick: *Leaves of Grass* by the American poet Walt Whitman.
>
> He then said to me: "The translation is not very good. At times, it is rather clumsy. However, at least it gives an idea of this poet, who provided the most significant formal inspiration to modern poetry. . . .
>
> "The formal quality of Walt Whitman's poetry has found an enormous resonance in the world. However, Whitman's significance actually lies elsewhere. He has brought together contemplation of nature and civilization, which are apparently diametrically opposed to each other, in one single intoxicating impression of life because he was always aware of the short duration of all phenomena. He said: 'Life is the little which is left of death.' Therefore he devoted his heart to each leaf of grass. It was this quality in him that enchanted me even at a very early age. In him, I admired the harmony between art and life. When the War between the Northern and the Southern States broke out in America, the war which more or less started the immense power of our machine world as we know it today, Walt Whitman became a nurse. He did what every one of us should be doing today. He helped the weak, the sick,

> and the defeated. He was a true Christian and therefore a measure of humanity—especially closely related to us Jews."
>
> [Janouch:] "So you know his writings very well?"
>
> [Kafka:] "Maybe not so much his writings as his life. Because this is actually his main achievement. What he wrote, his poems and essays, are just glowing ashes left from the fire of a consistent life and an active belief."[27]

Even Kafka, hardly a naive writer, fell prey to the temptation of the Whitman legend and was "enchanted" by it. He recognized clearly that nature and "the machine world," art and life, could not be brought into harmony as in earlier times.[28] He was aware of the epistemological problem posed by the dissociation of the perceiving self ("the short duration of all phenomena"). Nevertheless, he *wanted* to believe in the possibility of such a unity—which is denied by all his fictional writings. The short-lived solution is found in the poetic *Pathos* ("one single intoxicating impression of life") and in the "deed." From such a point of view, it is not poetry which is Whitman's "main achievement," but his "life." The question of why anybody should still want to become a poet, however, was answered neither by Kafka nor by the other expressionists propagating this thesis.

Of the many texts illustrating an expressionist reading of Whitman, one contribution by Ludwig Meidner, expressionist artist and co-editor of the *Neue Pathos*,[29] deserves special mention. In his "Painter's Salute to the Poets," he follows the call for more *Pathos*:

> Put down your brush, painter. Enough hours dripping with color on ponderous leather canvases. Soar up from the cave of your attic to the cloudy heavens and salute the poets! Closer, closer, you squadrons of fear and ecstasy. Closer, you, with large hats resting on maned heads.[30] You, with rattling flags on your hips; with pennants and ribbons on the shoulders. You, with the enormous legs, thunderers[31] through the millennia. You gigantic crocodiles, swimming, diving, panting in the sea of emotions; from your nostrils fountains of rapture are spouting. Your jaws wide open for love, complaints, and repentance. You white, towering elephants with wonderful winged trunks snuffling out what is necessary for humankind.[32]

Here, too, the step beyond. Away from the narrow attic of the painter, to the cosmos of the poets who know what is "necessary for humankind." And Meidner continues with characteristic expressionist volume:

> Welcome you, world poet Goethe, you, imposing Victor Hugo, and you, dear brother *Walt Whitman*! You, first and closest singer of humankind, torch, lifeblood, and comet of the new era! . . . Friedrich von Schiller, bravest, most

manly [poet] of all Germans! Herwegh, Freiligrath, Uhland! You, poets of the people, Desaugier and Béranger! You, Lamartine! Once more flow forth, Walt Whitman, youth, man, and hoary bard! You Southern mistral! You, poet of the foaming seas of cities! Verhaeren! You, Alfred Mombert, like the white sun: meteor above the mountains, so loved by me and celebrated in paintings and many resounding leaves!

Alfred Mombert, welcome![33]

Whitman and Whitman-enthusiast Mombert are the only italicized authors in this text, and Whitman is even mentioned twice. The *Pathos* of this address is extraordinary. What Schlaf was merely hinting at becomes a jubilant epiphany here: "You, first and closest singer of humankind, torch, life-blood, and comet of the new era!" It is as if the singer of humankind has fulfilled the high expectations of the new "O Man!"-poets.

The attempt to identify any one issue or element which would define Whitman's significance for the expressionist poets is futile. Like Nietzsche, Whitman inspired a characteristic *Lebensgefühl* in the expressionist generation.

In a manner akin to their appreciation of Rimbaud,[34] the expressionists understood Whitman's art and his life as one larger symbolic unity. At the outset of the expressionist decade, the Tyrolian expressionist Carl Dallago describes "Whitmann" in the journal *Der Brenner*: "Sturdy and broad, a giant of a man and he displays grand gestures like Millet. A man from the country with a transparent character, matured in the presence of large waters, wind, waves, next to the prairies, steppes, and virgin forests."[35] In German, Whitman was frequently misspelled as "Whitman*n*." These misspellings were by no means always typographical errors. Through this spelling—referring to the genuine, real, grown male—Dallago embodied one of the favorite expressionist views of Whitman: a "real man," pitting his strength against the dehumanizing forces of his time. The Whitman legends, now further embellished, lent themselves extremely well to such fantasies of an idealized new humanity.

Obviously, there were no limits to the exaggerations surrounding the Whitman myth. Dallago's mythopoeic description is outdone by the leftist expressionist Arthur Holitscher, writing for the important journal *Die Aktion*:

Walt, the chaotic symbol of his immense, unexplored continent, the column of fire at the entrance to a mysterious new age of the human race, the wild seer and obsessed [Saint] John [the Divine], this floodwave from nature deluging civilization, this veritable tornado of a human being, an eye gazing around far and wide like the eye of the lighthouse, open hand in whose hollow the elements are mating, ear directed upward, beating heart in which world affairs

> are pulsating, warm forehead of a giant, mildly bowed to the least of creatures, Walt, never born, forever alive, beginning and end, shocking outlook on times to come, beyond and upward.[36]

Is it possible to take such texts seriously? Given their great number, this question must be answered in the affirmative. The superhuman democrat Whitman is pitted against everything connected with civilization and tradition. Writing at the beginning of a new age which must indeed have seemed mysterious and threatening, the expressionists were not able to define the quality and the true issues of their time. So they deified a poet, "never born," in whose hands the elements were mating—Whitman is continuously revered as the creator of a new world, even if it is unclear what this new world might eventually look like.

This deified Whitman is precisely what emerges from Dallago's effusions. Following the presentation of the person and a few quotations, the special quality of "Whitmann" is defined:

> Such a great love for all things, those closest and those farthest away—such a profound brotherhood with the essence of creation has hardly ever been expressed by a poet. Feeling at home with this great man and recognizing him as my very own, I add: He was the greatest singer of human nature in its urge to create.[37]

The subjective recreation of the world was an important point on the expressionist agenda. This passage describing Whitman contains the key concepts of expressionism: love for one's immediate environment and the cosmos, brotherhood, essence, expression, singer, the urge to (re)create.

In an essay in *Die Aktion*, the critic Rudolf Kayser attempts to refute the "death of art" thesis. Art has become superfluous only insofar as it is an "expression of cultural reality":

> Actually, however, art is not the fulfillment, the synthesis of a culture, but transcends and overcomes it. . . .
>
> With hot hands, I am writing: "The new rhythm has the soaring power of intellectual conquest, the feverish ecstasy of a new barbarism. It is winged by fruitbearing decadence and birth-giving agony. A new beginning develops in front of our eyes. Already old ways are superseded. Art does *not* die in the hands of Walt Whitman and his successors. . . . "[38]

In attempting to transcend "cultural reality," art has assumed a revolutionary mission. "Rhythm," "ecstasy," and "barbarism" are the key words in the recreation of the world, at the beginning of which this critic places Whitman. Through

Pathos and "out of necessity," the expressionist recreates things out of chaos, Max Picard states with only a slight exaggeration. This is why the expressionist "loves" Whitman.

All this effusive material documenting the expressionist Whitman cult calls for a critical evaluation. As an early "activist" author, Whitman was obviously of overwhelming importance to the expressionist period. Greatly disturbed individuals needed lyrical reassurance (in a sophisticated version of wishful thinking) that the world was intact, whole, and manageable and that they could still act autonomously. The increasing alienation of the author in an increasingly uncomfortable society (owing both to the repressive political conditions just prior to World War I and to the worrying consequences of the industrialized-technologized-militarized society) inspired the desire to live in harmony with oneself and "humanity."

The image of Whitman, half imported and half constructed, lent itself very well to these intentions and was developed further by the expressionists. The tornado, the column of fire, the superhuman prophet—these images are defiantly set against the disintegration of the human individual as an entity, the disappearance of the self, its disintegration into the components of perception. Expressionist authors were experiencing this fragmentation and attempted to compensate for the loss of traditional "humanity" by creating giants and superhuman beings which best express the intensity and degree of this total alienation.

The examination of Werfel's prospectus for Wolff allows a similar conclusion. Although Whitman is—implicitly—given a reason to cry (pity for the wounded), it is really the feeling that counts, not the action. Kurt Pinthus, editor of a famous expressionist anthology, diagnosed correctly that "the quality of this poetry is founded on its intensity. Never in world poetry was there a cry so loud, so tearing and earth-shattering, the fall and yearning of an age."[39] Pinthus, who also refers to Whitman, gives a very fitting explanation of this "cry." A rebellious generation was tortured by family, social, and military hierarchies which they no longer wanted to accept. However, the expressionist *reaction* to this pain is not (as in the case of the naturalists) primarily political or social. The leftist connections of many expressionists were loose and usually not permanent.

In the following passage, published in 1918, Friedrich Bill launches a pacifist, antiwar protest. His solution, however, is not political rebellion but consolation in Whitmanesque *Pathos*:

> It seemed to me as if I had to die on the road. What I saw—and still see—hurt my eyes, what I had to hear hurt my ears. What they wanted me to do made me shiver. Walls were towering up in front of me, cheered by those who were

> not dashed to bits on them. Flags in the wind blocked the sun. I wanted to escape. My strength waned and I collapsed helplessly. Then you came, Walt Whitman, you took me into your strong, kind arms, you looked at me with your faithful eyes, and you spoke the following words whose balsam healed me.[40]

This remarkable text is followed by excerpts from "Song of the Open Road." The expressionist protest manifests itself in emotional intensity which becomes a weapon to be used against a nonresponsive, alien world.[41]

This art—typified in the expressionist "cry," Whitman's barbaric "yawp"—does not investigate human life in a social context, although it does take a critical stand toward society. It is much more concerned with the inner life of human beings. External life presents itself (in Picard's initial formulation) as chaos from which "things" must be recreated.

Kurt Hiller, one of the intellectual activists of the period, characteristically comments on the poet Franz Werfel: "Do you know why I love him [Werfel] so much? Because of his *empathy* [*Mitleid*]. Walt Whitman excepted (he, more of a farmer, more tanned . . .), there is nobody, nobody (among poets) who is so full of feeling and love for humanity as Franz Werfel."[42] Nowhere does Hiller say for whom or why Werfel displays compassion. Compassion as an emotion is an end in itself, a mood examined by the expressionist. No wonder expressionists focused on Whitman's "free rhythms," which, not being subjected to any "external" rules, could best transport "pure" emotionality.

One of the most famous expressionist poets, Ernst Stadler, was equally fascinated by Werfel. Commenting on "thousandfold life" as represented in Werfel, he exclaims: "From the thousandfold variety, there is yet always a way back to one's own soul, which recognizes itself in the external world by assuming its shape. Because there is more than just human sympathy, social compassion . . . there is actually something like spiritual transsubstantiation. On this foundation rests the new and more intense experience of life whose first prophets were Whitman and Verhaeren: intoxicated prophecy more than creative fulfillment."[43] This intensity of experience is, of course, a physical experience based on the human nervous system. The chief aim of messianic expressionist poetry is to create a feeling of *Pathos*, which becomes the basic tool of human perception.

The world as recreated in Whitman's name has a strongly regressive tendency. Kafka was impressed by the fact that Whitman could experience the essence of the world in one simple leaf of grass. Activism, in itself regressive when pitted against the intellect, is only a vestige of political action as it was known earlier. Finally, activism can be reduced to an emotion underlying this action. Previously,

Pathos was of necessity connected with a well-defined issue, concern, and goal; here it is unadulterated. Human feelings and emotions are "liberated" from the external world.

Because this sensibility rests essentially on the human body, a regression into essentially physical, sexual areas is only natural. This is reflected in Holitscher's image of the elements mating in Whitman's hand: the pulsation of history is essentially reduced to the human heartbeat. It was entirely natural that Whitman should be the model for such experiments—even if Europeans were frequently afraid to follow the master's lead.

I do not want to claim that Whitman's works and biographical fantasies in any way "founded" German messianic expressionism; in many ways, Whitman was an expressionist construction designed to serve specific aesthetic, cultural, and political aims by German-speaking writers. The social, ideological, and cultural *foundations*, of course, existed independently of the American poet. However, Whitman was able to become such a strong force in German expressionist poetry because he was so well suited to the atmosphere and the character of the period. The demands put forth by expressionist programs read like Whitmanesque poems. Secondary literature on Whitman and secondary literature on hymnic and messianic expressionism are frequently interchangeable; their similarity is stunning. Precisely because the American had experienced alienation in his own life, albeit not exactly in the contemporary, twentieth-century meaning of the term, expressionist authors were so successful in constructing "their" Whitman.

The activist construction of Whitman's person and the activist quality attributed to his poetry by German writers as well as the general "leftist" message the U.S. Whitman community had transmitted to the world explain the extraordinary interest that politically minded "revolutionary" expressionist German authors took in Whitman.

In his book *Der Mensch in der Mitte* (The Man in the Center, 1917) Ludwig Rubiner (1881–1920), a messianic expressionist on the extreme left, points out Whitman's "enormous voice of love for humanity" and calls the American a "political poet."[44] This voice Rubiner recognized as a model for his own poetry and echoed in a variety of poems, especially in his volume *Das himmlische Licht* (Celestial Light, 1916).

Other activists among the expressionist poets who reworked Whitman creatively are the French-German writer Ivan Goll (1891–1950), Karl Otten (1889–1963), the Slovak-Austrian-Jewish poet Hugo Sonnenschein (1890–1953), and Oskar Maria Graf (1894–1967). In Sonnenschein's work, Whitman's traces are obvious; he shares his enthusiasm with other poets in the Czech and Slovak area such as Franz Werfel, Max Brod, and Otokar Březina. His work, long forgotten, is presently being rediscovered.[45]

Another important representative of the messianic expressionists, Ernst Stadler (1883–1914), was also a Whitmanite. Helmut Gier has demonstrated Stadler's development toward expressionism ("antisymbolism") in connection with Whitman. He also points out the connections with the French (of great importance in Stadler's case) and with French Whitman reception.[46]

Johannes R. Becher (1891–1958), a fervent admirer of Whitman in his expressionist period who later became a staunch Marxist and minister of culture in the German Democratic Republic, is one of the most famous German Whitmanites. In his collection of poetry entitled *Die Schlacht* (The Battle), the future Communist enters into an imaginary dialogue with Whitman. After having produced what amounts to most authentic Whitmanesque poetry, he says:

> See, my dear brother Whitman . . . just today I have again opened your immortal book (. . . o, what a book . . .)—and then I felt as though our eyes rested on each other and our hands were touching—: o, immortal, melting, all-uniting eternal contact! It was as though a multitude of antennas, beams of rays, darted out of our bodies, touching all being, even the most distant objects.
>
> Dear Brother Whitman—: hope, incitement, absolute certainty, out of the steaming mass of the swaying army of your lines I feel confirmed.
>
> Yes, I almost said that I will take over your command for this century.[47]

Although Becher addresses Whitman as "brother," the militant Marxist takes a different approach toward Whitman: with the military imagery of the "swaying army of your lines," he ascribes a very interesting pose to Whitman; it is this pose with which Becher, calling for the foundation of a "socialist army," addresses his own reader. It is important to note that Becher qualifies ("almost") his speculation about assuming Whitman's command in the twentieth century, because he ultimately does not agree with Whitman, as he informs us, in politics, economics, and philosophy. An analysis of Becher's Whitmanesque poems shows us that the American was an inspiration, but no more. From his proto-Marxist position, Becher was not about to "touch all things" and transform the world into one large whole. Although he calls for "fraternal melting" and wants to be "not lonely, but / *everybody*,"[48] his world is an exclusive one. The persons in his catalogues are asked to "unite" *against* their enemies, "the demons of hell."[49] Whitman's all-encompassing, if naive, view of humanity is transformed into a biased, class-based catalogue, limiting membership in humanity to the exploited and the suppressed and ultimately calling for a revolution "by workers, students, soldiers."[50] In a leftist way, German elitism is being superimposed on Walt Whitman.

Another important expressionist author, although less well-known than Becher, is Armin T. Wegner (1886–1978). Like many other artists and intellectuals, Wegner entered World War I as a medic—a decision which was probably influenced by the example of the wound-dresser. In the course of the war, he developed an enormously broad internationalist vision. His attempt to combine an enlightened Marxist ethos with a Whitmanesque vision produced poems of a most remarkable originality. One of the most interesting is "Funkspruch in die Welt" (Radio Message to the World):

> To all, all, all! To the peoples of Europe and the peoples of America!
> To the steppe tribes of Asia, to the rice farmers of India and the peoples of the South Sea!
> To the stony jungles of the cities,
> To the loneliest of camel herdsmen, who prays in his tent!
> I lift my heart out of a buried well calling out to you:
> Drink! Drink! . . .
> Let me approach you with bared head, you peoples, touch your hands,
> Look into your eyes, deep, deep, like lovers after long separation,
> You lonely ones, who are buried, broken by silence,
> Who, exiled, roamed around the alien earth,
> You one-eyed, you mothers weakened by tears! You all, who were obsessed and lied to—
> O the smell of the scenes of carnage of this earth,
> Which rises through the filter of your hearts, you Reconverted ones, is sweeter than the smell of paradise.
> And you, most loved ones, from the prisons of all countries,
> Whose chains we loosened from the pale stalk of your hands,
> Must I not kneel down, to kiss your loins with tears of joy?
>
> O arms, embracing the globe!
> Love radiates from my ten fingertips.
> And the hair on my head, still, is a flame of love.[51]

This poem is a strange mixture of Lenin and Whitman. "To all" refers to Lenin's famous call to all the peoples and governments to end World War I and enter into negotiations for a just and lasting peace. But only the beginning of the poem is Leninist; it soon changes into a Whitmanesque catalogue addressing the disadvantaged in this world. Unlike Becher, Wegner's ultimate aim is not that of social emancipation but a new union and unity of the world on a nonintellectual, sensual basis. The last three lines quoted above show that the resolution of the conflicts will not come out of class struggle but out of a regression into the id. The final line of the poem confirms this strange utopia: "A broken vessel of love, streaming forth onto all fields of the world."[52] In "Funkspruch an die Welt," Wegner was able to approach Whitman's lyrical consciousness more closely than in any other work. In other poems, and in the case of other expressionist authors, the self is still too strong to submerge itself into the realm of the id.

The picture of creative expressionist Whitman reception would not be complete without the so-called late expressionists. Traditionally, German literary historiography marks the end of German expressionism in 1918; later efforts are at best considered epigonal. Paul Raabe has encouraged me to look into "late expressionist" writers as well and to dispense with value judgments implied in terms such as "epigones." A revision of the received periodization of German expressionism is necessary in order to include (good and bad) expressionist poets until 1925 and even beyond.

Important postwar expressionists include Anton Schnack (1892–1973), Friedrich Sieburg (1893–1964), Hans Schiebelhuth (1895–1944), Heinar Schilling (1894–1955), Walter Rheiner (1895–1925), and Georg Kulka (1897–1929). Their poetry is mostly characterized by the *Pathos* of the messianic expressionists. With the exception of Sieburg, they were on the left politically. Unlike prewar "visionary" expressionism, their work was influenced by the revolutionary period immediately following World War I. The tension between the utopian claims of their work and the reality of the revolution led to a strange, often contradictory, tone of expectation and despair.

Whitman's presence among these authors is pervasive. In Schnack's poetry, Whitmanesque symbolism abounds; in one poem we even find lilac, thrush, and star *together*. Heinar Schilling's poetry published between 1917 and 1920 speaks, with Whitmanesque *Pathos*, of the community of all humankind. Schiebelhuth's later interest in American literature (he became the German translator of such writers as Thomas Wolfe and Carl Sandburg) starts with Whitman. A poem by the Viennese poet Georg Kulka entitled "To Landauer's Spirit" is a small but highly impressive document of German Whitman reception. It contains the following two lines:

> You, who have been from the very beginning, you will grow ancient
> As Meister Eckehart, as blood friend Walt.[53]

Meister Eckehart was the German medieval mystic whom Landauer rendered into modern German, and "blood friend Walt" of course refers to Whitman. It is impressive to see how much a part of literary life of the period Whitman must have been if Kulka was able to refer to him simply as "Walt"!

Another interesting feature of creative Whitman reception in the expressionist period are poetic "confessions" dedicated to Whitman by German-speaking authors.[54] They depict Whitman as a giantlike prophet and model for expressionist poets. Sometimes it remains unclear whether such poetry aims to connect with the Whitman tradition poetically or whether it is merely supposed to convey—in a lyrical format—Whitman's significance to these poets. A particularly heady example is a poem by a relatively little known expressionist poet from Würzburg, Arthur Drey, published in the expressionist journal *Die Aktion*:

WALT WHITMAN

Swinger of the torch! Blazing titan of virgin primeval forest!
Your eyes kiss the world, and dream-caressing
The white sun of your hair flows over the sea—
Universal man!

Your heart is love between the struggling blocs
In the torn-open breast of bleeding brotherhood—
Children kneel down eye-tired before your youthful soul—
Dream!

Warm peace shines through your pale tears,
And the words of your dear lips are flowers—
Which we drink, healing spring—
Miracle!

Your ancient edifice grows, wild gold . . .
Pious lands spread out their gray hands
For the capture—Lonely, you stand on the brink of the world—
Prophet![55]

In many ways, this "answer" to Whitman consists of a series of clichés, which have their origin in late romanticism; some of the images, as daring and unusual they may seem at first, turn out to be flat and tasteless. The poem clearly reflects the cult around Whitman's person. Again we get an example of the significance of *Pathos* and emotionality. In a line like "warm peace shines through your pale tears," the reader is not informed why Whitman is crying or why peace should be the consequence of *pale* tears. With such lines, indeed with the whole poem, Drey attempts to work with the effect of pure *Pathos*; any form of logic has become obsolete.

Better expressionist poets such as Franz Werfel would be much more successful in their reworking of Whitman, but *Pathos*, as we have encountered it in "critical" reviews and in dedications to Whitman, remains a constant among most creative recipients of Whitman.

FRANZ WERFEL (1890 – 1945)

Next to Kafka, Franz Werfel is the most famous German expressionist internationally. Werfel's fame in the United States is mainly based on extremely successful prose works such as *The Song of Bernadette* (1941), a worldwide bestseller that was turned into a successful if not very good movie. However, this Austrian-Bohemian-Jewish (and finally American) poet, dramatist, and novelist deserves much more serious attention for ringing in the expressionist period with a volume entitled *Der Weltfreund* (The World's Friend), published in 1911.

There has been quite a bit of interest in Werfel in recent years.[56] As early as 1951, Frederik Schyberg referred to Werfel as "the most famous of them all [the authors who started to write in the Whitman tradition after 1910]."[57] Schyberg was the first academic critic to point out Whitman's importance to Werfel. His thorough knowledge of Whitman allowed him to recognize and describe important connections between the American poet and the Austrian.

For the majority of Werfel scholars, normally not very well versed in American literature, Whitman's influence on the early poetry is given lip service or is not mentioned at all. A typical example is Leopold Zahn's monograph, with the simple statement: "In terms of content and form, the *Pathos*-laden, sometimes rhetorical poetry of brotherhood reveals the influence of the American Walt Whitman. . . ."[58] Many authors of Ph.D. theses dealing with Werfel are unable to judge Whitman's role for reasons of method. Either they discuss Werfel exclusively in the context of German literature or their religious and mystical prejudices prevent sound philological work. New Critical approaches, finally, do not even raise such questions. Lore Foltin's survey of Werfel research summarizes briefly that Whitman's influence on Werfel is "questionable," and this seems to be the scholarly consensus up to the present.[59] Only Norbert Abels, author of the latest Werfel biography, has suggested that Whitman was a decisive literary experience for Werfel.[60]

One of the reasons for the failure of Werfel scholars to recognize Whitman's significance may well be their ignorance of Werfel's contemporary reception. Especially in connection with *Der Weltfreund*, Whitman was frequently mentioned by reviewers. In the influential *Neue Rundschau*, Felix Stössinger noted with a characteristic expressionist tone:

> Walt Whitman is the modern poet who has most forcefully invited reality into his art and from him originates the long line to German poetry and to Werfel by way of Verhaeren. . . . Whitman transferred his country's democratic principle from politics to the cosmos and became intoxicated by the mass character of all things, celebrating their equality. He had the power to search for unity in variety and he was not weakened but stimulated by his uninhibited sensuality in objects. . . . [Werfel "overtook" Whitman] by honestly loving rather than adoring this diversity. In him, we can observe the great progress of the individual in overcoming this lyrical Americanism, which we may ignore from now on.[61]

In spite of this premature abandonment, critic Richard Rieß, on the occasion of Werfel's second poetry volume, *Wir sind* (We Are, 1913), again recalled Whitman's example: "Werfel is characterized by the cosmic feeling and sympathy which captures us so powerfully when reading poems by the American Walt Whitman. His passionate poetic sympathy connects all things and all humans with his own person."[62] Kurt Pinthus, a critic, admirer, and friend of Werfel, who later escaped the Nazis and came to the United States, even called him "Whitman's brother."[63] And for Johannes Thummerer, the link between Werfel and Whitman even proves the former's "epigonal quality," for Werfel supposedly "came completely under the influence of Whitman, on whose ideas all his mature poems live." Werfel is said to be "dependent on Whitman even in the smallest nuances."[64] Such reviews indicate that the early Werfel was considered Whitman's "successor" in the German-speaking countries and that there was general agreement on Werfel's creative debt to Whitman.

The memoirs of several personalities important in Werfel's life confirm Whitman's impact on the early poetry. Johannes Urzidil, Werfel's younger expressionist poet-friend in Prague, wrote in the afterword to the 1969 Reclam edition: "Franz Werfel . . . was the first and most determined writer [to follow Whitman] in his earliest volume of poetry *Der Weltfreund* (1911) but also in his subsequent volumes *Wir sind* and *Einander* and altogether in the poetic rhythm of his whole life."[65] An even closer friend of Werfel's, Max Brod, executor of Franz Kafka's estate, wrote in his obituary for Werfel in 1945 that Whitman's influence could be seen in the first three volumes of poetry by Werfel.[66] And Werfel's publisher, Kurt Wolff, wrote in his memoirs that Werfel's poetry had its origin in Whitman.[67]

Such documents may be significant for a preliminary thesis regarding Werfel's link to Whitman; however, this investigation also seeks to connect Werfel's construction of Whitman with a comparative analysis of both authors' creative works.

In August 1918 Franz Werfel wrote about Whitman in a letter to his lover Alma

Mahler (1879–1964), the famous wife of three famous artists: Gustav Mahler, the composer; Walter Gropius, the *Bauhaus* architect; and Franz Werfel, the poet. (Alma never married her lover Oskar Kokoschka, the painter.) He proclaimed that Whitman "contains everything that is my knowledge, only in a different type of human being. . . . I did not come to know Whitman until much later, long after they started to say I imitated him!—I am happy that this soul through which I am so strongly confirmed has lived."[68]

This claim, in which Werfel refers to their kindred souls, is probably only partially correct. Werfel's attempt to emphasize his autonomy with regard to Whitman may well have had to do with his attempt to impress Alma. Decades later, in 1941, already in exile in the United States, Werfel said, probably more accurately, "I was seventeen or eighteen when Walt Whitman's *Leaves of Grass* fell into my hands."[69] This date suggests 1907 or 1908 and therefore Schlaf's translation, certainly not an English original edition, since he said in an interview for the *World-Telegram* in the same year: "Years gone by, I fell upon a German translation of Whitman."[70] From various correspondence we also know that Werfel followed new translations of Whitman poems published in journals and newspapers.

In several places, Werfel emphasized Whitman's significance for his own work. In his notebook of 1913, he stated that he wanted to connect with "realism, the Russians, Whitman," thereby contradicting his claim of not having known Whitman earlier.[71] In later, retrospective statements, he referred not only to Whitman's significance for his own poetry but to his effect on a whole generation: "In German-speaking culture, Walt Whitman and Edgar Allan Poe have had a decisive influence on the generation to which I belong and on myself."[72]

After his adventurous escape from his National Socialist enemies to the United States, Werfel had much occasion to reflect the significance of American literature for his own work. In a contribution entitled "thanks," published in English in Klaus Mann's exile journal *Decision* in 1941, Werfel explained:

> I can never forget those intoxicated days when my mind was inundated by this Mississippi of poetry. Until that time I had believed that there was an aristocratic hierarchy of objects suitable for poetry. But Walt Whitman taught me and my generation that in the realm of reality there is nothing commonplace; that in the simplest word, the commonest designation, the most shopworn idea there lies hidden an explosive poetic force surpassing a thousandfold that which is esthetically sanctified. Walt Whitman, this prophet of a cosmic democracy, taught us far more: that a mysterious, a divine stream of love fills the universe—a stream in whose embrace all creatures alike receive their religious value. And through his own mighty example he showed us that the poet can

> be the antenna of the stream. The example of this Homeric American continues to work upon a future yet unknown.[73]

According to this passage, Whitman's significance for Werfel expressed itself foremost in a revolution in poetics and lyrical conventions. Of course the naturalists had previously turned to the urban sphere, poverty, and other topics up to then considered unfit for poetry. But for Werfel the extent of this revolution by far exceeded the naturalist conception.

Werfel writes of his (poetic) consciousness being "inundated" by the "Mississippi of poetry." Already in a diary notice of 1916, he had called Whitman's poetry a "prophecy" and claimed that "the wealth [of poetic material] that *streams* forth from it [Whitman's poetry] is all too great and it is impossible to observe any other laws than its own."[74] In the New York speech quoted above, he spoke of Whitman's "verses resembling the broad streams of this [American] continent."[75] With the image of the stream, Werfel connects poetic lawlessness and a lack of conventions. The stream of Whitmanesque poetry cannot be controlled.

Traditional walls of propriety were torn down by an explosive poetry, an explosiveness found in the "simplest word, the commonest designation, the most shopworn idea." This is not just an emancipation of everyday life in poetry. Rather, in terms of their *effect*, these democratic poetics "surpass" traditional aesthetics with their normative hierarchies "a thousandfold."

When Werfel refers to Whitman's "poetic force," he is talking about the *effect* poetry has on the reader, suggesting that he was thinking in American literary categories. Traditional poetics was less concerned with effect than with the mimetic ideal, the imitation of ideal nature, or, in the Romantic tradition, the expressive function of literature. American writers, especially since Poe and Whitman, had given a good deal of attention to the calculation of effect, a category that now started to assume greater importance in Europe as well, especially in the poetry of messianic expressionism. At the conclusion of a sonnet by Werfel with the Whitmanesque title "Hundertfaches Dasein" (Hundredfold Being) we read:

> Am I not, where my name is mentioned, already close,
> Where I am felt, in two ways close?
> Because existence is the medium, effect [is] everything.[76]

The question of which objects might have the greatest poetic effectiveness of course endangered and eventually dissolved traditional hierarchies and "order" in poetry.

The victory of everyday life as a subject of poetry must be viewed with Werfel's newly discovered awareness of the poetic effect in mind. Whitman's lines in section 30 of "Song of Myself" belong here:

> The insignificant is as big to me as any,
> (What is less or more than a touch?)
> (*LG*, 58)

And, closely following, in section 31:

> I believe a leaf of grass is no less than the journey-work of the stars,
> And the pismire is equally perfect, and a grain of sand, and the egg of the wren . . .
> (*LG*, 59)

What Whitman referred to as "insignificant" had such "explosive" power because it did not fit received poetic conventions. Both Whitman and Werfel incorporated areas into their poetry which formerly could only be treated in prose—or which were not suitable subjects for literature at all.

Werfel took up this dedication to the realm of everyday life, to the "shopworn" idea, and developed it further in a most unorthodox manner. At the beginning of *Wir sind*, there is a group of poems under the collective title "Ein Gesang von Toten" (A Song by the Dead). Four lyrical subjects that act as speakers in these poems, personae of a special kind, are defined as emanation of *one* spirit: a statesman, a servant girl, a canary, and—a schoolbag. Death, the great equalizer, creates the conditions for an equal appearance of the four lyrical personae in this cycle of poems. The key experience of the—seemingly—inanimate schoolbag is as magnificent as that of the statesman ("There was a day, / when a King shook my hand," FWL, 75):

> THE SCHOOLBAG
>
> Once somebody lowered into me
> a chrestomathy.
> And then it happened, then I lived
> large, as never before.
> And as I existed consciously,
> The silence of my being cried:
> *We all are, all are here!*
> (FWL, 76)[77]

Contemporary reviewers were rather surprised to find an inanimate object become a lyrical persona. The anthropomorphization and animation of the object world, later a trademark of expressionist poetry with epistemological and socio-critical functions,[78] here is a consistent consequence of the desire to emancipate all things. Statesman, servant girl, canary, and schoolbag are all linked to a "spirit" which presents itself lyrically as Whitmanesque catalogue:

What else was I but a small dream,
Was Susa and was Capernaum?
A hero wildly fighting with niggers,
And an old woman,
Jumping into the water at night?
And always I am a place,
wind and animal of the stars
And am all four of you.
(FWL, 75)[79]

This omnipresent, all-encompassing spirit is linked to the creativity of the author. Just as the lyrical persona in *Leaves of Grass* expands to a "kosmos" (*LG*, 52), Werfel, according to Thummerer under Whitman's influence, "expands the limitations of his self by a kind of cosmic sympathy, a sympathy for the whole world."[80] In a sonnet entitled "Die vielen kleinen Dinge" (The Many Small Things), the two final tercets are programmatic:

What is in me and above me said roguishly:
"You yourself are what you can never have,
And you call it: wine, old man, Mitzi, roses!

You are one with it and will never understand it,
You love someone else, and thereby love yourself.
O you eternal beingless shape!"
(FWL, 36)[81]

Whitman formulated this with a similarly rejoicing voice, although more abstractly:

O the joy of my soul leaning pois'd on itself, receiving identity
through materials and loving them, observing characters and
absorbing them,
My soul vibrated back to me from them, from sight, hearing,
touch, reason, articulation, comparison, memory, and the
like . . .
(*LG*, 181)

These lines address the solipsistic extension of the self, the elimination of the borders between self and nonself, as the philosopher and Werfel-critic Martin

Buber formulated it for Werfel's early poetry.[82] Werfel, however, a later and more reflective author, makes Whitman's implicit epistemological problem explicit: by expanding the self, the whole world eventually becomes a mirror of the author's poetic consciousness. The narcissism of a line like "You love something else, and thereby love yourself," which is so characteristic of Whitman's whole poetry, is recognized as such by Werfel, even though it has not yet become a problem for him.

The expansion of the self leads first to a general eroticization of the world around the lyrical persona, later to its incorporation into the lyrical self. In Werfel's poetry this process is frequently sanctioned by the category of "love." In his lengthy statement quoted above, Werfel called Whitman a prophet of a "cosmic democracy" who teaches that "a mysterious, a divine stream of love fills the universe—a stream in whose embrace all creatures alike receive their religious value." In his New York speech Werfel said that Whitman "has taught us in completely new forms the *all-encompassing* dimension of his cosmic feeling of comradeship."[83]

The mystical dimension of Whitman's work here appears as a welcome quasi-religious superstructure of great interest to Werfel, the mystic. Werfel may have learned this from a wide variety of passages in the *Leaves* which cannot all be quoted here. In the famous section 5 of "Song of Myself" he could have read: "And [I know] that a kelson of the creation is love" (*LG*, 33). Or, similarly, only more extensively, in the introductory lines to "I Sing the Body Electric":

> I sing the body electric,
> The armies of those I love engirth me and I engirth them,
> They will not let me off till I go with them, respond to them,
> And discorrupt them, and charge them full with the charge of the soul.
>
> (*LG*, 93)

The category of "love" appears throughout Werfel's *oeuvre* and assumes an almost ideological quality. In the early poetry of the *Weltfreund* expressing (according to many paraphrasing reviewers) Werfel's "love for the world," this "love" is more prominent than in later works. But in his late novel *The Song of Bernadette* (1941), "love" still plays a decisive role when a naive heroine with her instinctive "capacity for love" rather than a theologically trained nun who is "unable to love" is rewarded with the Virgin Mary's blessings.

Regarding this "love" in Werfel's early poetry, Eva Cassirer states: "He [Werfel, Werfel's poetry] is filled with love, a place into which the world is projected in order to rise again in the essence of their being, the old woman, the nightly players in the women's band, the murderer and the canary bird and the old schoolbag. In him everything is connected and through him with God."[84] Love is a homogenizing force in an all too heterogeneous world, and it functions as an agency to standardize the world. Cassirer shows that this love can easily be interpreted in religious terms ("connected . . . through him with God").

Julius Kühn's words on Werfel's "love" suggest a great degree of cultural discomfort. In his essay "Der Dichter und das All" (The Poet and the Cosmos) we read: "Life today presents itself as a variety of things and beings that are *next* to one another, but our young people [here he includes Werfel] want—out of a very deep urge—to overcome and replace this by a state where everything and everybody are *together*: in the first experience of love."[85] The un- or disconnected and thus confusing multiplicity of the modern world is presented as a negative state which must be overcome and unified through the "love" of the poet.

The love for the cosmos and for humankind is the most important feature, indeed, the basis of the "O Man" rhetoric characteristic of the messianic expressionists, and Werfel was their leading representative, at least in the initial years. Did Werfel and his expressionist colleagues perhaps use this category as a pseudometaphysical notion, to satisfy a human psyche that was still used to a metaphysical order, to hierarchies and religion? Are this category and this rhetoric possibly indicative of a general cultural malaise whose origin the interpreter needs to explore by a close reading of Werfel's metaphors?

If we want to investigate this love rhetoric, we might profitably compare it with its origin in Whitman. In him, an American author less "laden" with tradition, the conditions and complications behind this rhetoric might be more easily recognizable. Moreover, a comparative interpretation also shows the significant differences between Whitman and Werfel.

Werfel's poem "An den Leser" (To the Reader), which has been called *the* programmatic poem of the early expressionist period,[86] lends itself particularly well to an interpretive comparison with Whitman's poetry. It was the final poem of the *Weltfreund* collection, representing a kind of summary of the lyrical theses of the volume.

TO THE READER

My only desire, o man, is to be related to you!
Whether you are black, an acrobat, or whether you are still dormant in
  your mother's womb,
Whether your young girl's song reaches across the courtyard, whether you
  steer your raft in the evening light,
Whether you are a soldier or a pilot full of endurance and daring.

Did you also carry a pop gun on a green strap when you were a child?
When it went off, a cork came out of the barrel.
My comrade, when I sing memories,
Don't be hardened, but dissolve, with me, in tears!

I have experienced all lives. I know
The feeling of lonely harpists in health spa bands,
The feeling of the shy governess in a family not her own,
The feeling of debutants, shivering for the first time on a stage.

I lived in the forest, had a job at the railway station,
Sat hunched over ledgers and served impatient customers.
A fireman, I stood in front of the boiler, my face overwhelmed with bright
flames,
And as a coolie, I ate garbage and kitchen scraps.

So I belong to you and all!
Please, do not resist me!
O, if it could once come to pass,
That we, brother, fell into each other's arms.[87]

The first line and the last stanza have become famous in the history of German literature. The poem reflects Werfel's admiration for Italian opera, one of the most interesting similarities in the personalities of the two authors. Their shared enthusiasm for opera is not a fact that has particular interpretive value, especially since Werfel probably knew little about Whitman's love for this European genre. But Robert Faner's book on Whitman's interest in opera and Adolf Klarmann's study of Werfel prove, along with Werfel's novel *Verdi: Roman der Oper* (1924), how much the *Pathos* of the Italian opera affected both authors and how the younger poet was able to identify with the older on the "musical" level of poetry.[88]

The similarities between this poem and many passages in Whitman, in terms of both form and content, are obvious. Werfel, like many other expressionist followers of Whitman, uses the long line, or rather a mixture of long and short lines. Although the rhymes are kept, there is a prose rhythm strongly resembling Whitman's "lyrical prose" (as Whitman's poetry was frequently referred to in German reviews). Werfel worked from a conception of organic form for lyrical "prophecies" which he had learned from Whitman: "Here a word on purely rhythmic prose: on a kind of poetry which rejects any spatial constraints and which is dominated by the laws of breathing. Its father, if I am not mistaken, is Walt Whitman, who renewed it out of the biblical forms. It is incontestable if it remains true to its task: prophecy."[89]

This observation marks the bridge to the thematic aspects of the poem. Somewhat in the tradition of Whitman's "Inscriptions" (contained in full in Schlaf's translation), Werfel's persona directly addresses the reader. The author assumes the pose of a prophet and presents, in a long introductory line, his dedication to humanity: "My only desire, o man, is to be related to you!" The immediate and direct turn to the reader is remarkable; in a Whitmanesque manner, the poet attempts to enter into quasi-physical contact with his reader, beyond the conventional poet-reader relationship.

In analogy to catalogues in Whitman's poetry—for example, "Song of Myself," sections 15 and 16, giving a cross-section of American society, or the multinational catalogues in "Salut au Monde!"—Werfel's poem offers a picture of the human community in its entirety. Werfel's persona extends its sympathies to all mankind and womankind; from blacks to the Asian "coolie," from the unborn to the shy governess, representatives of humanity of all age groups, sexes, professions, and geographical regions are addressed. The pilot, a representative of modern technology, derives from an area of life opened to poetry mainly by Whitman.

In stanza 3, the lyrical persona moves from approximation to identity, also a very typical Whitmanesque movement.[90] With the anaphorical words "The feeling" (a technique common in the *Leaves*), the lyrical persona identifies in a very emotional way with a group of individuals under psychological pressure. The harpist, the governess, and the debutants are of course not persons typical of Whitman catalogues but figures from Werfel's world, the Austrian-Bohemian bourgeoisie. The shy governess, especially, played an important role in Werfel's life and appears in a series of poems and novels.

In the fourth stanza, the speaker comes still closer to his figures. Whereas in the third he only "knew" about the lives of others, he now *lived* in the forest, *had* a job with the railway, and *ate* the garbage and kitchen scraps. The identification seems complete; a sort of mystical union as in many of Whitman's poems addressing the reader seems to be achieved.

But is this situation really identical with that of Whitman's poetry? For the American author with his remarkable degree of self-confidence, there is no doubt regarding the possibility of such a union, of the identity with his environment and his world.[91] At the end of the long catalogue in section 15 in "Song of Myself" we read:

> And these tend inward to me, and I tend outward to them,
> And such as it is to be of these more or less I am,
> And of these one and all I weave the song of myself.
>
> (*LG*, 44)

Or in the section following:

> Of every hue and caste am I, of every rank and religion,
> A farmer, mechanic, artist, gentleman, sailor, quaker,
> Prisoner, fancy-man, rowdy, lawyer, physician, priest.
> (*LG*, 45)

Does this high degree of optimistic self-confidence on the part of the American persona, who at the beginning of "Song of Myself" claims that "every atom belonging to me as good belongs to you," also exist in "An den Leser?"

The majority of critics have assumed that the poem actually *does* achieve identity between poet and humankind. In a letter to one Hayek, possibly Max Hayek, of 23 March 1925, however, Werfel states: "One who knows my books knows that these virtues [friendship to and kinship with world and humankind] are a *goal* for which one needs to fight with painful *yearning* and that it says nowhere that either I or any other human fulfill it."[92] With this restrictive disclaimer in mind, the poem needs to be reconsidered.

It is the persona's "only desire" to be related to the reader representing humankind, a goal that, according to the first line, has not yet been reached. The movement toward the "other," the identification with humankind in its variety is, judged from the point of view of the last stanza, a lyrical wish dream, presented in the past tense. While he claims to "belong to you and all," as affirmed in a Whitmanesque way in the last stanza, he also pleads, in a most noticeable German subjunctive (the "contrary-to-fact condition" as modern grammar would have it): "Please, do not resist me! / O, if it could once come to pass, / that we, brother, fell into each other's arms." Humankind seems to resist the persona, and it is unlikely that such a union will ever take place. Even *within* the poem, the universal community is revealed to be an unfulfilled fantasy—quite in contrast to Whitman's poetry, where it is mostly successfully realized.

This difference between Whitman's self-centered self-confidence and Werfel's doubt, between the "Kosmos" and the "World's Friend," shows that the American's ego is much better endowed than the Austrian's. This can be demonstrated in other poems by Werfel that lend themselves to easy comparison with Whitman's poetry. In a poem at the beginning of part 3 of *Weltfreund*, Werfel introduces the "Wanderer," a very Whitmanesque figure:

THE WANDERER FALLS INTO THE GRASS

> I am so tired, so tired from walking,
> I feel so heavy, so wonderfully heavy.
> Not tired am I, not heavy,

Only tired from walking and so wonderfully heavy.
I know the reason why:
Earth loves me, the pure soul, intimately
And pulls me violently toward her.
(FWL, 46)[93]

The mystical pose of the individual in the grass reminds us of "Song of Myself." But the certainty of Whitman's persona defining itself as *identical* with the earth ("My tongue, every atom of my blood, form'd from this soil, this air," *LG*, 29) is much more intensive than that of Werfel's "Wanderer," who needs to be violently pulled toward the earth.

In "Dampferfahrt im Vorfrühling" (Steamboat Ride in Early Spring), the lyrical persona describes the world on the riverbank, a series of pictures moving by in rapid succession. Clearly, this very optimistic poem suggests the desire to abolish the borders between perceiver and perceived world:

O dance halls on the shore, o brothers, o steamboat, ferry house, earth and
heaven escorting us!
I am a creature!—I am a creature!
And I spread my arms wide . . .
(FWL, 51)[94]

But the operatic gesture cannot convince the close reader of Werfel's lyrical claims: his arms are spread wide—but the steamboat moves on and the world stays out of reach.

Even in these seemingly optimistic works by Werfel, there is an obvious difference when compared to Whitman. The messianic expressionists, and others, admired Whitman because of the way he encompassed humankind and the cosmos with his *Pathos*-laden verses, representing the union between subject and world. Werfel himself said that Whitman contains "everything that is my knowledge, only in a different type of human being, in a bearded, Atlantic farmer! That is democracy, socialism, love for humankind as a *certainty of the soul*, the way I believe in them. . . . Awake, conscious of death, pleasure-loving, with manly, fatherly irony coming out of the sublime experience of union. . . ."[95] This all-encompassing love for humankind, the union with the world, was what Werfel admired in Whitman and what he wanted to imitate. His many attempts to do so, however, document his failure. The desire to view Whitman as "Yankee-Messiah" already implied, in fact documented, a state of inner disintegration, a split in the personality which could not be restored or "healed."

Whitman himself was hardly the harmonious, "whole" personality of Werfel's projection. From psychoanalytical studies such as Edwin Miller's, we know that Whitman's poetry is not a naive celebration of that which exists. Miller shows in Whitman's poetry the attempt "[to reconcile himself] to the anguish of loneliness. Out of this loneliness, Whitman wrote some of the world's loveliest lyrics."[96]

In his Whitman biography, Justin Kaplan has pointed out again to what a high degree Whitman's work is a reaction to a rapidly changed and changing, increasingly industrializing and urban society. Its amorphous and fragile, both fragmented and fragmenting, character impressed itself with great difficulties in the psyche of human beings used to an agricultural-rural existence.[97] Whitman's very American and radically democratic resolution of that conflict was to *sublimate* this crisis of society and consciousness through a kind of primary narcissism (in Freud's terminology). It is this narcissism that hides behind the rhetoric of love and cosmos. The "Self" is enlarged to cosmic proportions and makes possible a new identification between external and internal world. It deifies itself, and narcissism, often mistaken for and named "love," renders an otherwise alien and alienating world seemingly intact and whole.

In Whitman's poetry, Werfel and other expressionist poets encountered a comprehensive process of lyrical regression. The search for "union" with the "cosmos" leads the self to the "lowest" levels of human consciousness. The tactile sense, as the least differentiated human sense below cognition, therefore plays a central role. In an increasingly technological society, the self looks for communion with nonintellectual forms of life—animals, for example—because

> They do not make me sick discussing their duty to God.
> . . . .
> Picking out here one that I love, and now go with him on brotherly terms.
> A gigantic beauty of a stallion, fresh and responsive to my caresses . . .
> (*LG*, 60)

Or the persona descends to a still lower level of organic life: "If nothing lay more develop'd the quahaug in its callous shell were enough" (*LG*, 57).

In his poetry, Werfel attempted to follow this regressive model. In the afterword to *Wir sind*, he stated this explicitly: "Although these poems are [located] *deep down*, where truth is *just starting to learn to breathe*, I still consider them important for human beings, because they have a mission. They speak in many shapes and forms of only one thing. Of the *permanent consciousness of being, that is piety* (FWL, 137; emphasis added).[98] Permanent consciousness of being on a level "where truth is just starting to learn how to breathe" is hardly the traditional meaning of "piety." Here the regression to a lower level of "consciousness" becomes explicit, and a union that was lost is restored. "To be in any form, what is that?" Whitman asked. And he answered his own question with the recognition just quoted: " . . . the quahaug in its callous shell were enough."

Werfel attempted to imitate the message of salvation he saw in Whitman by copying the American's cosmic pose as brother to humankind, to the world of objects and animals. Whitman's love of rhetoric, his egalitarian program of regression (as shown in the example of the quahaug), serves as a model for the expressionist poet. However, Werfel's poetry also shows that, while he wanted to follow Whitman, the elitist European was unable to regress in the radical, democratic way of the American. Such regression, which would also imply social egalitarianism, seemed too high a price to pay for overcoming the tragic split between self and world.

This difference between Werfel and Whitman points to a basic difference between the two authors and the two worlds they came from. The opening of Werfel's persona to the world is—paradoxically precisely *because* the self maintains its autonomy—a less egotistical process. Whitman's relationship to the world, by contrast—in the sense "There was a child went forth every day, / And the first object he look'd upon, that object he became" (*LG*, 364)—is that of narcissism. This also holds true in view of the fact that Whitman's readers of the preexpressionist and expressionist period did not know of these categories and naively judged this to be an expression of a (Christian) love for the neighbor in accordance with Whitman's wound-dresser image.

In the course of his career, Werfel repeatedly followed his regressive tendencies, especially in literary representations of early childhood. His novel *The Song of Bernadette* can be read as regressive and must necessarily be interpreted from the viewpoint of sectarian Catholic propaganda. The novel shows the attraction this brand of primitivism still had for Werfel toward the end of his life in spite of the fact that the aged European could no longer share the American's opinion.

In spite of the egalitarian tendency and the many proclamations of unity with creation as a whole in the early poetry, the Austrian remained too much an elitist artist in the European tradition and a conservative individual to be completely "liberated" by Whitman, as he put it in the interview with the *World-Telegram.*

With the composition of *Der Gerichtstag* (Court Day, also Doomsday, completed 1917, published 1919) under the influence of the war, the egalitarian impetus in his poetry was replaced by a complex *Gedankenlyrik* (intellectual poetry). From then on, Werfel devoted his poetry more to traditional religiosity—rather than to Whitman, who in speaking of religion meant his own deified self.

The disintegration of the perceiving subject stops and the subject is partially restored; the alienation of the self in a world often recognized as hostile becomes an important theme of Werfel's poetry. Celebration of the universe is replaced by epistemological, philosophical, and cultural criticism. At first, traditional moral values were of little importance in his poetry and the morally indifferent category of "love" was a pseudo-value. Then the Austrian returned to standards of "good" and "evil" in a modified version, to "a religious attitude . . . increasingly emphasized by an ethical emphasis."[99] In a simplified manner, one might say Werfel had switched from (the early) Whitman to Dostoyevsky.

CHAPTER FOURTEEN

BEYOND EXPRESSIONISM

With the end of the expressionist period, the atmospherics of German literature changed dramatically. The tone, style, form, diction, and themes of expressionist poetry were remarkably similar to those of Whitman because of the expressionists' acquaintance with Whitman but also because of the parallels between the two societies at large. Wars (Civil War, World War I), the democratic process (the "second American revolution" as a result of the abolition of slavery and the Southern feudalist system, the revolutions in Germany and Austria in 1918), and the problems connected with the alienation of individuals in industrialized mass societies (in Germany later than in the United States) created similar social situations and prepared the ground for the German reception of Whitman as a mass phenomenon.

In the course of the 1920s, the mood in Germany, Austria, and Switzerland changed. The soberness of the *Neue Sachlichkeit* (New Objectivity, also New Sobriety) movement in literature and the arts, although it did not dominate the whole literary scene, was not very conducive to Whitman's *Pathos.* New Objectivity art also looked across the ocean to America, but to a pragmatic, economist America. After the German currency reform of 1924 which marked the end of the war and the postwar crises, the tone was decidedly antiutopian and anti-*Pathos*—i.e., anti-Whitman. Poetry became functional.

Given this context, it is not surprising that the creative reception of Whitman turned parodistic and ironical. The famous leftist satirical writer Kurt Tucholsky (1890–1935) was convinced of the significance and the value of Whitman's writing, as we saw from his letter to Bauer (see chapter 10).[1] After all, literary satire only works when it targets a literature that has in some ways firmly established itself.

Yet his biting satire and irony reveal as much antagonism as admiration for the American poet:

THE FIVE SENSES

Five senses God, the Lord, has given me, in order to find my way around
here on earth:
Five shining lanterns lighting my dark way;
sometimes one shines, sometimes the other—
never are all five directed to one and the same thing . . .
Shine, lanterns—!

What do you see, Walt Wrobel—? . . .
I see, next to the unfriendly man behind the office window, the dirty little
coffee pot, from which he takes a civilian sip every once in a while . . .
I see the honorable Mr. Appleton from Janesville (Wisconsin) on the
terrace of the Boulevard-Café, laughing cocottes throwing little balls at
him, but he sticks his wooden lower jaw hard into the air . . .
This is what my sight sees.

What do you hear, Walt Wrobel—?
I hear the chef in the kitchen of the French restaurant calling: "Ils
marchent: deux bifteks aux pommes! Une sole meunière!" And four
voices under the high white hats reply: "Et c'est bon!" . . .
This is what my hearing hears.

What do you taste, Walt Wrobel—?
I taste the lower crust of the fruit tart which my aunt has baked; regarding
the tart, it is a bit blackened below, this is where the dough got burnt, it
crunches in the mouth like sand . . .
This what my taste tastes. . . .

Five senses God, the Lord, has given me, in order to find my way around
here on earth:
Sight, hearing, taste, smell, touch.
Five senses for the immensity of all phenomena.
This world is imperfection, her lighting is imperfect. . . .

Shine, lanterns!
Stumbling, my foot is searching for the way, the lanterns are flashing.
With all five senses I take it in, and it is not their fault: mostly
it is
pain.[2]

Tucholsky's parody, of course, refers to the Germans' favorite Whitman poem, "Salut au Monde!" Tucholsky's point is clear from these excerpts. Whitman's spiritualized epistemological optimism—"My spirit has pass'd in compassion and determination around the whole earth" (*LG*, 148)—is shown to be unfounded; the wealth of all phenomena cannot possibly all be grasped by five senses. Paradoxically, the senses mediate mainly one thing: pain. The global panorama in Whitman's poem is replaced—as is characteristic of the atmosphere of New Objectivity literature—by ridiculous local observations from the author's everyday life. The presentation of this life, from Mr. Appleton to auntie's tart, is totally devoid of *Pathos*; it is petty-bourgeois, mean—and painful. At the very best, it is slightly humorous—something Whitman's poem is certainly not.

The only other significant writer between the wars who worked Whitman creatively into his own writings was Thomas Mann. In his famous novel *Magic Mountain*, a Whitman catalogue appears in French(!) in a central section of the novel where the protagonist Hans Castorp finally manages to declare his love for Clawdia Chauchat. This technique has the quality of a collage, slightly reminiscent of other modernist works such as T.S. Eliot's *The Waste Land*.

For months, Castorp has been hesitant about approaching Clawdia. Using Whitman's section 9 of "I Sing the Body Electric," he manages to address her directly as a sexual being.[3] The way Mann secretly slipped a Whitman catalogue in French into a declaration of love in a German novel, without ever mentioning Whitman's name, forms a prime example of Mann's famous ironical attitude toward his texts. The protagonist, Hans Castorp, a very repressed, very German character, could never have made this "physiological" declaration in German. In his letter to Reisiger, Mann said that the new Germany needs not only Goethe, but a good dose of Whitman as well. Is this young German in this ironical *Bildungsroman* learning from Whitman?[4]

But there is also another aspect to this use of Whitman. In the novel, Castorp's declaration of love is coupled with his reminiscences of a homoerotic relationship in his youth. Given Mann's awareness of the homoeroticism in Whitman's poetry, this passage also serves as an encoded way of suggesting Castorp's bisexual orientation.[5] These sections in *Zauberberg* are the only known cases of intertextuality with regard to Whitman in Mann's works. Mann used Whitman in a specific situation, but not at all as a literary model in the way the expressionists had done.

The strange creative reception of Whitman's poetry during the Nazi period is discussed in detail in the section on Whitman and politics (chapter 17). The fatal parallels between Whitman's tone and diction and that of some Nazi poets led to a blockade of creative Whitman reception which still exists, with some significant exceptions, today.

While exile writers used Whitman and Whitman poetry in their polemics against their Nazi enemies, the distance between their own writing and Whitman remained great. One notable exception is the Viennese poet Ernst Waldinger (1896–1970), who managed to escape to the United States in 1938. His volume *Zwischen Hudson und Donau* (Between Hudson and Danube, 1958), an example of "intercontinental poetry," has Whitmanesque qualities, especially in form and diction. Waldinger addresses Whitman several times by name, for example, in "Auf der Fähre" (On the Ferry),[6] a reminiscence of Whitman's "Crossing Brooklyn Ferry."

Susanne Araas-Vesely reports on the response to Whitman by Gertrud Kolmar (1894–1943?). Kolmar, a German-Jewish poet, was deported by the Nazis in 1943 and probably died in a concentration camp. Her poetry is one of the most interesting examples of anti-Nazi literature.[7]

Although the interest in Whitman after World War II was great and many German poets were fascinated by what they considered to be the internationalist message of Whitman's poetry, they remained fairly aloof from him. A poem by Jürgen Wellbrock (born 1949) addressed to Whitman is strongly critical of Whitman and Whitman's rhetoric. At the same time, as Wellbrock himself says, it testifies to the power of Whitman's voice and the necessity for every poet to come to terms with it. Wellbrock speaks of his "ambivalent" attitude to Whitman, whose expansiveness and freedom he admires but whose rhetoric and glorification of strength and body he rejects.

I CAN'T SING YOUR SELF
(For Walt Whitman)

You sing yourself, you singer and perfect soldier,
  and your song, carrying no address, meets a corpse.
    Sounds that are caught
in your frailest leaves,
knotted not in the old knot of contrairiety,
which you, chewing prairie-grass, have knotted
from haste and bones.

WRITING mocks the technique of your wrist:
you never sang the divine average.
Whoever touches you these days, touches a book,
moving in the hands of busy corpses.

The word "Democratic" I utter, if you will, calmly,
but my physiology has no boot-soles.
  Instead I am shooting again,
and the resulting crack is the song
to the curvature of your writing-finger
  (o how it's flattering me).

The same old laughter.

Do not announce what comes after you:
your own finalè drowned in the chords.
To know what it is to be evil
does not make us better.

Singer, you have blisters on your lips![8]

The poem is a clever montage of Whitman quotations which are famous in Germany. Each of them is refuted. No German poet has "talked back" in a more radical fashion to Whitman than Wellbrock.

In the GDR, the situation was somewhat different. A number of writers such as Johannes R. Becher, Arnold Zweig, Kurt Barthel, Volker Braun, Karl Mickel, Wilhelm Tkaczyk, Paul Wiens, Peter Gosse, and others seem to have been willing, although with great hesitation, to use Whitman to convey their own messages and sometimes the ideological message of their state. Yet they make sparing use of this vehicle.

In a purer form, Whitman's ideological function in the German Democratic Republic appears in a poem by Gabriele Eckart (born 1954), then a high school student:

TO WALT WHITMAN

searching for meters I met you,
                    Walt Whitman.
i know, if you lived today and here,
you would sing with endless astonishment—
reveal the gigantic themes
                    in hymns,
you would
  sing of the surging crowds
                    passing through the cities,
    rejoicing in the applause of the light façades,

sing of the millions of faces,
flushed with enthusiasm
high above banners of the blood
of fallen fighters,
sing of the gigantic combines,
like silver birds,
hurrying across the furrows,
sing of the students on the benches
of the endless chestnut avenue,
calculating the coming hundred years,
sing of the lilac, giving shade to the
children,
they know not Lincoln but build
in the sand
rockets and castles that do not
remain illusions,
sing of the breathing of cities,
growing into the cosmos,
sing of the people on their flat roofs
high above, waving to the sun with red scarves,
sing of the meadows flooded with flowers,
carrying the lovers.
but you are dead, Walt Whitman,
therefore be my teacher; teach me your meters!
i will sing instead of you![9]

In recent years, Eckart has emerged as a talented and successful lyricist and prose writer. At the time she wrote this poem, she was still quite young and her ideological environment obviously had strong control over her, even though the poem, upon closer examination, does reveal a certain critical potential.[10] Her "search for meters," in the course of which she encountered Whitman, already points to the original poetry she would write in the future. By the mid-1980s, Eckart had become a dissident persecuted by East German political intelligence and eventually removed to the United States.

The case of Roland Kluge (born 1944), another GDR poet, is quite different. The Whitman address of this part-time poet (a physician by profession) deals with the frequent attempts to pronounce Whitman dead. Yet, to the poet writing in the "mid-age" years of tranquillity and "maturity," Whitman is still as provocative as ever. Kluge writes that "for somebody who was forced to live in a walled-in country, it can be a revelation to see the upright posture of a human being: self-determination instead of other-directedness, sensuality instead of prudishness, love of truth rather than hypocrisy. . . . To me, Walt Whitman was a great help."

WALT WHITMAN'S SPIRIT,
SO OFTEN PRONOUNCED DEAD

In these middle years   these
Years of maturity
When time seems to be
Inexhaustible
And my hands dive into it
As into mountains of grains of wheat

I encountered you   encountered
Your voice   indomitable
There
Where there is smoke and the rolling of the
Cities
Where humans touch each other
Exchanging their electricity

You love masses   substance
To chew between teeth   to taste
Bodies   to clasp with deepest
Breaths   Splendid
Counsel of our capability to love
A Niagara   not to be shouted down or
Hissed down

The herds of buffalos
Fill America's plains as if with thunder
You seize the continent from coast to
Coast   spirit
Foaming around the Capitoline Hills
In the remotest citadels of power
Dashing the oceans
Foam of your words

Comprehending the Cosmos as Great
Camerado

Perceiving the same
Song
In the nameless leaf of grass
As in the inexhaustible semen
Of the galaxy
Are you still trickling forth
From the broken plant
Invincible wolf's-milk[11]

With the end of the German Democratic Republic as a state, very specific conditions for a prolonged creative Whitman reception have come to an end. It seems as though the pluralistic character of life and culture in the West, which is likely to dominate the whole country, has discouraged the creative reception of writers such as Whitman whose appeal is so strong that it excludes the possibility of mixtures of styles and themes. With the advent of postmodern literature, writers have also become much more conscious of their intertextual practice, a process which has certainly not aided Whitman's creative reception.

Furthermore, in an age of a potential nuclear holocaust and global ecological catastrophes, Whitman's universal optimism becomes somewhat tedious. Only a new attitude toward his poetry, which would probably have to be prepared by an interpretive enterprise that stressed the cultural criticism implied in Whitman's work, might change this situation. Whether this will occur, possibly in conjunction with the creative powers of the newly emerging gay rights movement, remains to be seen.

POLITICS

While the democratic-republican tradition in the United States reaches back to 1776 and earlier, most German-speaking Europeans (with the notable exception of the Swiss) were still fighting feudalist structures in their societies at a time when industrialization had already caused the emergence of the socialist movement. Justifiably or not, "America" had been the battle-cry of the German-speaking left throughout the nineteenth century, while European conservatives, especially authorities charged with keeping their subjects from emigrating, eyed developments in the New World with distrust.

It is therefore not surprising that Germans read Whitman's appeal to democracy in a much more politicized way than American readers. Betsy Erkkila (*Whitman the Political Poet*) has traced Whitman's political views and defined his construction as a "political poet" through his life and poetry. However, she says little regarding the *reception* of these views. Indeed, if Whitman's political "message" had been "understood" in the United States, Erkkila would not have had to write her book *defending* Whitman as a political poet. In Europe, however, Whitman's political positions, allusions, and implications were well understood, sometimes too well, judging by some of the over- and misinterpretations discussed in the following chapters. But in the eyes of most German readers, Whitman was a natural political poet who had taken strong political stands.

There is much disagreement over the question of whether Whitman can be considered a political radical or not. Possibly Traubel's leftist-socialist convictions steered the Whitman-movement in a direction Whitman himself would have been uneasy about. But Traubel's championship of leftist ideas was not the only reason Whitman appealed to political radicals in Europe. Whitman's strong and passionate rhetoric, his unconventional diction, and his refusal to buy into poetic conventions seem to have fascinated political activists in general, and not only on the left. Naturally, his status as a "poet of democracy" made him more interesting to the left than to conservatives. But, as chapter 17 shows, the extreme political right, too, attempted to utilize Whitman's strong appeal to German readers, albeit with much less success.

CHAPTER FIFTEEN

WHITMAN AND THE MARXISTS

In discussing Max Hayek's Whitman translation, I have already described a very specific wartime context which gave rise to the Social Democratic interest in the translation of Whitman's works. However, Social Democratic journals noticed Whitman much earlier than 1915. As early as 1904, the *Sozialistische Monatshefte* carried an article on Whitman by Johannes Schlaf. In this article, William O'Connor's image of the "Good Gray Poet" and wound-dresser was highlighted.[1] In 1905, a Whitman essay by the socialist critic Stefan Großmann appeared in the Viennese Social Democratic *Arbeiter-Zeitung*.[2] In 1907, Richard Scheid discussed O. E. Lessing's German translation of Traubel's *Chants communal* (German title *Weckrufe*) alongside Whitman's poetry and emphasized the importance of these authors for the development of a genuine American socialism.[3] The Austrian "proletarian" author Maurice Reinhold von Stern (1860–1938) made the extraordinary and, for his time, singular attempt to characterize Whitman as a "collectivist poet"—thereby anticipating Soviet and some Hispanic constructions (especially Anatoly Lunacharsky and Pedro Mir).[4]

In 1908, an interesting essay discussing socialist tendencies in American poetry appeared in the German Social Democratic weekly *Die Neue Zeit*: "Walt Whitman is *the* American poet in whose works all currents of a preproletarian socialism, born out of an enthusiasm for democracy and out of confidence in its consequences, found their strongest and most sublime expression. . . . And not of European democracy, whose every step is hampered, restrained, whose unfolding was hindered by old traditions and strong remnants of reactionary classes. . . ."[5] This passage is remarkable in that it makes allowances for the specific quality of American democracy, which—in contrast to the European version—was not hampered by remnants of feudalism (excepting, of course, the system of the antebellum South which was eliminated by the Civil War). In this way, the author claims to recognize a "magnificent view of a distant dawn [in Whitman's visions of a radical democracy] which seemed to foreshadow socialism."[6]

In 1910, Hermann Bahr conducted a Whitman evening in a Viennese workers' education organization:

> He [Bahr] ended by saying that Whitman celebrated organization, that he was the singer of the term 'comrade.' . . .
>
> Bahr concluded the evening with a reading of Whitman poetry . . . whose anticonventional tendency in the best sense of the term was . . . frantically applauded by the audience.[7]

It is unclear in which way Bahr thought Whitman celebrated "organization" (referring to the structure of the Social Democratic Party),[8] but the quote shows an attempt to use Whitman even in day-to-day political work. Moreover, there is an indication that Whitman's poetic "anticonventionality" was considered "antibourgeois," somehow representing the new aesthetics of a new literature of the working class.[9]

Whitman reception during the war years, with their uneasy mixture of pacifist fantasies and attempts to justify involvement in the war, was dominated by the right wing of the Social Democrats. At the same time, however, there were some attempts by leftist Social Democrats and by non-Marxist leftists to use Whitman for antiwar purposes as well.

Clara Zetkin's socialist women's journal *Die Gleichheit* (Equality) carried a few poems by Whitman and Traubel.[10] One of the poems published was "Come Up from the Fields Father." It is not hard to imagine the effect of the following lines on the women readers of *Die Gleichheit* during World War I, most of whom had a husband, a son, or a brother to worry about:[11]

> Open the envelope quickly,
> O this is not our son's writing, yet his name is sign'd
> O a strange hand writes for our dear son, O stricken mother's soul!
> All swims before her eyes, flashes with black, she catches the main words
> only,
> Sentences broken, *gunshot wound in the breast, cavalry skirmish,*
> *taken to hospital,*
> *At present low, but will soon be better.*
>
> (*LG*, 302f.)

A Whitman volume strictly guided by pacifist interests was published in Switzerland in 1919,[12] containing Whitman diary entries and letters to his mother that are clearly directed against the war. They stress the American's abhorrence of militancy and violence and contain no apologies whatsoever. The selection shows the intention of the Alsatian expressionist author René Schickele as editor and Gustav Landauer and Ivan Goll as translators to create an uncompromisingly pacifist book. Quite in contradistinction to this aim, Franz Diederich (see chapter 7 above) quoted Whitman's civil war diary entries and interpreted them as supposedly harmonizing "human wars and cosmic peace"[13]—thereby, of course, making war seem inevitable and even constructive.

The loss of the war, coupled with economic depression and widespread starvation, produced a highly revolutionary and explosive situation in Germany and Austria. The success of the Bolshevik revolution in Russia and a Soviet Republic even in nearby Hungary radicalized the political climate. On the extreme left, the small but well-organized Communist Party pushed the Social Democrats to abandon their policy of compromise with the existing state. The monarchs were forced to abdicate and new republics were created which promised welfare and social security for the working masses.

In this situation, the meaning of Whitman's message was reinterpreted by the Social Democrats. The poet of war changed now into a poet of peace, democracy, and socialism. The theoretical journal of the Austrian Social Democrats, *Der Kampf* (The Struggle), edited by Friedrich Adler, explained Whitman's timeliness for the Social Democratic cause: "Walt Whitman's time has only now arrived. He is the poet of our day, he is the poet of the years to come."[14] Whitman was soon constructed as a prophet for the new republics that had just been established in Central Europe.

Whitman's egalitarian discourse found its way into Social Democratic interpretations: "*En masse*, that's the word of democracy. No state is less valuable than the next, no race inferior to the next, no man, finally, better than the next. Even the lowest will rise; those who are last in line will come to the front. Everything that is created is divine, nothing is imperfect."[15] This passage, with obvious biblical overtones (Matthew 19:30), shows the emerging leftist fascination with "masses" and mass phenomena. Whitman's mythical "en masse" (although meant as part of a dialectic between the "mass" of the people and the individual, and not in a collectivist spirit) must have been of paramount interest to German leftists.

Most leftist commentaries on Whitman and Whitman's poetry during the postwar period included a socialist-religious rhetoric which may have bewildered solid Marxist atheists. *Leaves* was celebrated in a hymnic, religious tone and was said to be "the bible of democracy: her [i.e. democracy's] powerful breath drifts through these forceful utterances and prophecies, the idea of equal rights and equality of all human beings and races, no one less divine than the next. The democratic idea in its purely human, timeless strength is presented with incomparable magnificence."[16]

A look into the leftist (including Communist) press of the period, however, shows that such religious overtones were common: "The religiosity of the nondenominational, the love of the new heathen, the exultant love of life by a godless dreamer of the earth rushes in blessed choirs through his [Whitman's] creations."[17] In a world still massively influenced by organized religion and religious thinking, Whitman's poetry served as a kind of ersatz metaphysics for those socialists who wanted to pass for atheists but were still psychologically grounded in the divine. Thus, religious belief disappeared; religious rhetoric, however, remained. It comes as no surprise that Whitman also fulfilled these requirements. In his later poetry, often quoted by the socialist press (for example "The Mystic Trumpeter"), he stressed the "religious-spiritual" nature of his own poetry.

In the period of stabilization following the postwar "revolutionary" years, Whitman continued to find his way into the party press, but the revolutionary interpretation of his poetry was replaced by more conventional, sometimes even conservative readings. The women's section of the Social Democratic *Vorwärts*, for example, claimed to be investigating Whitman's attitude toward women. Following the questionable thesis that "poetry of all countries and peoples [has always been] a more or less faithful mirror of women, their souls and desires, their love and suffering," the male contributor summarizes Whitman's attitude:

> Walt Whitman, finally, the American socialist[!] and famous author of the book of poetry *Leaves of Grass*, whose 32nd anniversary we are celebrating this year, says of women:
>
> "The female contains all qualities and tempers them,
> She is in her place and moves with perfect balance,
> She is all things duly veil'd, she is both passive and active,
> She is to conceive daughters as well as sons, and sons as well as daughters.
>
> As I see my soul reflected in Nature,
> As I see through a mist, One with inexpressible completeness, sanity, beauty,
> See the bent head, and the arms folded over the breast, the Female I see."[18]

Taken by itself, this section from "I Sing the Body Electric" sends a strange message. In Whitman's original context, the emphasis is on the physical quality of the human being, the liberation of the human body. When Fischer isolates this passage and interprets it as Whitman's central statement on womanhood, it is reductionist: women are reduced to the traditional sex role, including child-bearing.

It seems ironic that a writer associated with the party championing equal rights for all should distort the emancipatory view of women in Whitman's poetry by quoting a passage out of context and in a misleading way, but it reminds us that in spite of the fact that male European leftists fought for the formal, legal emancipation of women and were successful in procuring voting rights for them, they were unable to accord to them an equal status in their own *minds.*

The American writer was also offered as a model of identification for young socialists. A didactic article in a Social Democratic youth magazine suggested to its readers: "Yes, you [young reader] are Walt, the great, strong brother of life, a man confident in the future, affirmative of the present, the creative son of the world, moving forward!"[19] During the twenties, Whitman was also repeatedly quoted in the *Jungsozialistische Blätter*, where he was usually presented as a progressive American writer. An excerpt from "Paumanok" even appears on the title page of one issue.[20]

When Hayek's Whitman translations were collected in two volumes in 1919 and 1921,[21] Whitman entered the libraries of Social Democratic Party organizations, trade unions, and institutions of continuing education for workers. But Hayek's translations, growing out of the war experience, were not particularly suited for these purposes. As the edition produced in the German Democratic Republic shows, a selection with an emphasis on the "revolutionary Whitman" would have been entirely possible, but poems such as "Europe" or "To a Foil'd European Revolutionaire" were not included in Hayek's edition. Nevertheless, Whitman became an important factor in organized working-class culture.[22]

The Social Democratic Party had moved far away from its original revolutionary positions and become a part of parliamentary democracy. In this way, Whitman became a poet of the party, recited on festive occasions, but of little concern for the party's ideological orientation. The official printed program of an evening devoted to working-class poetry in Heilbronn in the southwestern part of Germany, for example, included two Whitman poems: "When I Peruse the Conquer'd Fame" and "The Mystic Trumpeter." Section 8 of the "Trumpeter" (the final section) concluded the evening.[23]

Compared to the wide-spread interest in Whitman on the part of the Social Democrats, the groups further to the left seem to have had little use for Whitman in the 1920s and 1930s. In the party paper of the (leftist) Independent Social Democrats of Germany, *Die Freiheit* (Freedom), there is an article identifying Whitman as representative of a "preproletarian socialism,"[24] without, however, any noteworthy political message. In her reception study of U.S. literature in the Communist German press prior to 1933, Helga Lumer found only one reference to Whitman—the poem "Years of the Modern" in the Communist daily *Rote Fahne.*[25] This is surprising because the first Soviet commissar for education, Anatoly Lunacharsky, was very interested in Whitman as a poetic and moral force in the construction of socialist society.[26] His remarks on Whitman as a collectivist poet, however, probably never reached Germany before 1945.

This Soviet championship of Whitman became a significant factor in Whitman's reception in the Soviet-occupied zone of Germany between 1945 and 1949 and the German Democratic Republic after 1949. Many of the Communist exiles who, persecuted by Hitler, had fled to the USSR encountered Whitman there. Moreover, some prominent Communists who were to obtain high positions in the GDR had been Whitmanites in their youth.

This is especially true of Johannes R. Becher, who, as we have seen, was an ardent Whitmanite in his younger expressionist years. In addition to his creative adaptations of Whitman discussed earlier, Becher showed surprisingly strong political interest in Whitman. His poetry proves how much influence Whitman exerted on some individual radical leftists. In a poem weighing the poets of the *décadence* against Whitman, Becher writes:

> But tirelessly, again and again,
> *Whitman*, long by himself, pushing
> a hymnic paean, like one of these moving shields
> in front of him, against the nations still warring—
> ha!—against their innumerable cannons.
> (—!But you, poets of decay! . . .
> Stylized rot is pouring
> from the containers of your works. Brightly,
> the pus-moon is crawling up the corridor of your
> veins.[27]

Here, Whitman, the American, is favorably contrasted with the authors of decay and *décadence* (i.e., European authors). The Marxist Becher was fascinated by American mass society; using Whitman's mass rhetoric in his own poetry, he calls for a "Socialist Army" (the piece was written around the time of the Russian Revolution of 1917):

> Let us subordinate ourselves, once and for all, consciously, full of belief: o most splendid, most glorious of all deeds, let us willingly discipline ourselves. En masse: what a word: what magic! What magic! What a flow, what a word: en masse! . . . Let us join![28]

Becher hardly understood the difference between Whitman's idealistic, visionary conception of "masses" and his own political view, but he did see American "mass society" as a phenomenon which was important to the socialist experiment. In 1924, he wrote:

> From two countries, the beacons flare up to you, German people, on your march. From America. From Russia. . . . from the anonymous Russia of 150 million workers and farmers, from Lenin's Russia, and Gorky's Russia. . . . [And . . .] from the America of Whitman and Sinclair, and, I dare say, from the "America of Chaplin." From an America with power eyes, steel skin, from an electric America which will one day be the technologically most perfected bulwark of the world, controlled by the working masses.[29]

Becher, one of the leading German exiles in the USSR during World War II, eventually became minister of culture in the GDR. Through him and other comrades, Whitman received a significant position in the official and unofficial cultural life of the GDR.

In 1947, Whitman was already included in propagandistic booklets used by the blue-shirted Freie Deutsche Jugend (Free German Youth) and referred to as "America's great poet of liberation".[30] The cultural weekly founded by Becher, *Sonntag* (Sunday), regularly carried articles on Whitman, frequently suggesting that bourgeois society, uncomfortable with Whitman's revolutionary poetry, had persecuted him: "Bourgeois morality has always accepted confessions by individuals in literature without indignation, even if they expressed the most perverted vices. It only became uncomfortable when an author's word managed to get a hold on a reality which those who dominate society claim the right to mystify. As soon as a literary confession is replaced by an address to the world's realities, as soon as the poet's 'I' appeals to the readers' 'we,' public hypocrisy is mobilized. It persecuted Whitman into his old age."[31] This idea of an almost systematic repression of Whitman's writings by bourgeois American society and its state is frequently expressed in GDR literature on Whitman. Whitman did lose his Washington position as a result of "public hypocrisy" (even though he received a new position soon enough), of course, and the publication of his books was made difficult (in at least one case) by legal action.

What GDR commentators failed to understand is that this did not amount to the persecution of a politically dangerous author by the "system." Whitman was incomprehensible to most Americans in the nineteenth century and there was little danger of an identification between the poet's "I" and the readers. Whitman's poems were not commonly read by his compatriots as revolutionary texts. What the American public did understand were the sexually explicit passages—and the reaction was one of "healthy" indignation.

In the passage quoted above, the prominent use of the term "reality" points to another misunderstanding. If Whitman was to be accepted into a Marxist system, he *had* to be a "realist" of some kind. GDR criticism often addresses Whitman as a realist, in line with other realist-"naturalist" authors such as Jack London, Upton Sinclair, and Theodore Dreiser. In such a *tour de force* of literary history, even Emerson could become a "pioneer of realism in American literature."[32] In Hans Petersen's afterword to Arendt's GDR edition of Whitman in 1966 we read: "What [in Whitman's *oeuvre*] was frequently interpreted as an experiment in depth psychology on the part of an egocentric personality with his own self [as an object] is really the starting point for the discovery of the world, the cosmos, the infinity of space and time and the human individual, which are defined as a pantheistic unity."[33] It was obviously important for Marxists to reinterpret Whitman's extreme subjectivity as quasi-"objective" and "realistic."

The special quality of Marxist conceptions of "realism," however, is that they are didactic. "Realism" is never just the photographic reproduction of an outside world; it is always also a world as it ought to be. As the commentaries of a number of critics suggest, Whitman's "realism" is really the conception of an ideal, better world, for which the American fought with revolutionary fervor: "Whitman had little interest in 'absolute poetry,' in art for art's sake. His poetry was to excite readers for a better life, to kindle their enthusiasm for his idea."[34] From this vision, it is only a small step to an awkward didacticism. Even Whitman's early temperance novel, a work its author hardly took seriously, is employed for this argument: ". . . especially for young people, he wrote a tale entitled 'Franklin Evans, or The Inebriate.' Whitman, the excellent schoolmaster, wanted his works to be useful. . . . in each poem, Whitman wanted to present something moralistic, i.e., something useful to humanity. . . ."[35]

In this way, some GDR critics constructed an author who almost completely fit the desired ideological coordinates of their own state. That Whitman idealized America did not matter. America was made to fit Marxist ideology by emphasizing that at that time "American democracy . . . was as young as he [Whitman] was, when he first reached for the pen. Liberalism still had revolutionary passion and vital energy; revolution, human rights, freedom, rejection of class differences—all this amounted to a tradition which Whitman later called the 'good old cause.' "[36] By the time Whitman "reached for the pen," America had already experienced its first economic crises and, in the course of expansionist policies, had already lost its political innocence. The image of a pure, shining, young democracy coupled with the idea of a "democracy-turned-sour" after the Civil War is a myth, but served to integrate Whitman into Marxist-Leninist conceptions of the United States.

The question remains why Communists in the GDR were so interested in Whitman in the first place? Why (apart from personal reasons of individuals like Becher) was Whitman so widely accepted in the GDR? Why were his poems and even his prose almost always available and why was he mentioned so frequently? There are essentially three reasons. First, there was the revolutionary "tradition" of Whitman's German reception. The American-Soviet Americanist Maurice Mendelson even suggested, using information furnished by John Spargo, that Marx himself liked Whitman, especially "Pioneers! O Pioneers."[37] Critics in the GDR did not go quite as far. But there was the initial interest of Freiligrath, a revolutionary and friend of Marx, as well as Whitman's reception by revolutionaries all over the world: the Soviet writer Vladimir Mayakovsky, the Turkish writer Nazim Hikmet, Pablo Neruda, and, of course, Becher himself. For Friedemann Berger, Whitman even became the "father figure of modern literature."[38]

A second set of reasons can be traced to Whitman's historical significance as an author writing at a time when bourgeois society was still young. The "first worker's and farmer's state on German soil" (the GDR's self-definition) understood itself as continuing the best traditions of humankind. These "best traditions" were often defined as cultural achievements by revolutionary classes of all ages. Of course, Hawthorne, Melville, or Poe might have qualified as well (and they were, indeed, widely published in the GDR), but they did not have Whitman's apparent bright optimism, his positive image. In this view, Whitman as a revolutionary writer of the bourgeoisie anticipated revolutionary writers of the emerging socialist society.

Closely connected with this is a third reason. Whitman's construction as a revolutionary poet obviously coincided with Communist ideals of what a revolutionary writer should be like. The GDR poet Kuba wrote: "Just as the poetry of Walt Whitman, the singer of young bourgeois America, deals with the human individual, Vladimir Mayakovsky, writing for the young working class, focuses on the new society in his poetry."[39] Sometimes it appears as though GDR critics appreciated in Whitman the kind of optimism which they missed in their own writers.

Whitman was not only mythologized for the purpose of providing a context of revolutionary world literature for the writers of the GDR, who frequently felt cut off from the rest of the German-speaking world. He also lent himself to multiple applications as a commentator on the relations between the United States and the socialist countries. During the Cold War, the East German literary journal *Neue Deutsche Literatur* published a passage by Whitman under the title "Walt Whitman contra McCarthy."[40] One year later, in 1955, the International Peace Council, often considered a Communist front organization, recommended that the anniversary of the first edition of *Leaves* be commemorated. In the USSR, a large Whitman celebration was held in Moscow. On 6 November 1955, the GDR followed this up with an official celebration at Weimar, the city of Goethe and Schiller, in the course of which GDR Americanist Karl-Heinz Wirzberger spoke of the "sluggishness . . . of [present-day] Americans with their full stomachs," which he compared unfavorably with Whitman's revolutionary energy.[41] In the early period of détente, Arendt's Whitman edition closed with the optimistic preface Whitman had written for a Russian edition of his works, where the poet deals with the common interests of "You Russians and Us Americans." In the late sixties and seventies, Whitman became, much less aggressively than in the early years, a "prophet of a better America."

A final fascinating aspect of Whitman's reception in the GDR is the fact that he not only received official support but was also widely read by young people; official and popular interest coincided in a strange way. Many young readers in the GDR, unable even to get to West Germany let alone to the United States, used Whitman in order to undertake a literary voyage to a country that had so many mythical connotations. Whitman was therefore a rare and important cultural bridge between the United States and the GDR.

CHAPTER SIXTEEN

THE ANARCHIST WHITMAN

The term "anarchism" conjures up secret associations, violence, bombs, and assassinations, but these widely held connotations derive from a propagandistic effort based on the uncharacteristic activities of only a few anarchists in a few countries. Quite in contrast to this popular myth, most anarchists emphasize their unconditional pacifism and their ardent desire for personal freedom. In their opposition to power, bloodshed, and coercion, they differ notably from Communists of any kind.

As early as 1902, the colorful anarchist journal *Der arme Teufel* (Poor Devil), which had such important personalities as Erich Mühsam and Gustav Landauer among its contributors, published poems and prose pieces by Whitman.[1] A poem by Mühsam and part of Whitman's 1855 preface introduce the programmatic first issue:

> This is what you shall do: Love the earth and sun and the animals, despise riches, give alms to every one that asks, stand up for the stupid and crazy, devote your income and labor to others, hate tyrants, argue not concerning God, have patience and indulgence toward the people, take off your hat to nothing known or unknown. . . . (*LG*, 714f.)[2]

This is a Whitman quotation indeed worthy of an anarchist publication.

Much more intensive anarchist interest in Whitman began immediately after World War I. In the discussions surrounding war and peace in the revolutionary period, anarchist writers interpreted Whitman in a significantly different and much less convoluted way than the Social Democrats. Anarchists did not have to turn Whitman from a "poet of war" into a "poet of democracy." Rather, they employed for their own purposes the anarchist tendencies in Whitman's works, such as demands for disobedience, decrease of (governmental and other) authority, and rule of "love" and "intellect."

Freie Jugend (Free Youth) for example, a "youth journal for anarchist socialism" published in Berlin, related Whitman's life and work directly to postwar revolutionary events in Germany. The following hymnic call served as introduction to Whitman's poem "To a Foil'd European Revolutionaire":[3]

> You, German youth,
> will also hear his ardent calls,
> just as in 1853[!] his compatriots, North America.
> This man opened his mouth, without having
> the permission of an authority.
> He wrote and printed his "*green leaves*"[!]
> (title of his work) without degree, without
> having been examined by professors.
> From *life*, not books, he became wise,
> through himself.
> Carpenter and son of a carpenter, like
> Jesus
> full of ardent love for *everybody* and *everything*, like
> Jesus
> a fighter against *all* repression.
> Enemy of the state: out of love for *order* among humans.
> Enemy of the church: out of religion and conscience.
> *One* authority only he accepts for human beings:
> their own conscience.
> As there has never been another authority.
> Not in the time of Jesus, who went to Jerusalem
> in order to be crucified.
> Not in the time of Karl Liebknecht, who was murdered
> by our servants of war
> The great heroic deed of the German Republic.[4]

Very much in accordance with the ideal of a repression-free, anarchist socialism, this piece questions all established order and authority in Whitman's name. Unlike the vague presentation of Whitman in the Social Democratic youth magazine, this anarchist journal addressing young people takes a clear and radical point of view. Freedom of speech (opening one's mouth without permission of an authority) is only one, relatively harmless, demand. The *Freie Jugend* goes on to reject the entire established system of education. Instead of reading books, human beings should immerse themselves in life itself (a strange thesis when supported with a poet whose work is not exactly characterized by brevity). This is the expressionist interpretation of Whitman translated into the realm of politics. The well-known analogy to Jesus is radicalized, and the love for everybody and everything (including the world of things) is supplemented by a battle "against all repression." State and authorities are held responsible for disorder and unscrupulousness; their abolition would therefore lead to, or better, *restore* "order among human beings" and "religion." What sort of a "conscience" could possibly replace authorities remains vague.

The most interesting aspects of this text are the parallels between the crucifixion of Jesus and the murder of Karl Liebknecht, a German Communist leader who was considered a martyr. In this German context, the poem "To a Foil'd European Revolutionaire," in which Whitman recommended himself as the voice of "every dauntless rebel the world over" (*LG*, 370), became a defiant obituary. The German translation even reinforces Whitman's *Pathos.* The English line "And stakes his life to be lost at any moment" (*LG*, 370) becomes in German "Und setzt ein sein Leben, ums *gern* zu verlieren, jeden Augenblick" (*gladly* stakes his life to be lost at any moment); "cause" in the original becomes "*große* Sache" (*great* cause; all emphasis added).

The poem's immediate context in the anarchist journal offers further insight into this reading of Whitman. Immediately following the poem, on the same page, there is a *Pathos*-laden call to comrades in the Communist Party entitled "Blood or Spirit?" It emphasizes that Communists and anarchists have identical ideals: "Communists! We want what is most necessary! We are serious! One does not play with ideas, one fights for them. We want the same [as you]."[5] However, the anarchists condemn force and violence as a means in the political struggle:

> But: Your way is the weapon! Your way is dictatorship! That is blood! That is power! Against blood, against power you have fought. Now you want to shed blood toward power. . . . *Somebody will have to be the first to renounce blood and power if blood and power should ever be driven from this world.* To take up weapons is miserable weakness. . . . Don't hate, *love*! Love begets love! Hatred begets hatred! Don't ape others! *Be* free! Not blood but intellect![6]

If Whitman's "Foil'd Revolutionaire" celebrates "defeat, poverty, misconception, imprisonment," and finally also death, because even "death and dismay are great" (*LG*, 371), then Liebknecht, killed by representatives of the old order, is by analogy turned into a martyr. Communists are asked to join the nonviolent activism of the anarchists. This construction of Whitman is quite different from that of Social Democrats, who attempted to use an idea such as "dismay is great" as a way of coming to terms with their guilty conscience in the postwar years. Anarchists do not question the revolutionary aim, the new society, but rather the effectiveness of a strategy of power and violence as the means to that new social order.

Whitman's reception in other anarchist publications is consistent with *Freie Jugend*'s use of his work. There are frequent Whitman translations in the Viennese *Neue Erde* (New Earth), a magazine fighting for the "fastest and most complete construction of socialist society founded on complete freedom."[7] For *Neue Erde*, Whitman was a "precursor of a fraternal life, of a great, emotional, supranational human community, a lover of all things, including the painful ones."[8] The program as well as the style of *Neue Erde* reminded Hermann Bahr strongly of Whitman[9]—and this was no coincidence. Connected with a movement that wanted to establish rural working-class colonies in order to come to terms with starvation and unemployment, *Neue Erde* also published a "Green Manifesto" in which its author, Leberecht Migge, calls for a "new colonization of the country"—in a "poetic-scientific-dithyrambic style, the origin of which lies in Whitman":

> I see:
> *The Green Land of Youth, of Health and*
> *of Happiness,*
> the fresh, virgin land.
> But, citizens, men and women,
> this happier existence does not come of its own accord: it must be fought for!
> Each individual must fight (with him/herself).
> Each individual must build (his/her own future).
> Each individual must help (his/her neighbor),
> *Help, Build, Fight!*
>
> Come closer
> You strong individualists
> You freest of nature's beings
> You youngest of *Wandervögel* and to Free-Germans[10]
> You nimblest of players and athletes
> You most successful of gardeners and farmers
> You funniest of musicians
> You artists, thinkers, and poets
> join in:
> Create a new life. Create new energy. Save your country!
> Muster courage, German, nothing is lost yet.
> Your people will live,

Your people will rise,
Your people will lead.
Long live
the new ideal of Germans, the new general idea:
The Country![11]

Again we see how Whitman's poetic form and *Pathos* were used for a topical issue of the day—in this case the call for rural colonies by the urban working class.

Beyond such issues of the day, *Neue Erde* also turned to Whitman for broader political purposes. In the issue of 1 May 1919, just about the time when Gustav Landauer, anarchist and member of the Bavarian Soviet Government, was murdered in a prison in Munich, *Neue Erde* published "To Him That Was Crucified." Whitman's identification with Jesus (who is not explicitly mentioned in the poem) seems to have a programmatic significance for the anarchist movement: "I specify you with joy O my comrade to salute you. . . ." In spite of violent threats from all sides, it is necessary to maintain the strategy of peaceful agitation:

> We hear the bawling and din, we are reach'd at by divisions, jealousies, recriminations on every side,
> They close peremptorily upon us to surround us, my comrade,
> Yet we walk unheld, free, the whole earth over, journeying up and down till we make our ineffaceable mark upon time and the diverse eras,
> Till we saturate time and eras, that the men and women of races, ages to come, may prove brethren and lovers as we are.
>
> (*LG*, 385)

Obviously, some of Whitman's poetry lent itself effectively to anarchist agitation. Unlike the Social Democrats, whose post-war readings of Whitman were at best indirectly political, the anarchists included Whitman in the political discussion of the day. With Landauer's translation (discussed above), anarchism even made a major contribution to the history of Whitman reception.

CHAPTER SEVENTEEN

WHITMAN ON THE RIGHT

It is surprising how few negative reactions against Whitman came from the conservative side. Given the enthusiasm with which he was embraced by leftists, conservative as well as religious groups would have been entirely justified—from their point of view—in rejecting Whitman and especially the cult around his person. Yet I have only found one such document, an article in the conservative Lutheran journal *Der Alte Glaube* (The Old Creed), which, though it acknowledged changes in modern life, concluded that they were inadmissible from a theological point of view:

> We are utterly unable to follow Whitman's revolutionary trombone any further and we also do not share his democratic spirit. Any revolution is a transgression against the existing order, against reality. . . . While Whitman says: "Resist much, obey little!" the Bible holds . . . "Let every soul be subject unto higher powers. For there is no power but of God: the powers that be are ordained of God." . . . It seems to us more than questionable whether this wild fighter against divine and human order may seriously be glorified as the greatest author since Goethe. Where in Whitman is the ennobling function of poetry?[1]

From this point of view, there is some justification for rejecting Whitman's reversal of all values. His poetry, especially when accepted as a kind of ideology or creed, indeed amounted to a destruction of the foundations on which traditional religiosity was based. That the body of negative criticism, especially from religious quarters, is so small is thus actually surprising. Given the increasing secularization of the age, it seems that Whitman's religious rhetoric was more important to many Christians than the critical implications of his works.

Further to the right, enthusiasm for Whitman was equally scarce, although those documents that do exist are very revealing. In my discussion of the German-nationalist Whitman translation by Wilhelm Schölermann (1904), I have already shown that Whitman could indeed be used by the nationalist right. In the same year, a frightful example of an ultra-"Germanic" Whitman interpretation was published in the anti-Semitic journal *Der Hammer*:

> A German heart can get nothing out of Levitical sophistry. Prophetic rhythms must again resound through German lands.
>
> We stood before the academics like silly schoolboys, permitting ourselves to be told that only thinking about thinking and nothing else is wisdom. No, our spirit is a tool to grasp life, devoted to fighting and loving.[2]

Here the admiration for Whitman "with his invigorating, refreshing thoughts" turns into anti-Semitic antiintellectualism.[3]

The anonymous author, calling himself "Samitasa," has been identified as one Willy Schlueter, who specified his ideas in a letter to the editor of *Der arme Teufel*: "I will gladly admit that . . . I believe it is high time for a heroic and free Young-Germanism in the spirit of Emerson, Walt Whitman, and Lagarde. . . .[4] The main point is that those willing to bear responsibility, the collaborators in the construction of a joyful race of the future, may gain ground, that the intellectual senescence that today often poses as science not kill the new spirit of Balder."[5] Schlueter's article and letter indicate the *possibility* of a nationalistic-Teutonic reception of Whitman, which, fortunately, never developed to any significant degree.

Yet there were attempts by critics operating during the Nazi period to make use of Whitman. After the Nazi takeover, the right-wing Whitmanite Heinrich Lersch (see below) was once asked whether he thought Whitman could be of use for National Socialist ideology. He shrewdly replied that he thought Whitman would have a lot to say to the Nazi period if the word "democracy" were replaced by "Volk" ([German] people) wherever it appeared,[6] implying that there were dimensions to Whitman's poetry that could indeed appeal to Nazi ears, a statement that would be shocking to most Whitmanites, both inside Germany and outside.

In the *Volkserzieher* (Educator of the People), a radical anti-Semitic journal which was in its thirty-seventh year in the year the Nazis took power, one Heinrich Kästner wrote an article entitled "Walt Whitman, the Prophet of a New Humanity," shortly after Hitler had come to power: "Already in the last century, a man of rare greatness departed from the course determined by machines, technology, and capitalism, which humanity still follows today. It was a man who anticipated centuries of human development and became a prophet of a future race."[7] The antimodernist impulse characteristic of National Socialist ideology and strategy is the driving force of Kästner's article. Even the typical pseudorevolutionary anticapitalist rhetoric appears prominently. Dissatisfied with "machines, technology, and capitalism," but not really interested in revolution, Nazi ideologues searched for "solutions" to the general human dissatisfaction with modern life. Such solutions always pointed to the past, even if they were said to anticipate future centuries. "Whitman restores to humans an open mind for everything that is alive and gives them the energy and strength to manage their life and their death. This unique person [Whitman] has deeply felt the divine character of a fully lived life which man has abandoned and turned into a servant of his daily needs."[8] Through the replacement of this divine feeling of life (referring to the individual's mystical relationship to the *Volk* and to the environment) by the intellect and through its functionalization in a technological environment, humans have destroyed their "pure relationships of their lives to the world and to things."[9] Through the demystifying methods of science, "man" has embarked in a wrong direction.

The mystical-irrational dimension Nazis took over from Christian religion was used in very rational and calculating ways, as is obvious in such quotations. To complete this microcosm of National Socialist ideology, Kästner ends his Whitman essay (in which the term "democracy" does not appear) with a sentence that could hardly have been misunderstood in May 1933: "We do believe in a perfect human race exemplified by one man."[10] Whitman as Führer?

Some six years later, Hans Flasche undertook an investigation of the "German spirit in the Anglo-Saxon philosophy of history." Although he pretended to retain academic objectivity when analyzing the foundations of Whitman's philosophy, passages like the following are all too close to official Nazi diction: "[Whitman's] immediate intuition of vital values strongly emphasizes nature, *Volk*, race, blood, soil as important forces. Whitman has a high estimation of the individualism of a person, but he always places the individual in the community of the *Volk*."[11] This passage contains key terms of the National Socialist ideological rhetoric that had become fully integrated into public German discourse by 1939. For the misinterpretation of Whitman along Nazi lines, the perverted use of such terms as "people," "race," or "blood" was a prerequisite. There is nothing wrong with such terms unless they signal intolerance, repression, and inhumanity. Integrated in the biologistic universe of Nazi ideology, even a poet like Whitman could become the victim of a perverted reading and turn into an unwitting accomplice of Nazi aims.

Another interesting misrepresentation concerns Whitman's stand on war. Whitman's war poetry was so remarkable because it was in essence pacifist war poetry (supported biographically through his work as a nurse). Flasche puts it in different terms:

> Man and woman should not remain confined in their limited individuality. They must always be conscious that they are descendants, links in a long chain, that they beget and bear children and thereby maintain the racial and folkish values. The highest racial values that are passed on include bravery, valor, heroism. Those who gave their lives for the Fatherland must be accorded unanimous gratitude. From their graves, energy rises for new deeds. The memory of the sons who shed their blood for the fatherland is the holiest legacy of a people, even holier, in some ways, than national literature and art.[12]

The way in which the scholar of literature belittles the value of his craft in comparison with the warring caste is touching—and entirely appropriate to the time the essay was published, at the beginning of World War II. But the quotation also shows why such a perverted reading of Whitman remained an exception: while the terms and some of the concepts used here *can* be found in his poetry, they go against the tenor of the *oeuvre* as a whole. As Whitman states in "As I Ponder'd in Silence," *Leaves* is concerned mostly with war "*for the Body and for the eternal Soul*" (*LG*, 2; emphasis in original). The direct National Socialist claim upon Whitman was doomed because it reflected neither the spirit nor the text of the American.

The various attempts to recruit Whitman for German nationalism and Nazism could be overlooked as mere aberrations were it not for an indirect impact Whitman had on Nazi culture which is much more significant: the Whitmanesque poetry of some of the so-called *Arbeiterdichter* (worker poets). Although this is arguably a case of creative reception involving Whitman's adaptation in German literature, its function is so blatantly ideological that it needs to be discussed in the present chapter.

The ongoing discussion among German critics and literary historians about whether there is a literature specifically relating to the working class, a proletarian literature, has also dealt with the question of whether this literature is by, for, or about workers. The group of writers we are concerned with here were, technically speaking, workers, at least for a time. Their thinking and identity, however, betray a lower-middle-class background—their "fall" into the working class was the result of impoverishment. Their intended audience was not primarily workers but the middle class; the theme of their writing was usually related to work, to the living conditions and environment of workers—but with a special twist.

The political background of these poets is diverse: some were anti-Marxist from the very start, others came from the Social Democratic Party, but none of them were leftists in a strict sense. They abhorred naturalist writing of the kind produced by Zola, Hauptmann, Holz, or Schlaf as "poetry for paupers."[13] They especially rejected the concept of class struggle, which to them was defensive and apologetic. Rather than fighting for a classless society, they demanded social recognition of workers and their acceptance into (bourgeois) society.

It should be remembered that the official name of the Nazi Party was Nationalsozialistische Deutsche Arbeiter Partei (National Socialist German Workers' Party). The Nazis, although extreme anti-Marxists, did call themselves socialist and did define their roots as working class. In their rhetoric, they were also "anticapitalist," although not in the Marxist sense, but in the context of their anti-"plutocratic" and anti-Semitic world view.

According to Nazi ideology, it was Marxists together with "capitalists" who had degraded the proud German worker to the status of a "proletarian" without any feeling of self-esteem. The solution to the "question" of the worker offered by the Nazis was mainly psychological: workers had to adopt a new identity; society, rather than looking down on workers as members of a lower class, had to accept them as important and equal members of the community. In this way, the actual reasons for social degradation, human alienation, and economic impoverishment of the working class, which derived from the industrialized and technologized society, were obscured. Nazi ideology carefully and skillfully appealed to the psychological dissatisfaction of an impoverished class, suggesting that the solution to their problems lay in a return to old values. Essentially, they promised workers a return to their former preindustrial status as artisans.

Capitalism, therefore, was not to be overthrown, but educated. The representatives of "international high finance" such as Jews or Freemasons needed to be "weeded out" and replaced by a class of truly German "employers" who would accord due recognition to workers, treat them "fairly," and pay them "honest" wages. This solidarity was to emerge from a shared feeling of nationhood; the fact that all members of the society were Germans was to ensure mutual benevolence.

The *Arbeiterdichter* had independently arrived at these very same conclusions. Most of them, including the two figures discussed in greater detail here—Heinrich Lersch and Karl Bröger—reacted enthusiastically to World War I. They welcomed the general national fraternization expressed in the emperor's announcement that he knew no more parties (and classes), but only Germans. At the beginning of the war, Bröger wrote a poem whose final five lines became famous throughout Germany:

We always have loved you
but never called it love.
But your greatest peril revealed in a splendid way
that your poorest son was also your most faithful one
Be aware of this, o Germany.[14]

Pathos-laden, this poem imploringly demands that German society, which in the face of the war crisis had been saved by the German worker, by "the poorest" but "most faithful son" of the nation, reaccept workers into the national community (*Volksgemeinschaft*).

For the *Arbeiterdichter*, the idea of a national community and simultaneous abolition of class barriers (as naive as this may sound) was not just a wartime necessity but also a peacetime ideal. "Denk es, o Deutschland" not only means "Be aware of it" but also "Do not forget." After the war, these poets believed, the country should be restructured using the model of the army. The ideal of a pseudo-classless national community should be extended to the work place. They demanded a "work community" (*Werkgemeinschaft*) which would ensure social *inclusion*, rather than *exclusion* of workers. To National Socialist critics, this was welcomed as the "breakthrough of the [German] worker to his people."[15] Workers would again be able to "experience" what it means to be a part of their nation; the work they render for their nation would thereby acquire new meaning.

In reality, of course, this did not remove the alienating and frustrating work conditions that laborers were subjected to. No factory in Nazi Germany was closed down and converted into a craftshop. Quite to the contrary, the Nazi takeover, due to the increase in military production, sped up technological progress. Therefore, in addition to creating a fictitious harmony between the classes, it was also necessary to instill in workers' minds the belief that their work was not alienating and degrading, even if in effect it was. This required a mythicization of work[16]—turning the steel worker into a blacksmith, the textile worker into a tailor, and so forth—that is, recreating the earlier guild spirit by using its diction, although its basis had long disappeared in the course of industrialization. A poetry that performed all of these ideological tasks would seem to be hopelessly overtaxed. Unless, of course, one had Walt Whitman as a model.

Heinrich Lersch (1889–1936), a boilermaker, first became known throughout Germany by the following couplet:

A free German does not have to be forced:
Germany must live, even if we must die![17]

These lines, and poems in a similar spirit, were included in a book published in 1916 in a large popular edition. The book, entitled *Herz! Aufglühe dein Blut: Gedichte im Kriege* (Heart! May Your Blood Glow: Poems in Wartime), was introduced by a motto from Whitman:

> Thou reader throbbest life and pride and love the same as I,
> Therefore for thee the following chants.[18]

That Lersch would introduce a highly nationalistic book published during the war with a motto from a foreign author is unusual and can only be explained by the close affinity the author felt with Whitman. The two Whitman lines anticipate the central concern of Lersch's poetry, the condition of the worker-poet, who is appealing to the middle-class reader for equal consideration. Whitman's yearning for a close relationship between author and readers here becomes a highly politicized issue.

The fascination Whitman's poetry exerted on Lersch is evident in his well-known book *Mensch im Eisen* (Man in Iron, 1925), a long, lyrical autobiographical presentation of the life of a blacksmith. *Mensch im Eisen* shows how an alienating and alienated reality of everyday work is overcome through the worker's integration into "life." The working environment is mythicized through Whitmanesque rhythm and diction. The elemental power of fire plays a special role in this literary blacksmith's shop:

> Coals onto the glowing fire, blaze up, magnificent [flame]!
> Sun of the blacksmith, rise!
> Blaze up higher, flame! Fire of Peace!
> Shine, burn, warm, glowing fire of work and love!
> Lighthouse we used to steer our course,
> while we, shipwrecked soldiers in the rocking rowboat of hope, were
> lost on the blood sea.
> Flare up, golden light of the work day! You Easter candle,
> Light after the long Holy Weeks of War-Golgotha;
> Evening and morning star! Consolation after a sleepless night;
> You are the column of fire, showing the way to the Promised Land.
> Flame! Provider, you ripen the ears on our fields, sowed by the farmer.
> Flame! Consumer of all impurities, death, death of all bad thoughts;
> Just as the wild beasts avoid you in the night of the jungle,
> Bad thoughts avoid the blacksmith standing in your light![19]

The attempt to establish a metaphorical relationship between this occupation (the blacksmith's is a largely preindustrial profession) and nature (agriculture) is obvious. In this idealized work place, the worker identifies with his labor. In these lines, the echoes of Whitman are as strong as in the following passage, where Lersch's rejection of industrialized modes of production becomes obvious:

Let us live with the elements
Fire, Water, Air, Earth, with the symbols of active life:
Fire! Anvil! Hammer!
Blessing! Blessing! Blessing!
Our children are becoming young men, maidens,
brotherly-sisterly.
They will discover their Fatherland, and behind it the
earth.
They will discover their power, will wake up and look
toward freedom with wonder . . .
One day, the bold young men,
against the machines, the motors, against us,
they will lift the old hammers to destroy the rule of
the machines,
so that their souls may again be free.

(*MiE*, 60)[20]

These lines clearly demonstrate the workers' malaise. The solution, however, is anachronistic: the future will bring a return to the past. The old hammers will destroy the machines and recreate the old, nonalienated world of handcraft and trade.

Such lines reflect Whitman's rhetoric, but certainly not his spirit. At first glance, poems such as "Song of the Broad-Axe," recalling elemental work situations, seem to fit here:

Weapon shapely, naked, wan,
Head from the mother's bowels drawn,
Wooded flesh and metal bone, limb only one and lip only one,
Gray-blue leaf by red-heat grown, helve produced from a little seed
sown . . .

(*LG*, 184)

The forger at his forge-furnace and the user of iron after him,
The maker of the axe large and small, and the welder and temperer,
The chooser breathing his breath on the cold steel and trying the edge with
his thumb,
The one who clean-shapes the handle and sets it firmly in the socket;

The shadowy processions of the portraits of the past users also,
The primal patient mechanics, the architects and engineers . . .
(*LG*, 187)

These lines show how Whitman was able to inspire Lersch. On the surface, in rhetoric and presentation, there are strong similarities. In contrast to Lersch, however, Whitman never took anti-"modern," antiindustrial positions. Rather, he attempted to synthesize the earlier, pastoral conception of America on the one hand with industrial and technological progress on the other.

Lersch mythicizes not only the work place, but also the loving community of employer and worker. Without mentioning existing hierarchies and class differences, boss and workers are presented as an eroticized Whitmanesque collective:

We are forging.
The young apprentice and myself.
The young man is working the bellows. Up, and down
his girl-like[!] arms are moving.
I stand and take care of the fire. . . .
The youth and I are looking into the flame. We are not looking around us, neither left nor right, until he turns his head and looks in my face.
I look back at him. We say nothing and smile. Because each of us feels the joy that is rising.
Joy, originating from the red flame and sinking into our hearts. Like a secret only the two of us know, a secret that binds us together. That ignites friendship wordlessly and increases it. Friendship of joy originating from the flame. We are again looking into the fire, the youth and I, and are silent. But we both know our happiness comes from this fire.
(*MiE*, 62)[21]

Of course, there are many passages in Whitman poems such as "Song of the Broad-Axe" where work is eroticized and charged with sexuality. But in Lersch's text, Whitmanesque camaraderie has a negative political function: it is designed to *hide* hierarchies, class differences, and dependencies in the work place by presenting an ideal relationship between "master" and "apprentice"—perfectly rounded off by homoerotic overtones.

In obvious Whitmanesque diction, the master presents himself as a caring comrade and protector:

My workers are my friends.
They want no master other than myself.

I share their small and large worries. Am godfather of
their children and witness at their marriages.
I hear their opinions and am delighted when they impart
a new and beautiful thought.
From the secrets of their hearts I receive all
mysteries of earthly life.

I no longer need books.
In their lives, there is immense drama, and their fates make pure and true
novels. The verse-making of poets is chatter, when I compare it to my
young apprentice telling me the secrets of his Sundays with his
young woman.
(*MiE*, 64f.)[22]

Through such lines, the persona of *Mensch im Eisen*, the blacksmith, approaches Whitman's universal persona. In Whitman's original text, identification with others is a literary vision, sometimes even with a humorous effect; if it has a political function, it is egalitarian-democratic. With Lersch, the political function is to obscure authority and make it invisible. The employer as omniscient and ubiquitous lyrical persona! The authoritarian solution of the "proletarian question" by the Nazis is clearly demonstrated in this text.

Mensch im Eisen is not devoid of criticism, and there are pessimistic passages where the reality of industrialist society shines through. However, Lersch's conception of the future, clothed in Whitmanesque lines, dominates the book. Whitman would have embraced the following lines:

Everything in the world is perfect: the sun, the stars,
the tree, the animal, the leaf of grass, everything is perfect in itself.
How can I permit myself to be the only thing that is imperfect?
More imperfect than any other part of creation?

Nothing is absolutely necessary.
But one thing is: that I am happy!
That I am happy and that I can sing at my work.
(*MiE*, 102)[23]

Lersch even introduces a Whitmanesque figure into his work. When the book's persona, once again laden with psychological problems, wanders through the mountains, he meets a "bearded man":

He was thirty-seven years old, born in America,
worked in all professions, a vagabond, who had walked around the earth,

> had lived with Indians, Negroes, Islanders,
> and now worked only during the winter months,
> in the distant city as sports instructor.
> After long resistance I entrusted myself to him and asked him to heal my body.
> (*MiE*, 170f.)[24]

In spite of some initial hesitation, the persona of *Mensch im Eisen* eventually becomes the "comrade" of this Whitmanesque figure:

> And I finally did become his comrade.
> He taught me my body, the old Adam,
> taught me the laws of the body.
> And I saw: The laws of all eternal things are identical; of sea and cloud, stars and flower, animal and stone, man and earth: the all-powerful laws of spring and fall, summer and winter, the unshakable laws of coming and going, life and death. And he taught me, the great camerado, to feel the currents carrying the cosmos in their blowing breath, he taught me to become a part of the living world and I shared in the force moving this earth, the suns and the stars; from which everything alive constantly renews itself in eternal rebirth.
> (*MiE*, 173)[25]

Tutored by this pseudo-Whitman, the persona is reborn:

> A child, I discovered myself anew!
> Once more the meadows were resplendent in early fall, the roar of the waterfall and the turning of stars in the evening became music. And I rose and fell with the great breath of the world.
> (*MiE*, 174)[26]

In these passages, the connection of *Mensch im Eisen* with *Leaves of Grass* becomes unmistakable. Lersch was very important to the National Socialists, and his poetry was often reprinted (for example, in songbooks of the Hitlerjugend [Hitler Youth] and the Bund Deutscher Mädel [League of German Maidens]). He himself went on extensive reading tours throughout the Reich and on the occasion of his death propaganda minister Joseph Goebbels, aware of Lersch's contributions to Nazi society, donated an official wreath. Of course, Whitman (though not one of the writers whose books were burned, certainly not one who received special official support) could not be used for propaganda,[27] but the fact that a prominent National Socialist poet connected his own work to Whitman is an extraordinary phenomenon.

After his rebirth, the persona of *Mensch im Eisen* is capable of enormous achievements and spreads his vision of a new world:

> We liberate the woman from the suffocating kitchen,
> deliver her from her low station as servant, from her responsibility for the
> saucepan,
> raise her to her station as playmate[!] of the man,
> as mother of children, as sister of men.
> We liberate peoples
> from their anxiety over food and space.
> See, they return, the dehumanized slaves, damned to be pariahs, now
> they return, these people, to the East, whence they came.
> (*MiE*, 175)[28]

These are brutal and violent lines. It is highly questionable whether the status of women will be raised by permitting them to leave the kitchen and concentrate on the marital bed and on motherhood—but it certainly anticipates the Nazi solution. And the "liberation" of the peoples from the "East," their "return" to the "East," is nothing else than a cynical prediction of the German eastward expansion, the *Drang nach dem Osten*. Did Whitman deserve such a successor, and did he do anything to provoke such a following?

Karl Bröger (1886–1944), a second *Arbeiterdichter* who was important to the Nazis, has already been mentioned. Closely connected with the Social Democrats, he was much less involved with Nazi propaganda than Lersch. In recent years, in fact, there have been several attempts to exonerate him.[29] These studies emphasize the many years of Bröger's Social Democratic affiliation but also note his role and the character of his poetry during the Nazi period.

In 1922, Bröger wrote a very enthusiastic review of Whitman's *Leaves*:

> Walt Whitman's work is a strong inner consolation and an even stronger hope. The male character of this pioneer of new worlds disperses the fog of the hypocritical and mendacious literature written by *literati* which covers our time thickly and oppressively. A luster breaks forth from Whitman's work which outshines the somber present. Walt Whitman presents an overwhelming example of what democracy will become once the word has been removed from

> its discursive political meaning and is tied to all the fibers of the living human being. The American visionary evokes the best virtues of a male era which will have to return if the world is to be worth living: [to have] energy for the largest as well as the smallest [things], an open mind for the moment and its immortal values, love, reaching out toward that which is closest and that which is furthest, comradeship in spirit, unfortunately lost to us for the present time!
>
> Today we need books with the energy and power to set our "Yes, but" against the course of time. Walt Whitman's works are such a source of power.[30]

Some readers of the *Frankfurter Zeitung* must have liked this sexist review. Bröger does not comment at all on the meaning *Leaves* had for the German left. Instead, he wants to take on sociopolitical reality with "sources" of "consolation." In contrast to Thomas Mann, whose letter to Reisiger appeared in the same paper, Bröger does not seem to worry much about concrete problems of democracy, but empties the term of its political meaning.

Given Bröger's enthusiasm for Whitman, also documented in a variety of other statements around this time, it is not surprising to find Whitmanesque passages in his creative work as well. One example will suffice: "Der blühende Hammer" (The Blossoming Hammer). This is a poem about a hammer suddenly sprouting with twigs and blossoms:

> Here!—at the naked twisted shaft
> the effects of a secret miraculous force.
> Twigs are sprouting forth
> already the first leaves,
> and in the bed of the crown,
> already the first blossom, swayed by the wind.
> A second, a third has blossomed,
> soon all the branches are full
> with red roses, sending greetings far
> into the celebration of spring . . .
>
> Around the blossoming hammer, hand in
> hand,
> are the brotherly workmen from city and
> land.
> They all come to see the miracle,
> and exultingly the story is told:
>
> "Now blossoms the hammer in our hand,
> Labor reigns freely in our land!"[31]

In this seemingly innocuous little poem, already published at the beginning of World War I, social change occurs through the mythologizing of "work." The blossoming hammer is strongly reminiscent of Whitman's axe, "Gray-blue leaf by red-heat grown, helve produced from a little seed sown" (*LG*, 184). The brotherly workmen do not have to move one finger for their liberation; the existing power structure remains untouched. For the National Socialist critic, the final lines of the poem are even a "visionary anticipation of the May festivities realized by the Third Reich, overcoming partisan hatred and homicide [the allusion is to the May Day demonstrations of the Marxist parties and leftist unions] and reaching a point where honest joy is found in work."[32] Even a quotation from a speech by the Führer himself is given: the Nazi May celebrations are a "glorification of the national awareness against the international subversion of morals."[33]

The line leading from Whitman to the *Arbeiterdichter* and, finally, to the Third Reich should not be exaggerated. Whitman, certainly, cannot be held responsible for being used by poets like Lersch and Bröger whose poems ended up in the songbooks of the Hitler youth. Parallels exist predominantly in the rhetoric (masses, collectivism, community). Whitman's mode of addressing individual professions was a significant lyrical parallel to the corporate ideal of the National Socialists, who preferred to divide their society horizontally into labor groups rather than admit to the reality of a vertical class division. The mythicization of labor and work place could not eliminate class antagonisms and alienation, but it could make them appear irrelevant for a time. Whitman's nature mysticism and his rejection of traditional religiosity fit Hitler's myth of *Vorsehung* (providence). Whitman's emphasis on the physical character of humans and nature resonated with Nazi slogans of *Blut und Boden* (blood and soil). Whitman's idealistic *Pathos* and his praise of motherhood also were echoed by Nazis. Even in Bröger's cycle of poems entitled "Phallos," published in the "monthly for the future of German culture," *Die Tat* (The Deed), Diederichs, its German-nationalist conservative publisher, was able to see the signs of a new race, "as it will once be reborn in the Germanic spirit."[34] The stagnation in German Whitman reception in the years since the end of World War II is a result not only of the general distrust of *Pathos* in literature and the other arts, but also of the uneasiness caused by the many specific parallels between Whitman's poetry and that of the National Socialist songbooks.

Even the many German exiles who wanted to use Whitman as an ally in the antifascist struggle were confused by a *Pathos* which reminded them all too often of the propagandistic discourse of the system from which they had escaped. Klaus Mann, Thomas's son, idolized Whitman, and, in 1941, authored a long article on "The Present Greatness of Walt Whitman," attempting to prove that Whitman would have taken an antiisolationist anti-Nazi stand and would have wanted the United States to join the allied powers. Yet even he, one of the most enthusiastic German Whitman admirers, had to admit to himself:

> We have learned to be more skeptical and restrained about the "splendid day-rise of science" and the magnificent modernism of our enlightened age. Nor do we share any more Whitman's exuberant admiration for everything colossal—masses of men, masses of land, masses of steel or water or words. The cruel experiences of our times are more likely to teach us that neither *quantity* nor technical *progress* as such have any moral value; that everything depends upon the spirit in which they are to be employed. They may be employed "for the sake of the Soul," or for the sake of evil and destruction.
>
> What seems to be the weakest spot in his philosophy is his way of simplifying the character of man and of ignoring the elements of madness and infamy so profoundly inherent in human nature.[35]

The "cruel experiences of our times"—and the cruel sounds and rhetoric that time produced. German readers had become uncertain about Whitmanesque poetry in the course of the Third Reich and this has remained true until the present.

On 19 June 1942, the German anti-Nazi exile Friedrich Sally Grosshut evoked Whitman in an antifascist spirit in the German-language weekly *Orient* published in Haifa, Palestine:

> America has risen in order to realize athletic democracy, the finale, to assist freedom. The Statue of Liberty greets the ships, the airplanes leaving the American coast in order to assist allied nations and countries in the common cause. From the noise of the factories and the shipyards, from the hammering of the shipbuilders and the thundering motors of airplanes, emerges Walt Whitman's immortal song. The song of human greatness, devoted to love of life, a song of the will to order and to the building of a victorious future democracy.[36]

The *Pathos* is Whitman's, but—with all due respect to Grosshut's political intention and integrity—is it not a little bit also the *Pathos* of Lersch's *Werkgemeinschaft*?

CHAPTER EIGHTEEN

THE GERMAN SIXTIES

Given the leftist traditions in Whitman's German reception, it is surprising that Whitman's poetry was not recalled more frequently during the political upheaval of the late sixties. Possibly Whitman's influence had become more indirect. Günter Grass said that Whitman's influence was felt *through* writers in the Whitman tradition such as Allen Ginsberg.[1] Ginsberg spoke, in Whitmanesque ways, more to the time and was therefore more appreciated; the Ginsberg reception thereby becomes part of the German Whitman tradition.

During the sixties, however, Günter Grass himself made a very clever, direct, and highly political use of Whitman. In 1965, Grass decided to support the Social Democratic candidate for the West German chancellorship, Willy Brandt, against the conservative candidate, Ludwig Erhard. On his own initiative, the famous author of *Tin Drum* organized a campaign tour under a Whitman motto: "Dich singe ich, Demokratie" (For You, O Democracy). In one of the earlier speeches, he explained:

> I have never before given campaign speeches and for weeks now, I have been feeling something new: stage fright. . . . But an American colleague has helped me: Walt Whitman. He lived from 1819 until 1892, had a flowing biblical beard, a large breath reaching from the East to the West Coast, from Long Island to California. His legacy is his book *Leaves of Grass.* Endless songs, touching on every region and every profession, on the individual and the masses of people. These songs have given the United States of America a poetic constitution which is still in force today. Walt Whitman, a Lincoln of the language. Somebody who sang Democracy. Courage and humor led him to say:
> "O such themes—equalities! O divine average!"

> Walt Whitman shall be our pedestal. On the foundation provided by him, as citizen among citizens, we will build: "For You, O Democracy!"
>
> This motto, with which my friends and I are starting out this exciting trip, was taken from the following quote by Walt Whitman: "For you these from me, O Democracy, to serve you, ma femme! For you, for you I am trilling these songs."[2]

The fact that Grass turned Whitman into the patron saint of his private election campaign does not necessarily prove Whitman's great popularity, but it certainly suggests the fascination he still exerted on German literary activists of all kinds. Retrospectively, Grass wrote about his Whitman campaign:

> I drew up my first campaign speeches in the summer of 1965 in America at a safe distance from Germany. It was a few weeks prior to my first campaign trip. In these years I had, apart from many other interests, an intensive reading relationship with Walt Whitman's poetic panoramas of epic proportions. Thus his address to democracy was an obvious choice as a motto for me. Certainly, there was also a political consideration: to counteract the cheap political ingratiation with America on the part of the right as well as the primitive anti-Americanism [of the left].[3]

By appealing to the American singer of democracy, it was possible to challenge the conservative parties' monopoly on the United States, which was of eminent political importance because it allowed them to maintain their usual claim that the Social Democrats were "anti-American." Grass also wanted the German left to rethink its position on America, which was frequently laden with emotional prejudice. He wanted to show the German voters the spirit of the "other America"—in order to get closer to "another" Germany. The results of the elections, however, did not fulfill Grass's hopes. The Social Democrats gained a few points on the conservatives, but Ludwig Erhard again became chancellor. Willy Brandt would not head the West German government until 1969.

One final example given of a political application of Whitman is offered as pure speculation. In spite of the stagnation in Whitman's reception after World War II, Whitman and Whitman's "aura" were still present in German culture. The case of the *Arbeiterdichter* demonstrates how traditions can move in strange directions. But if the right person at the right moment takes up a sound which is still present in many heads, its success is guaranteed.

The most famous and most often republished poem by Whitman in the German language is "Salut au Monde!" Section 9, in Reisiger's translation, contains the following lines:

> Ich sehe die Städte der Erde und bin ihr Bürger nach meinem Belieben,
> Ich bin ein echter Pariser,
> Ich bin ein Bewohner von Wien, Petersburg, Berlin, Konstantinopel,
> Ich bin aus Adelaïde, Sidney, Melbourne,
> Ich bin aus London, Manchester, Bristol, Edinburg, Limerick,
> Ich bin aus Madrid, Cadiz, Barcelona, Oporto, Lyon, Brüssel, Bern,
> Frankfurt, Stuttgart, Turin, Florenz.
> Ich gehöre nach Moskau, Krakau, Warschau und in den Norden
> nach Christiania oder Stockholm und nach sibirisch Jrkutsk oder in eine
> Straße Islands,
> Ich lasse mich nieder in all diese Städte und hebe mich wieder aus ihnen.

It was an unforgettable moment of American political rhetoric in Europe when, in 1963, John F. Kennedy, promising the West Berliners that the United States was going to ensure their survival in spite of the tightening grip of the East, proclaimed: "Ich bin ein Berliner."

SEXUAL POLITICS

Some German reactions to the early editions of Whitman's poetry showed that reviewers and German readers were rather astonished over the explicitness with which Whitman presented not only the human body, but also the variations of sexual experience. It is not surprising, therefore, that groups committed to liberating the human body and human sexuality attempted to enlist Whitman for their causes. While this section deals with a number of such emancipatory groups and subcultures, it remains only a survey. Future research will no doubt turn up more examples for such readings of Whitman.

CHAPTER NINETEEN

HOMOSEXUALITY

The German debate on Whitman's homosexuality is connected to the debates in the United States, Great Britain, and France through the person of Eduard Bertz, who assumed a number of interesting roles including that of a man of letters and a sexologist.[1] In addition to providing insight into a very specific dimension of the German reception of Walt Whitman, it is also a chapter in the history of the legal and human emancipation of homosexuals in Germany.

In 1897, Magnus Hirschfeld, a Berlin-based physician, founded the so-called Wissenschaftlich-humanitäre Komitee (Scientific-Humanitarian Committee), an organization designed to assist homosexuals via scientific, medical, and legal efforts. Its most important task was the support of a legal initiative calling for a liberalization of article 175 of the German penal code regulating homosexuality. It demanded that

> sexual acts between persons of the same sex as well as such acts between persons of different sex (homosexual as well as heterosexual) are punishable only
>
> if they are performed using force,
> if they are performed with persons below the age of sixteen
> or if they are performed in a way so as to cause public nuisance. . . . [2]

This petition, which was eventually defeated in the German Reichstag, was supported by a large number of personages from public life. The list includes not only doctors and lawyers but also academics, artists, and writers; it is a veritable checklist of the German-speaking intellectual elite at the turn of the century: Gerhart Hauptmann, Otto Brahm, Max Liebermann, Hermann Bahr, Otto Julius Bierbaum, Richard Dehmel, Otto Erich Hartleben, Karl Kautsky, John Henry

Mackay, Max Nordau, Rainer Maria Rilke, Arthur Schnitzler, and many others. In 1899, the list of the signers was published in volume 1 of the *Jahrbuch für Sexuelle Zwischenstufen,* the committee's yearbook. It also contained the names of Johannes Schlaf and Eduard Bertz, identified as a writer living in Potsdam. In the course of the first two decades of the twentieth century, these two men, assisted by many others, would become engaged in a most violent, disagreeable, yet highly interesting and revealing debate on Whitman's homosexuality, the first public discussion of this topic anywhere. In addition to his Whitman translation and his creative response to Whitman's works, this discussion marks Johannes Schlaf's third major (albeit less convincing) contribution to the German reception of Walt Whitman.

Eduard Bertz (1853–1931) was born in Potsdam near Berlin. He studied at a number of German universities but apparently never received his Ph.D.[3] After a stay in England, where he became a close friend of the English novelist George Gissing, he went to the United States. He lived for a time at Thomas Hughes's utopian Communist community in Tennessee, later returned to Great Britain, where he published a successful novel (a "boy's story") in English, and finally ended up back in Germany, where he frequently changed his place of residence. Bertz wrote a number of works of fiction, popular science, and popular philosophy, all of which are forgotten today. He is, as Hans-Joachim Lang states, "as nearly a man without a biography as it is possible for a modern author to be."[4]

Bertz's most important experience during his stay in the United States seems to have been his introduction to Whitman's works. In 1889, the *Deutsche Presse,* the official publication of the German Union of Writers (Deutscher Schriftsteller-Verband), published an article by Bertz, then its assistant editor:

> My acquaintance with the writings of the most curious and most profound of all American poets amounts to the most important benefit of my stay in America. Indeed, it is one of the most fortunate events of my life. When I feel all of humanity's misery, when neither profane nor holy books can solve my inner conflict, all I have to do is open one of the volumes by the old, eternally young Walt Whitman. Then I feel how there is a force emanating from his every page which fills me with joy, a healthy, fresh abundance of life, electrically flowing from the strong heart of this most spiritual man of nature. . . . I love him.[5]

Bertz mailed a copy of this birthday greeting to Camden. The accompanying letter, written in English, was published by Traubel:

Dear Sir,
Dear Poet, Friend, and Master,

. . . those few lines will at least serve as an unambiguous testimony of my deep and true devotion to you. . . .[6]

It is the characteristic language of the enthusiast wanting to join Whitman's inner circle.

Believing himself to be the only German who held an interest in Whitman since Freiligrath, Bertz must have felt on the defensive when Schlaf's articles on Whitman started to appear in the 1890s, especially since Schlaf, knowingly or unknowingly, had ignored Bertz's article. Bertz finally wrote a letter to Schlaf which more than hints at his mortification:

What you say about the poet I read with sympathy, I had only silent regrets about your word that since Freiligrath nobody ever again was concerned with Whitman here in Germany. . . .

Because one person has indeed professed himself with unequivocal words, namely myself.[7]

This letter shows that Bertz's regrets are more than just "silent." In spite of some conciliatory words, even this very first contact with Schlaf expresses rivalry. Bertz still uses the rhetoric of the Whitman Fellowship: he "declares" himself "unequivocally" for Whitman—the characteristic formula of the disciple.

Since Bertz later attempted to downplay the duration and degree of his initial enthusiasm, it should be noted that he wrote articles linking himself to the cult as late as 1901.[8] In 1903–1904, he was still offering his good services to the Whitman Fellowship.[9] There is no reason to believe that Bertz's attitude toward Whitman had changed by 1905, the publication year of his work on Whitman, which opened the bitter fight over the American poet.

Bertz's 1905 "study" appeared in the scientific-humanitarian committee's *Jahrbuch*. The oversized article, some 125 pages long, was entitled "Walt Whitman: Ein Charakterbild" (A Character Sketch). Offprints were bound separately and one copy sent to Schlaf with a handwritten dedication. Bertz probably sent this copy quite innocently and hardly expected the violent reaction by Schlaf and the Whitmanites. The article was part of a series of sketches of famous homosexuals carried by the *Jahrbuch*, including such figures as Michelangelo, Oscar Wilde, and the German poet August von Platen. The journal of the German homosexual movement published such articles in order to prove the important contributions of homosexuals to the social and cultural life at large: ". . . nothing is as well-suited to removing prejudice and to paving the way for a fair examination as the recognition of the fact that many of the great men and women had this disposition. They were not in the least prevented from benefiting their fellow human beings more than thousands and thousands of normal [i.e., heterosexual] individuals."[10]

In a later publication, Bertz spoke of the importance of extensive "case studies" in the field of "sexual psychopathy."[11] Thus anybody who attempted to "ridicule such scientific and educational work on moral grounds" or denied Whitman's homosexuality antagonized Bertz.[12] This was true of Schölermann, who had "defended" Whitman against "charges" of homosexuality and whom Bertz accused of "terrorism" for his insistence on the norms of society.

In this article (unlike in earlier contributions), Bertz also criticized the Whitman cult: "An equation of Whitman with this ideal image [Jesus Christ] proves a pathological form of extravagance."[13] This criticism has to do with a strategy of modesty adopted by the committee in order to improve the lot of the homosexuals: "A small minority which has hitherto been persecuted and outlawed by the heterosexual majority first has to seek toleration by the majority. Anything beyond that amounts to fanaticism which fails to reckon with the facts."[14] This may seem all too modest by the standards of today's gay liberation movement, but it fits very well the framework and the horizon of the movement at the turn of the century, attempting to wrestle *toleration* of homosexuals and a *legal* (rather than comprehensive) emancipation from the heterosexual majority.

Attempts to interpret homosexuality as a "general human characteristic" or even as a political program were deemed strategic mistakes because they might provoke the heterosexual majority.[15] Bertz himself was certainly not willing to abandon the differentiation between "normal" (i.e., heterosexual) and "deviant" behavior. Similarly, the medical disciplines working toward an emancipation of homosexuals retained the opposition of "normal" and "abnormal"—as shown by a term such as "psychopathology."

The rest of Bertz's study is irrelevant to the present investigation. It attempted to prove Whitman's homosexuality by using a number of categories characteristic of the sexological discourse of the period (including the size and the shape of Whitman's ears). From Bertz's point of view, this pseudoscientific reasoning was employed not to antagonize Whitman, but to assure his continued identification with the homosexual community. Any attempt to deny Whitman's homosexuality was considered an affront against the homosexual cause at large and was thought to hurt the chances of a successful passage of the petition under parliamentary discussion in 1905.

Schlaf, far from being able to understand the complexity of the issue, simply felt under attack. In spite of his signature on the petition, he was unwilling to admit to homosexuality in his idol. Moreover, the lack of social acceptance of homosexuality endangered the continued existence and further expansion of the Whitman movement. In a characteristic case of homophobia, Schlaf believed he had to "defend" Whitman against Bertz. He could not comprehend the strategy of Bertz, who wanted to honor Whitman as a superior specimen of homosexuality by calling him a "noble urning" who suppressed his active sexuality. Nor did Schlaf understand (or approve of) Bertz's strategy of recruiting Whitman for the battle for the emancipation of homosexuals. Schlaf's answer to Bertz's article was a venomous pamphlet, revealing the author's lack of knowledge about many specific matters concerning Whitman. Nevertheless, he posed fundamental questions which are entirely justified, especially with regard to the role and possible abuse of "science" in such a case.[16] He criticized Bertz for adapting his "scholarly" findings to the needs of his "cause": for Bertz's purposes, Whitman *had* to be a homosexual. Schlaf also poked fun at Bertz's application of Magnus Hirschfeld's model with its four groups of "stigmata" supposedly characteristic of homosexuals. Schlaf's weakness was that he attempted to refute *all* of Bertz's theses—those related to Whitman's "conspicuous" external appearance and to his ancestry as much as the "internal" evidence in his biography and poetry. Schlaf was determined to hold on to Whitman's heterosexuality, including the well-known cultist-religious elements designed to lift Whitman to the stature of Christ.[17]

Bertz, told that his study was inadequate as well as senseless, became enraged. His answer, a book-length work entitled *Whitman-Mysterien*, equaled Schlaf's pamphlet in spitefulness. He now accused Schlaf of hurting the homosexual cause. Schlaf should have known that his pamphlet was "directed against the legal battle, which he himself had supported with his signature a while back. He has consciously put obstacles in the way of this humanitarian cause supported by himself; indeed, he has frivolously disparaged the scientific discipline serving this cause" (*WM*, 17). According to Bertz, Schlaf presented the worst possible prejudices against the "outlawed homosexual race" and attempted to appeal to the general public's prejudicial instincts in his pamphlet.

Thus far, Bertz's line of reasoning and his attitude are consistent and understandable. Subsequently, however, there is a surprising and decisive change in his evaluation of Whitman's person itself. Proceeding from the assumption that "homosexuality can never be accepted as a standard variant [of sexual behavior] but . . . only as a pathological phenomenon . . . a symptom of degeneration" (*WM*, 101), he admitted: "Through the systematic study of the 'Leaves of Grass' I had become convinced that he [Whitman] expresses a pathological anomaly of the sexual urge in the Calamus-Songs and in related poems. This was a painful recognition . . ." (*WM*, 10).[18] Bertz claimed to have noticed this as early as 1889, the year of the publication of his article in the *Deutsche Presse*! He explained his prolonged silence on the matter by his "consideration for Whitman" (*WM*, 11)—a feeling he doubtless would have denounced as "terrorism" had it occurred in anybody else.

As we have seen, Bertz was initially indeed far from being critical of Whitman. When he failed in his endeavor to become the official representative of Traubel's Whitman Fellowship in Germany, mainly because Traubel banked on Schlaf rather than Bertz, he decided to devote his comprehensive knowledge about Whitman to the homosexual movement. He had been affiliated with the committee since 1899, possibly earlier. The records in the *Yearbook* show that he was an active member. In each list of donations, his full name or his initials appear. He had a warm personal relationship with members of the committee, including Hirschfeld himself.[19] Thus he was firmly committed to the efforts of the homosexual movement in Germany, although it is unclear whether he himself was gay.

His failure to become the German Whitman representative required a new orientation with regard to his efforts on behalf of Whitman. Turning into a specialist for sexual questions, he had to abandon his cultist jubilations and adopt a sober but "humanitarian" scientific language. This led to a collision with Schlaf as well as other members of the Whitman community in Germany and abroad, in the course of which Bertz changed his attitude toward Whitman altogether. The conflict altered his social consciousness and moved him closer to conservative positions.

Why did Bertz feel he had to discontinue championing Whitman following his recognition of Whitman's "true" sexual leanings? The recognition alone would not necessarily mandate rejection. He himself explains his position with the standard argument about protecting young people: "There is a moral peril in the way fanatics turn a pathological way of feeling into a gospel, even a religion, and poison the normal male youth with such erroneous doctrines. Therefore I have stressed emphatically that a clarification of this issue involves the greatest public interest, '*because harm and confusion are caused by the dissemination of an unhealthy idea under the guise of health and deliverance*'" (*WM*, 109; emphasis in original).[20] If it took Bertz himself years to discover this unhealthiness (from his stay in the United States in 1882 until 1889), how could it endanger the "normal male youth"? And if it did so indeed, how could Bertz, who prided himself on being well-versed in ethics, allow young people to be exposed to the danger for another sixteen years—only to "protect" Whitman, who had died in 1892?[21] There is just one explanation for Bertz's erratic and contradictory behavior: paranoia.

In a letter to the British physician W. C. Rivers, the author of a pamphlet entitled *Walt Whitman's Anomaly*,[22] Bertz wrote in 1913: "Your book on 'Walt Whitman's Anomaly' came to me as a most valuable aid, and I beg to express to you my sincere gratitude. . . . I have been persecuted by the Whitmanites with the utmost hatred, and the obstinate denial, in those circles, is still so strong, that a confirmation like yours, especially as you are an Englishman, moves me to great rejoicing."[23] First owing to their vocal protests, then due to an even more oppressive "conspiracy of silence,"[24] Bertz obviously suspected a conspiracy on the part of the Whitmanites. In *Whitman-Mysterien*, he complained that Binns, Traubel, Schlaf, and others intentionally hushed up Whitman's homosexuality (see *WM*, 161ff.). Moreover: "At times, Schlaf acts as if there was no reason for a cover-up in the case of Whitman and his followers. But the reason is very obvious. The Whitmanites as a movement, as a sect, know very well that the admission of homosexuality would be fatal to their cause in America. Whitman himself already knew this" (*WM*, 163).[25] According to Bertz, Schlaf would have made "an immortal fool" out of himself had he admitted Whitman's homosexuality and then proclaimed "a degenerate to be a superman" (*WM*, 103f.). These statements explain some of the potential explosiveness of the discussion. Public acceptance of Whitman's homosexuality by the Whitmanites might have terminated the successful Whitman cult with its dogmatic interpretation of Whitman as a model human being. This had to be prevented at all costs.

Schlaf, rather naive about the explosive background of these questions, communicated with his French colleague Bazalgette. The French Whitmanite argued with strong words:

> Thanks to our friend Stefan Zweig, I knew [about] Bertz's study on Whitman. I have ordered the book and I will receive it soon. I don't know yet what this Dr. has written, but I suppose, according to what I have heard about it, that this is one of the stupid anomaly hunters of whom there are so many at present. I know very well what *manly love* means in Whitman and he must be stupid if he is accusing the man who is *maybe the most normal [person] ever to appear on the planet* to be inverted. I am happy that you are preparing a response to that animal who amuses himself by dirtying what he does not understand. Do you know the sensible page *Havelock Ellis* has written on Whitman concerning this question in his book *Studies in the Psychology of Sexual Inversion*? This could maybe help you for your answer to Dr. Bertz, *if you want it*, I could copy the passage and send it to you.[26]

After he had read Bertz's article, he continued in a second letter: "I have had the study by Eduard Bertz in my hand. That is a stupidity, just as I expected. These people of the Lombroso-Kraft-Ebing [*sic*], Nordau school are so busy in denouncing the sexual inversion and the foolishness in the world that they are forgetting to look at themselves to discover how alienated they are themselves! We should treat these idiots with nothing but disdain and mockery. And it is good if a writer like you tells one of them his truths."[27] Bazalgette was sincere about everything he wrote, but it did not give the complete picture. Bertz and Krafft-Ebing had no desire to "denounce" homosexuals—quite the contrary. They wanted to improve their lot. But the whole discussion was detrimental to Whitman's image and therefore had to be hushed up.

Ernest Crosby, a homosexual himself, wrote to Schlaf following the receipt of his pamphlet:

> My dear Schlaf:
>
> I have read your new brochure with the greatest interest, and I am glad that you are defending Whitman's reputation so bravely. Only last month I saw Traubel at Boston, where he was preparing a new volume of recollections of W. W., and he showed me the draft of a letter of Whitman's to Symonds (from which Symonds has printed only abstracts,) and which is a strong argument on your side of the case. In it Walt expresses his horror that such things should have been thought of him.[28]

And even Binns, who implied that he knew the truth when he called the question "about Calamus + Doyle" "one of the most difficult of all,"[29] wrote to Schlaf: "I am glad you continue fighting Whitman's battles in Germany."[30] There was concerted international support for Schlaf's effort.

Given the obstinate denials from many quarters of the globe, it is not surprising that Bertz thought of himself as a victim of a conspiracy on the part of Whitmanites *and* homosexuals who attempted to disguise their "unhealthy idea" as idealistic poetry and covertly sell it to the world.[31] He began to suspect that even Schlaf was a homosexual and in 1907 unsuccessfully attempted to elicit information about Schlaf's sexual orientation from Arno Holz.[32] As paradoxical as it may seem, Bertz felt persecuted by the very objects of his humanitarian efforts. And what would Bertz have said, had he known about the following entry in Schlaf's private diary?

> I dreamt a very lively dream last night: I went through a large city with the aged Walt Whitman, arm in arm. This was an unspeakably beautiful feeling of bliss. The feeling of a magnificent male body, arm in arm. An unspeakably immediate feeling of pleasure, peace, a most inconceivable satisfaction. The blissful and holy feeling of a perfect human being with a completely harmonious inner balance.[33]

Bertz, filled with rage, did not stop with the *Whitman-Mysterien.* Shortly afterward, he completed an extensive volume on Whitman entitled *Der Yankee-Heiland: Ein Beitrag zur modernen Religionsgeschichte* (The Yankee-Messiah: A Contribution to Modern Religious History). Supposedly, this book was the result of many years of Whitman research;[34] however, its rhetoric is characterized by the spitefulness and hatred typical of his battle with Schlaf. The book, an all-out attack on the person and the work of the author, was the most vituperative charge against Whitman in the history of the German reception of the poet. According to the *Yankee-Heiland, all* aspects of Whitman's life and work were determined by his "deviance." In order to bolster this argument, Bertz even recruited the "psychopathologists" Cesare Lombroso and Max Nordau, who were openly hostile to Whitman.[35] Systematically, he deconstructed the myths of the Whitman legend. Instead of being a perfected human, Whitman was now a congenitally afflicted paralytic and homosexual. Whitman's much-praised efforts in nursing wounded soldiers were denounced as the lecherous pursuits of a pederast. Whitman's claim that he was paralyzed as a result of his strenuous nursing duties was denied as self-deception (*YH*, 30 *passim*). According to this new, negative Whitman legend, the author's natural posture and naiveté were nothing but a "well-studied role" (*YH*, 23). His "typically American" biography, which led him to try out a multitude of professions, revealed inconstancy and vagrancy (a view also held by Lombroso). His general laziness even explained his lyrical form: apparently, Whitman's long and unrhymed lines required no artistic effort (see *YH*, 36).

Apart from this attempt to destroy Whitman's image, Bertz also claimed to have proven the complete internal inconsistency of Whitman's *Weltanschauung.* He was a "totally nonphilosophical type" (*YH*, 200f.), unable to recognize the contradictions inherent in his work. Bertz was particularly outraged over Whitman's and his disciples' attempt to start their own scientific religion (see *YH*, 77)—to which he traced Whitman's extraordinary popularity in Germany (see *YH*, 86). He contrasted Whitman's sensualist "mysticism" with positivism, failing to understand the inner relationship between physical (sensualist) "perception" and the physical, "scientific" methods of positivism.[36] Bertz's most serious charge, however, was the suggestion that Whitman was probably a sexually active homosexual—not, as he had said earlier, a "noble urning." With this "argument," he appealed to the very same "terrorist" tendencies he pretended to fight.

In spite of the fervor that went into his two books, Bertz was unable to destroy the image of the "Good Gray Poet," even though he did have some effect on the views of others toward Whitman. The only German critic who "abandoned" Whitman was O. E. Lessing, and this was more a result of Lessing's new apprenticeship to Arno Holz. Lessing adopted Bertz's idea about protecting the "straight" population: "The 'passionate attachment of man to man' from which Whitman expects future salvation has an erotic quality. Whitman owes significant artistic advantages to this deviant predisposition and to his feminine receptivity. But this excludes him from the ranks of 'educators of humanity.' This is a fact which the Whitman propagandists will have to accept."[37]

There was a more enlightened point of view. Gustav Landauer took a position above the bickering. To him, Whitman's homosexuality was a fact which had little to do with his appreciation of the poet, prophet, and mystic. The issue of homosexuality was "merely a product of the culture [*Kulturprodukt*]."[38]

From the point of view of Whitmanites, the net result of the discussion must have seemed highly satisfactory. Schlaf's cheap pamphlet reached a wide audience and probably even strengthened Whitman's image—of course, at the expense of homosexuals. Schlaf was given the opportunity to publicize his views in his mass-market edition of Whitman's poetry. The reactions of the expressionist authors as well as the socialist ideologues were the result of Schlaf's cultist image of Whitman. Bertz's portrait of a homosexual, paralyzed individual deeply divided with himself, had it taken hold in the culture, would not have permitted Whitman's emergence as an idol of expressionistic messianism and Whitman could never have been promoted to the rank of the "wound-dresser" of World War I. Even the authors for whom Whitman's homoeroticism *was* important (such as Thomas Mann) were put off by Bertz's "scientific" attitude toward a topic which affected them personally.

Echoes of the battle were also heard in the United States, where the Whitman Fellowship soon had matters under control. The *Nation* thought it "curious that a renunciation of allegiance so frequently turns into a denunciation of its object"[39]—referring, of course, to Bertz. *Current Literature*, stating that "the puzzling personality of Walt Whitman is now one of the favorite topics of the [psychosexual] school,"[40] implicitly took Schlaf's side of the argument. In the *New York Times*, Amalie von Ende admitted that Schlaf's enthusiasm might have been slightly exaggerated, but in the end she fully supported his zeal: "It is true that there was an undue amount of extravagant phraseology in these and other estimates of Whitman, but it impressed and convinced the younger generation reaching out toward other worlds and other ideals than those of their fathers, and perhaps the growing popularity of the American writer caused some alarm among the more conservative and patriotic spirits."[41] Among these conservative and "patriotic" spirits she obviously also included Bertz. A certain anti-American feeling in Bertz's book "makes this attack upon Whitman appear as a mere pretext to sound a warning against the Americanism into which some unbiased spirits in modern Germany are drifting. To one familiar with certain nationalistic movements in that country the book has an undercurrent of insincerity which falls very unpleasantly upon the ear."[42] Thus she managed to distract attention from the central question and, just seven years before the outbreak of the world war, accused Bertz of chauvinist anti-Americanism.

Léon Bazalgette, in his French biography of Whitman, agreed with Schlaf: "The unusual and impassioned character of these attachments of man to man naturally provoked the surprise of some commentators and incite special writers to place the poet as a sexual anomaly. The novelist, Johannes Schlaf, has definitely replied to the more recent and copious of these psychopaths [i.e., Bertz!]."[43]

Some eight years later, the debate resurfaced in France.[44] It started with a literary hoax by Guillaume Apollinaire concerning Whitman's funeral. His article in the *Mercure de France* hinted at an orgy involving homosexuality and provoked a large number of letters to the editor.[45] In this fight, the Whitmanites around Bazalgette opposed a second group that was convinced of Whitman's homosexuality. Bertz took an active part in the discussion by submitting numerous letters to the editor, but nothing new emerged from this debate. Bazalgette managed better than Schlaf to explain the irrelevancy of the discussion by calling attention to the autonomous and creative character of art.

What Robert K. Martin has called "Bertz's own inner confusions" were also the confusions of sexology attempting to approach the "problem" of homosexuality from a medical point of view.[46] It is the internal conflict of a discipline which still clung to anachronistic normative categories and values. While understanding and appreciating the problems homosexuals faced in a repressive heterosexual society, the developing science still referred to homosexuality as "misfortune." Sixty years later, following the difficult but partly successful struggle of gay liberationists, a gay critic such as Martin can comfortably speak of homosexuality as an "option."[47]

The debate surrounding Whitman's homosexuality shows to what extent "nonliterary" categories influenced the German reception of Whitman—and to what degree they, too, involved literature and fiction. Bertz's strategy of supporting homosexual emancipation through his Whitman article was definitely legitimate: although his positions were absurd at times, we must note that he was the first international critic who did not attempt to ignore or obscure Whitman's homosexual dimension. This strategy inevitably came into conflict with Schlaf's attempts to promote Whitman's works as an answer to the social, philosophical, and epistemological problems of his day, in spite of the fact that Schlaf himself was in principle sympathetic to the homosexual cause. Bertz's attempt to explain all of Whitman on the basis of sexual instincts reminded Schlaf too much of the narrow-minded "philistine" naturalism he himself sought to escape.

From the point of view of "Whitman propaganda," Schlaf's defense of Whitman was absolutely necessary. As shown by the 1906 German homosexual scandal surrounding Count Philipp Eulenburg, to which the public reacted in an extremely conservative and defensive way, Whitman would have been severely discredited by such a revelation. Eulenburg (1847–1921) was a diplomat and a close friend and confidant of emperor Wilhelm II. His encouragement of the absolutist tendencies of the emperor and the use of his friendship with Wilhelm to assist his friends and political allies drew much criticism from German liberals. In 1906, Maximilian Harden, editor of the magazine *Die Zukunft,* started to attack the political influence of Eulenburg and his circle. When Eulenburg refused to step down, Harden's attacks became more explicit, focusing on Eulenburg's alleged homosexuality and his interest in spiritist practices. The emperor was forced to dissociate himself from Eulenburg and others involved in the scandal and the monarchy as an institution was dangerously shaken by the outcry of public condemnation. According to recent research, Eulenburg was bisexual and his relationship with the emperor possibly had homoerotic dimensions not understood by Wilhelm.[48] Just as in the Schlaf-Bertz controversy, this case related politics and sexual politics in strange ways. The liberal (Harden) used the homosexual issue against conservative tendencies in a fashion extremely detrimental to the cause of homosexuals. If Bertz had prevailed, German reception of Whitman would have taken a different and, at least at that time, decidedly more narrow turn.

CHAPTER TWENTY

WANDERVOGEL AND NUDISTS

The Wandervogel was a youth movement in Germany and Austria that started at the turn of the century and lasted well into the twenties. Broadly speaking, it called for the liberation of young people from the constrictions of home and parents, school and teachers, and the urban environment at large. It cultivated outdoor feelings through the organization of hiking trips and tours. Such outings, which sometimes lasted days or weeks, emphasized a feeling of community through shared experience such as hiking, cooking, and singing. In principle, these activities were to be self-managed by young people—with individuals in their late teens or twenties as leaders of groups of younger people. Politically, the movement was extremely heterogeneous. While there were large segments with a German nationalist and anti-Semitic orientation, segments to whom the Nazis later successfully appealed, there were other groups that developed in a leftist, Marxist direction, especially after the horrific experience of World War I.

It is not difficult to imagine that this movement looked at the author of "Song of the Open Road" with some interest,[1] and it comes as no surprise that a beautiful edition of that poem in Hans Reisiger's translation was published in a separate edition with several woodcuts by a Wandervogel artist, Wilhelm Tegtmeier, by a publishing house specializing in publications for the German youth movement.[2] On 7 February 1921, three Whitman poems were on the title page of a journal related to the movement, *Freideutsche Jugend*, and Karl August Wittfogel, later a Communist and prominent sociologist, reported on meetings where Whitman poems were recited.[3]

In spite of this interest in the American poet, Whitman did not become a cult figure among the Wandervögel, at least as far as we can gather from documents available to us today. This may have to do with the fact that homoeroticism and homosexuality seem to have played a not unimportant role in the movement and that Whitman's homoeroticism might have appeared dangerously "loud" to the Wandervögel involved. One of the ideologues of the movement, Hans Blüher, wrote a lengthy history of the erotic foundations of the movement in which he suggests as much, although he was vehemently contradicted by other members of the movement.[4]

However strong a role homoeroticism or homosexuality—and through it Whitman's poetry—may have played in the Wandervogel, there are a few interesting documents proving the physical appeal of Whitman's poetry in the movement. During the years 1921–1922, Hermann Hesse and others edited a short-lived journal related to the nonnationalist wing of the youth movement. In this journal, Wandervogel Herbert Grünhagen (1897–1989) wrote an article on Walt Whitman, describing his own initiation into Whitman's work in the year 1920:

> One afternoon, I sat on my desk all by myself. The sun was shining. It was completely quiet. I was tired of the endless discussions, the meetings, all the theoretical stuff. During the winter, I had read Weininger. Weininger, who destroys what he really wants to recognize as holy, out of grief over himself and his age. . . . There, suddenly, this book with three seals opened in front of me, and a stream of joy and premonition went through me. The spasms and blurs in my brain, the doubts, everything fell off me, sank down, a large and strong hand tore all the rags off my body and all the junk off my soul, I was completely naked. And the hand lifted me into the air and held me on its broad robust surface. There I lay, the head fell back, the legs sank down, no more cramps in my limbs. And I drank sun and wind through my mouth and skin.
>
> This is, roughly, how it was. And since then, the book has hardly ever left my pocket. Often it closes and its words sound as though coming from far away. I touch it and still don't find it. But once you have breathed this air you can never again fall back into former times; romanticism and neoromanticism, classicism and naturalism, machine, brain, technology, pretense, fever and cold, doubt and spasms never again completely dominate you. Civilization races by outside. Haste, impatience, propaganda, clichés, insults, pressure never again blind you completely.[5]

This experience is summarized under the subtitle "Man of the Future." The liberated, mystical state, Whitman's person, and especially his unwillingness to be tied down to one profession—all of this fits the context of the youth movement. In addition, there was the outdoors. Grünhagen explains in his article: "We leave the constraints of school. We hike. We put on shorts. We rediscover popular songs. We sing. We sleep in the hay. A few people. Seemingly a very trivial thing."[6]

Yet the youth movement amounts to "the beginning and origin of a new race of men,"[7] and Whitman is intimately connected with it.

Grünhagen, born in 1897, died only recently in northern Germany. Over the years, he had put together a large collection of books by and on Whitman. In 1988, he expressed his belief that the Wandervögel should have put Whitman on their flags and could not understand why they did not. But he also believed they knew more about Whitman than they ever admitted. When former members of the movement met in 1947, Grünhagen, who, as a leftist, was forcibly retired by the Nazis, tried to remind them of their former ideals. When he talked about Whitman's views on obedience and freedom, some participants, obviously ashamed of their political attitudes during the Nazi period, called out: "We do not want to hear about Whitman!"

We do not know whether Grünhagen, as a result of his Whitman experience, shed his clothes in actuality or merely metaphorically. Whitman's impact on the Austrian and German nudist movement, however, is documented. This movement has its origin at the turn of the century. Originally connected to the many "alternative" lifestyles promising a better and more fulfilling existence, it was adopted by the labor movement and became one of its more interesting forms of cultural expression. Designed to liberate the body and to destroy traditional religious hang-ups, it was a far cry from the fashionable and voyeuristic nudist mass tourism on today's West European beaches. As opposed to the commercialized nudist tourism, the nudism of the twenties was a lifestyle, almost a philosophy.

Whitman probably played a far larger role in this movement than is possible to demonstrate today (the Social Democrats' interest in Whitman comes into play here). There are references to articles on Whitman in journals that are presently not available. One interesting article, however, can be found in a 1927 edition of *Die Freude: Zeitschrift für freie Lebensgestaltung* (Joy: Journal for Liberated Lifestyles). The article is interspersed with nudist photography and advertisements for relevant literature such as *Bathing in Germany* (promising fifty-six nude photographs). About Whitman, the author Franz Rinskofer writes:

> [For Whitman,] nature is the basis for all further contact with his environment, a principle of constructive life, "realization" [of the human potential] itself. Since Rousseau and Goethe, nobody has experienced nature as profoundly as Whitman. . . . Each of the possibilities of experiencing nature he fully enjoys. Air and wind, for example, offer an eternally changing play of sensations. They must be enjoyed because Whitman is "in love" with the atmosphere:

> "I will go to the bank by the wood and become undisguised and naked,
> I am mad for it to be in contact with me."
>
> Whitman is a strong epicurean and remained so his whole life. A diary entry shows us what true pleasure was for him: He has, for example, discovered the "free exhilarating ecstasy of nakedness" and defines it as becoming conscious of an "inner never lost rapport we hold with earth, light, air, trees etc." A philosophy of sybaritism flashes [through his poetry]. Pleasure as the highest level of awareness of sensations, enhancement of a budding psyche.[8]

Of course, Rinskofer quotes from Schlaf's small pocket edition. This use of Whitman suggests how the American poet may have appealed to numerous German subcultural groups. The American bard provided the groundwork for interpretation and justification of a variety of lifestyles, even if the full extent of such adaptions of Whitman is as yet unclear.

The examples in this chapter demonstrate how Whitman's by now mythical figure and poetry were very consciously employed in the sexual politics surrounding the liberation of the human body and the physical dimension of human beings. For homosexuals, Whitman provided a new language which helped them to formulate and develop their homosexual identity; for nudists and possibly Wandervögel, to "mainstream" their subcultural identity. While these are sometimes very "literal" readings of Whitman's works, providing lyrical blueprints for specific lifestyles, they clearly antedate modern readings of texts as bodies and vice versa and show how Whitman contributed to the development of more liberated attitudes both to human sexuality and to texts.

CONCLUSION

A GERMAN "WHITMANN"

In his complex article discussing the relationship between German and American (intellectual) culture, the German-American Germanist Frank Trommler defines "totality" as a traditional goal of German philosophical, literary, and academic endeavors.[1] By this he means (among many other things) a yearning for a restitution of a holistic life, free from alienation, reification, or transcendental homelessness. The humanities and the cultural establishment, in this view, have a social responsibility to reflect and, if possible, rectify the various undesirable conditions and situations Germans find themselves in. In contradistinction, the central metaphor for the American academy (and, we may hypothesize, also for the cultural establishment) is the frontier. Science and art are always supposed to be at the "cutting edge" of human development.

Trommler's thesis provides us with a starting point for a summary evaluation of a phenomenon as complex as the German reception of Whitman. What we have seen in the previous chapters—and I have refrained from drawing any generalizing cultural (or cross-cultural) conclusions, preferring to present and analyze individual phenomena first—must indeed seem paradoxical. Whitman was positioned in the aesthetic and political avant-garde by German commentators. Yet, at the very time they praised him for his modernity, their construction of Whitman reflects values which were clearly antimodern.

In the preceding chapters, we have observed the many ways in which Whitman was constructed with the aim of healing German wounds.[2] Like Santa Claus, with whom he shares his beard, Whitman was expected to fulfill the (partly infantile) wishes of each of his admirers. Each of them wrote away for a present in one way or another connected with a desire for totality. To Knortz, Whitman was going to deliver democracy (a people no longer divided into ruler and ruled); to Rolleston (in that sense a "German"), new synthetic, antipositivistic, antiscientific ways of behavior and thinking; to Schlaf, an epistemological harmony based on a new unity of self and world; to Schölermann, a recovery of a "Germanic" identity by bringing back together work and emotions; to Landauer and the anarchists, a lifestyle based on a combination of manual and intellectual labor. Reisiger and Mann hoped for a unified nation based on homoeroticism; the exiles for a return to their homeland or at least an end of their strongly felt cultural split; the East Germans for a connection of their own isolated culture with the tradition of world culture. Whitman's *Pathos*, frequently strengthened in the German translations, is a precise lyrical expression of that yearning for totality.

Almost all German readers of Whitman, regardless of their politics, their social and geographic origin, or their professional activity, looked toward the restitution of some previously existing state or values. It obviously did not matter whether they identified themselves as progressives or not; indeed, a case could be made that leftist ideologues focused as much on previous states of society as those on the right. Marxists, holding on to the integrity of the human individual, are thereby revealed as last-ditch defenders of a traditional humanistic world view. In the German construction of Whitman, the avant-garde poet was brought (or forced) together with the figure of the healer. This matter was not made any less confusing by the fact that Whitman, especially in his later life, proclaimed *himself* a healer and that Traubel made this the central message of his Whitman cult. America marketed Whitman in the fashion of painkiller drugs, although not necessarily to cure the symptoms of the European yearning for totality.

As only Hermann Bahr, among all German-speaking writers and critics, understood and appreciated for a limited period, Whitman was indeed a modernist on the cutting edge of the avant-garde. He was an innovator in many ways, not only the first to appropriate the (American) frontier lyrically, but also genuinely curious what he would find there. No matter what he or Traubel would say about them, his "universal" catalogues are really appropriate reactions to a modern pluralist society, and his seemingly primitive optimistic judgment of this society reveals nineteenth century American attitudes at their most characteristic.

European Whitman readers, to simplify matters slightly, were curious about Whitman's frontier mainly because they were hoping that at that frontier they were going to find a society, a state of being, even an epistemology, which they had lost. Instead of appreciating Whitman's dialectics of the One and the Many, they were hoping—in a pseudo-pluralistic fashion—to reduce the many to one. Johannes R. Becher's seemingly Whitmanesque catalogue includes only one part of humanity—and this part is to be forced into a "Socialist Army" to liberate humankind.

Whitman's astounding German popularity is based on two factors: the one-sided interpretation of the lyrical message promising totality and such promises actually made by Whitman (in his wound-dresser pose) or by the Whitmanites. The frontier Whitman always looked toward was of interest to German-speaking readers because it promised them a return to a holistic life, to totality. Once they had actually confronted it, however, Whitman's poetry inevitably carried them in a different direction, one they were frequently unable to follow.

While Whitman was originally constructed as a healer, his subversive modernity was soon felt (although not necessarily understood) by his German advocates, supporters, and imitators: unknown or unexpected side-effects of the medicine. Characteristically, this happened more quickly in the creative reception, where authors actually experimented with Whitmanesque models, than in reviews or articles, where commentators could stick to their claims and hopes without testing them.

The creative reception which prevents a linear construction of a German Whitman shows a pattern of temporary fascination with Whitman followed by an eventual withdrawal. In their creative works, both Schlaf and Holz took up Whitmanesque models, but failed to implement them radically. Schlaf's hesitant *Frühling* remains on the level of the human individual without regard for society as a whole. Holz's main quarrel with Whitman (in addition to his disdain at being regarded as the poet's disciple) was the American's low level of abstraction. Becher defined his "break" with Whitman at the point where the latter was no longer compatible with his class-based (and thus essentially antiuniversalist and anti-egalitarian) ideology. And Werfel, at first echoing Whitmanesque optimism over a universal egalitarian democracy, soon withdrew into traditional (European) religiosity from which he only occasionally departed in later years.

Does this mean that the German-speaking Whitman reception was essentially a failure from an intercultural point of view? Did the recipients, in reading Whitman, never manage to reach beyond the cultural limitations of their culture? Was Whitman's construction an idiosyncratic, monocultural endeavor? The many examples of critical and creative reception have already shown that this was not the case. Precisely because of the subversive (hidden) quality of his modernity, Whitman could become a particularly effective agent for change. The opposition of frontier/totality (or egalitarianism/hierarchy or any number of similar oppositional pairs) does not represent a permanent, unchangeable pattern. Rather, Whitman introduced a language of the frontier which Europeans slowly learned. In this way, he contributed to the still-far-from-complete process of the cultural "Americanization" of Europe.

Whitman, whether or not all or even a majority of his advocates liked it, suggested a language for talking about modernity. To include technology in poetry, for example, helped to make an important aspect of modern life acceptable to a society longing for totality. Poetry, we should not forget, was one of the important ways Europeans managed to relate their own subjective individuality to the greater whole. (This is one of the reasons why Whitman's poetry became so much more famous than his prose.) In fact, by joining poetry and prose (as he seemed to be doing), he connected lyrical aspirations to totality with the drab and fear-inspiring reality of prose.

Whitman also "taught" German poets (Schlaf, Holz, and the expressionists) a language in which they could address the disintegration of the individual, a language that would allow a positive evaluation of a process which traditionally appeared threatening to Germans and Austrians. Whereas the "abstract" expressionists withdrew into lyrical anxieties, "messianic" expressionists, in Whitmanesque ways, started to experiment with pluralism outside and *inside* the human individual. If Thomas Mann, as seems to be the case, actually learned through Whitman to accept his own conflicting sexual tendencies as a part of his personality, we can see how far this experimentation with pluralist lifestyles actually went.

Whitman provided examples for poets and nonpoets alike of how to (linguistically) appropriate the democratic idea for themselves. Through Whitman—as Reisiger, Hauptmann, and Mann understood only too well—the democratic ideal would become a personal concern for human individuals, a precondition if it were to survive as a system.

Most importantly, however, Whitman provided a lyrical discourse on internationalism. It is no suprise that his poem "Salut au Monde!" became his most successful, most widely translated, read, and imitated work. Even Tucholsky's parody of it in his "Die fünf Sinne" only satirized the failure and/or banal way in which this internationalist discourse was accepted into German poetry and the German public discourse.

Whitman's future reception in the German-speaking world will start here. As Central Europe internationalizes as a result of regional integration and through the influx of millions of immigrants from southern, southeastern, and eastern Europe as well as many other parts of the world, his international poetry will no longer mediate the *Pathos*-laden appeal to "international brotherhood" but will be of interest to an emerging multicultural, truly pluralistic society.

A new, non-*Pathos* reading (and translation) of Whitman might lose much of what was characteristic of the old German Whitman. But, in a democratized fashion, this *Pathos*, formerly expressing both the bridge and the distance to other nations, might very well change into a multicultural reading of the texts where the reader feels not on the outside but on the inside, as a part of one multicultural world that has overcome outdated oppositions such as East-West or North-South.

It is conceivable that a new intercultural aesthetic might emerge from his poetry, appropriate to the new quality of Central European societies as a whole. I began this study by suggesting that Whitman's reception was predominantly an intercultural phenomenon. This case of an intercultural collaboration in the reception of one author may eventually emerge as a characteristic paradigm for the future artistic and cultural development of Central Europe as a whole.

NOTES

INTRODUCTION

1. Except where noted, this study uses the term "German" in its most inclusive sense, incorporating all German-speaking countries and cultures of East-Central Europe, without, however, wanting to negate the significant cultural differences among them.

2. Robert C. Holub, "American Confrontations with Reception Theory," *Monatshefte* 81/2 (1989), 214.

3. For a comparative analysis of the identity and self-definition of academic institutions in Germany and the United States, especially with regard to literary scholarship, see Frank Trommler, "Über die Lesbarkeit der deutschen Kultur," in *Germanistik in den USA: Neue Entwicklungen und Methoden*, ed. Frank Trommler (Opladen: Westdeutscher Verlag, 1989), pp. 222–259.

4. See Michel Foucault, "What Is an Author," in *The Foucault Reader*, ed. Paul Rabinow (New York: Pantheon, 1984), pp. 101–120.

5. See Eberhard Scheiffele, "Affinität und Abhebung: Zum Problem der Voraussetzung interkulturellen Verstehens," in *Das Fremde und das Eigene: Prolegomena zu einer interkulturellen Germanistik*, ed. Alois Wierlacher (Munich: iudicium, 1985), pp. 29–46.

6. The disruption caused by World War I and the disappearance of the American Whitmanites as an organized group after Traubel's death in 1919 has changed this interaction somewhat; Whitman's German reception has maintained its interactive quality, however, as shown, for example, by the interest of German exiles in the United States.

7. See also my article "Collaborators in the Great Cause of Liberty and Fellowship: Whitmania as an Intercultural Phenomenon," *Walt Whitman Quarterly Review* 5/4 (1988), 16–26.

8. Munich: Fink, 1991.

9. See Alphonso C. Smith, *Die Amerikanische Literatur: Vorlesungen, gehalten an der Königlichen Friedrich-Wilhelms-Universität zu Berlin* (Berlin: Weidmannsche Buchhandlung, 1912), pp. 265–287.

10. Thomas K. Smith, "Whitman's *Leaves of Grass*: Style and Subject-Matter with Special Reference to *Democratic Vistas*" (Ph.D. thesis, Königsberg, 1914).

11. Edward Thorstenberg, "The Walt Whitman Cult in Germany," *Sewanee Review* 19 (1911), 71–86.

12. Grace Delano Clark, "Walt Whitman in Germany," *Texas Review* 6 (1920–1921), 123–137.

13. Anna Jacobsen, "Walt Whitman in Germany since 1914," *Germanic Review* 1 (1926), 132.

14. Gay Wilson Allen, "Walt Whitman—Nationalist or Proletarian," *English Journal* (college edition) 26 (1937), 52.

15. Harry Law-Robertson, an American, completed a Ph.D. thesis on the subject in 1935. His study *Walt Whitman in Deutschland* (Giessen: Münchowsche Universitäts-Druckerei, 1935), some ninety pages in length, is characterized by its National Socialist context and hardly manages to transcend anti-Semitic and anti-Communist ideological limitations and is thus especially weak in its evaluation of many (Jewish) German expressionist poets. Another American who completed his Ph.D. in Europe, Edward Allan McCormick, was equally unable to understand the significance of the Whitman phenomenon (*Die sprachliche Eigenart von Walt Whitmans "Leaves of Grass" in deutscher Übertragung: Ein Beitrag zur Übersetzungskunst* [Bern: Haupt, 1953]). In his New Critical search for the "ideal translation" of Whitman's poetry, he overlooked "imperfect" translations, which are nonetheless very instructive with regard to specific variants of German Whitman reception. McCormick's claim to be able to "penetrate" and understand the peculiarity of Whitman's language (a position from which he judges the various Whitman translations) remains speculative.

A third dissertation, by Vincent P. Cosentino ("Walt Whitman und die deutsche Literaturrevolution: Eine Untersuchung über Whitmans Einfluß auf die deutsche Dichtung seit Arno Holz" [Ph.D. thesis, Munich, 1968]), attempts to demonstrate Whitman's impact on German expressionism. Cosentino's cursory study is also speculative, and his lack of any archival work led to factual errors which undermine the validity of the study as a whole. Moreover, a lack of familiarity with Whitman and Whitman scholarship, a problem most Germanist works suffer from, is painfully obvious.

16. Monika Schaper, *Walt Whitmans "Leaves of Grass" in deutschen Übersetzungen: Eine rezeptionsgeschichtliche Untersuchung* (Frankfurt/M. and Bern: Lang, 1976).

17. Frederik Schyberg, *Walt Whitman* (New York: Columbia University Press, 1951), 248–327; Gay Wilson Allen, *Walt Whitman Handbook* (Chicago: Packard and Company, 1946); Marianne Misgin-Müller, "Die Rezeption der Literatur der USA in der deutschen sozialdemokratischen Presse (1890–1933)" (Ph.D. thesis, Humboldt-Universität, Berlin, 1975).

18. Betsy Erkkila, *Walt Whitman among the French: Poet and Myth* (Princeton, N.J.: Princeton University Press, 1980).

19. M. H. Abrams, *A Glossary of Literary Terms*, 5th ed. (New York: Holt, Rinehart and Winston, 1988), p. 129.

20. Ibid.

21. W. V. Ruttkowski and R. E. Blake, *Literaturwörterbuch in Deutsch, Englisch und Französisch/Glossary of Literary Terms . . .* (Bern and Munich: Francke, 1969), p. 20. "Pathos," in *Metzler Literaturlexikon: Stichwörter zur Weltliteratur*, ed. Günter Schweikle and Irmgard Schweikle (Stuttgart: Metzler, 1984), p. 324.

22. Ibid.

23. Stefan Zweig, "Das neue Pathos," *Das neue Pathos* 1 (1913), 4.

1. FERDINAND FREILIGRATH, ADOLF STRODTMANN, AND ERNST OTTO HOPP

1. Walt Whitman, "Europe, The 72d and 73d Years of These States," *Leaves of Grass: Comprehensive Reader's Edition* [*LG*], ed. Harold W. Blodgett and Sculley Bradley (New York: New York University Press, 1965), pp. 266f.

2. *Poems by Walt Whitman*, ed. William M. Rossetti (London: John Camden Hotten, 1868). We do not know whether Rossetti and Freiligrath knew each other. Nothing in the published papers of the Rossettis or of Freiligrath points to a personal acquaintance. As Freiligrath was well connected in England, however, a personal encounter is entirely possible.

3. The quotations from this essay are taken from the English translation arranged by William D. O'Connor. It appeared under the title "Walt Whitman" in several American magazines, including *New Eclectic Magazine* (Baltimore), 2 (July 1868), quotation on 325f. Originally published in *Augsburger Allgemeine Zeitung* (Wochenausgabe), no. 17, 24 April 1868, pp. 257–259:

Walt Whitman! Wer ist Walt Whitman?

> Die Antwort lautet: ein Dichter! Ein neuer amerikanischer Dichter! Seine Bewunderer sagen: der erste, der einzige Dichter, welchen Amerika bisher hervorgebracht. Der einzige spezifisch amerikanische Dichter. Kein Wandler in den ausgetretenen Spuren der europäischen Muse, nein, frisch von der Prärie und den Ansiedlungen, frisch von der Küste und den großen Flüssen, frisch aus dem Menschengewühl der Häfen und der Städte, frisch von den Schlachtfeldern des Südens, dem Erdgeruch des Bodens, der ihn gezeugt, in Haar und Bart und Kleidern.

4. Walt Whitman, "Gedichte," trans. Freiligrath, *Augsburger Allgemeine Zeitung* (Wochenausgabe), no. 24, 12 June 1868, and no. 25, 19 June 1868, pp. 385f. Freiligrath's selection included "Eighteen Sixty-One," "Rise O Days from Your Fathomless Deeps," "Bivouac on a Mountain Side," "A March in the Ranks Hard-Prest," "A Sight in Camp in the Daybreak Gray and Dim," "As Toilsome I Wander'd Virginia's Woods," "Over the Carnage Rose Prophetic a Voice" (all from *Drum-Taps*); "Old Ireland," "Old War-Dreams," and "Bathed in War's Perfume." Nine of the ten poems dealt with the Civil War; all ten were in the original *Drum-Taps* or *Sequel to Drum-Taps*.

5. Monika Schaper, *Walt Whitmans "Leaves of Grass" in deutschen Übersetzungen*, p. 42.

6. Freiligrath, "Whitman," p. 327: "[Nach der Lektüre wird unser] herkömmliches Versemachen, unser Zwängen des Gedankens in irgendwelche überkommene Formen, unser Spielen mit Kling und Klang, unser Silbenzählen und Silbenmessen, unser Sonettieren und Strophen- und Stanzenbauen uns fast kindisch bedünken. Sind wir wirklich auf dem Punkt angelangt, wo das Leben, auch in der Poesie, neue Ausdrucksweisen gebieterisch verlangt? Hat die Zeit so viel und so viel Bedeutendes zu sagen, daß die alten Gefäße für den neuen Inhalt nicht mehr ausreichen? Stehen wir vor einer Zukunftspoesie, wie uns schon seit Jahren eine Zukunftsmusik verkündigt wird? Und ist Walt Whitman mehr als Richard Wagner?"

7. Freiligrath to Vollmer, 12 June 1868, in Wilhelm Buchner, *Ferdinand Freiligrath: Ein Dichterleben in Briefen*, 2 vols. (Lahr: Schauenburg, 1882), vol. 2, p. 382.

8. Wilhelm Vollmer to Freiligrath, 4 June 1868, Goethe-Schiller-Archiv, Weimar.

9. Whitman to Rudolf Schmidt, 16 or 20 January 1872, quoted in Horace Traubel, *With Walt Whitman in Camden*, 2 vols. (New York: Rowman and Littlefield, 1961), vol. 1, p. 407.

10. "Is Walt Whitman's Poetry Poetical?" In *Notebooks and Unpublished Prose Manuscripts*, vol. 4, *Notes*, ed. Edward F. Grier (New York: New York University Press, 1984), p. 1517.

11. W. D. O'Connor to Whitman, 16 September 1868, quoted in Traubel, *With Walt Whitman in Camden*, vol. 2, pp. 431f.

12. Freiligrath to his daughter Käthe, 2 December 1868, in *Freiligrath-Briefe*, ed. Luise Wiens (Stuttgart and Berlin: Cotta, 1910), p. 167. A transcript of O'Connor's letter to Freiligrath, dated 14 November 1868, was made available to me by Florence Bernstein Freedman, New York. The original, formerly part of the Bliss Perry Collection, is now lost.

13. Ibid.

14. Ibid.

15. Ibid.

16. Freiligrath to Käthe, 2 December 1868, p. 168.

17. "Walt Whitman," *Fortnightly Review* (London), 15 October 1866, pp. 538–548. Freiligrath mentions Conway by name.

18. Traubel, *With Walt Whitman in Camden*, vol. 2, p. 389 (entry for 27 September 1888).

19. *Amerikanische Anthologie*, ed. and trans. Adolf Strodtmann (Leipzig: Bibliographisches Institut, n.d. [1870]), pp. 149–154.

20. Adolf Strodtmann, "Einleitung," in *Amerikanische Anthologie*, p. 15.

21. Ibid., p. 11.

22. Ibid.: "mit welcher seine Verehrer die reimlosen, oft nur durch einen wilden Rhythmus die dichterische Form wahrenden Streckverse dieses literarischen Sonderlings als unvergleichlich hohe Meisterwerke des Genius preisen."

23. Ernst Otto Hopp, *Unter dem Sternenbanner: Streifzüge in das Leben und die Literatur der Amerikaner* (Beneath the Star-Spangled Banner: Excursions into Life and Literature of Americans) (Bromberg: Fischer, 1877), pp. 116f.

24. Free rhythmic, rhymeless poetry was known to German readers from biblical psalms, from works by the eighteenth-century poet Friedrich Gottlieb Klopstock (1724–1803), and from various Romantic poets of the nineteenth century, including Heinrich Heine.

2. KARL KNORTZ AND THOMAS WILLIAM ROLLESTON

1. T. W. Rolleston came from the Irish circle of Whitman enthusiasts at Trinity College in Dublin led by Edward Dowden. Inspired by the Irish nationalist movement,

this group was part of the British Whitman tradition which had influenced Freiligrath earlier.

2. For more information on Knortz, see Horst Frenz, "Karl Knortz: Interpreter of American Literature and Culture," *American German Review* 12 (December 1946), 27–30.

3. Whitman to Rolleston, 20 August 1884, in *Whitman and Rolleston: A Correspondence*, ed. Horst Frenz (Bloomington: Indiana University Press, 1951), p. 92.

4. Karl Knortz, "Geistige Turnerei," in Karl Knortz, *Deutsches und Amerikanisches* (Glarus: Vogel, 1894), p. 137.

5. Karl Knortz, *Walt Whitman: Vortrag gehalten im Deutschen Gesellig-Wissenschaftlichen Verein von New York am 24. März 1886* [KK] (New York: Bartsch, 1886).

6. Johannes Schlaf, review of "Walt Whitman, der Dichter der Demokratie: Von Karl Knortz," *Das literarische Echo* 2 (1899–1900), col. 65.

7. William D. O'Connor, "The Carpenter," *Putnam's Monthly Magazine* n.s. 1 (January 1868), 50–90.

8. Knortz, *Deutsches und Amerikanisches*, p. 137.

9. "Wenn er nun aber doch hin und wieder den Namen 'Gott' gebraucht so versteht er darunter im Grunde nichts Anderes, als sein eigenes moralisches Gefühl, das er in Menschen und Natur hinein gelegt hat, und bewahrheitet somit auch den alten Satz, dass die Götter Fantasiegebilde der Menschen seien."

10. "Die traditionelle Scham ist durch die Vertreter der christlichen Religion, welche den menschlichen Leib, von Luther Madensack genannt, zum Urheber aller Sünden stempelte, zu einer lobenswerten Tugend aufgebauscht worden; nun aber kommt ein vom Geiste des Griechentums durchdrungener Dichter."

11. "Scham und Moral bestehen nicht in einem umgehängten Kleide. Whitman feiert das Geschlechtsleben im Interesse des menschlichen Fortschrittes, im Interesse des physischen wie moralischen Wohlbefindens."

12. "Als begeisterter Amerikaner und entschiedener Fortschrittsmann verlangt Whitman, dass Kunst, Poesie, Philosophie und Erziehung vom demokratischen Principe durchdrungen seien und auf die Zukunft gestaltend wirkten"; "Der amerikanischen Gesellschaft fehlt das erhebende und stärkende moralische Element und dieses derselben einzuflössen ist Aufgabe der neuen Litteratur."

13. "Whitman's Dunkelheit [ist] durchaus nicht zu entschuldigen, denn derjenige Dichter oder Philosoph, der da glaubt die Welt mit neuen Gedanken beglücken zu können, sollte dieselben auch in eine solche Sprache kleiden, dass sie wenigstens einem einigermassen gebildeten Menschen der Gegenwart verständlich sind."

14. "Der Dichter und der Mann der Wissenschaft sollen eins sein, sodass ersterer also nicht mehr seine Gedanken an fantastische Erzählungen zu reihen braucht, sondern dem Uebernatürlichen Valet sagen, sich auf realen Boden stellen und somit einen weitergehenderen und mächtigeren Einfluss auf seine Zeit äussern kann."

15. "Der Dichter Amerika's muss *modern* sein und ohne das Gute und Schöne seiner europäischen Kollegen zu ignoriren, auf eigenen Füssen stehen. Er muss der Sauerteig sein, der seine Nation und dann mit Hilfe derselben die ganze Welt moralisch, politisch und litterarisch durchsäuert."

16. Rolleston to Whitman, 4 June 1881, in Frenz, "Karl Knortz," p. 31.

17. Ibid.

18. See Rolleston to Whitman, 27 September 1883, in which he gives a humorous account of his slightly confused audience, in Frenz, "Karl Knortz," pp. 77f.

19. T. W. Rolleston and H. B. Cotterill, *Ueber Wordsworth und Walt Whitman: Zwei Vorträge gehalten vor dem Literarischen Verein zu Dresden* [TWR] (Dresden: Tittmann, 1883).

20. "Geisteseroberungen dieses wunderlichen Zeitalters"; "d[er] moderne[n] Menschheit, mit ihrer furchtbaren Energie, ihrer beispiellosen Vertiefung in der Dialektik und ihrem grenzenlosen Muth in Wort und That"; "In England bekanntlich beschäftigt man sich hauptsächlich mit den Gesetzen der Erscheinungen, der Weise ihres Entstehens und wie sie einander bedingen, im allgemeinen mit dem, was man ihre äußere Wirkung nennen kann."

21. Rolleston to Whitman, 14 February 1882, in Frenz, "Karl Knortz," p. 57: "von dem Thun, sondern von dem Sein . . . [dem] Inhalt des Seelenlebens"; "Die deutsche Philosophie hält also immer am Centrum, an der denkenden Seele fest und verliert sich nicht in die Beobachtung." This comparison, originating with Freiligrath (see preceding chapter) will be echoed by Thomas Mann.

22. "Der größte poetische Vertreter von dem, was man gewöhnlich für ein Hauptmoment in der deutschen Philosophie hält"; "alles glaubenden Geist der Demokratie zu versöhnen vermag, der die ungeheueren, verworrenen, geistigen Bestrebungen des Jahrhunderts in sich auffaßt, ihre wahre Richtung hervortreten läßt und das kraftlos Zerstreute durch die unerklärliche Macht einer magischen Selbstheit der gewaltigsten Wirkung fähig macht."

23. "Wenn das Wissen, das Hineinsehen in das Leben der Dinge uns wirklich lieber ist als die leere Bekanntschaft mit Namen und Erscheinungen, welche gewöhnlich als wirkliche Kenntniß angenommen wird."

24. "Die Unabhängigkeit der ethischen Begriffe."

25. "Daß ein neues Verhältniß zwischen uns und dem Gegenstand des Glaubens auf irgend eine Weise herbeigeführt werden sollte, kraft welches er nicht mehr blos ein Name für uns ist, ein logischer Schluß, eine Ueberlieferung, sondern ein Ding, eine Wirklichkeit werde, etwas, das die Tiefe des Bewußtseins berührt."

26. "Lebendige geistige Wahrnehmung"; "die Dinge täglicher Erfahrung in ihrer Wirklichkeit wahrzunehmen, [das] *ist* Religion und *erzeugt* die Ethik" (emphasis added).

27. Richard Blunck, *Der Impuls des Expressionismus* (Hamburg: Harms, 1921), p. 38: "Die Religion des expressionistischen Menschen, die Bindung, die er zwischen sich und dem All weiß, ist ethisch, Bewegung, ewige Forderung, dynamisch: nichts Festes und Fixes. Nicht ist das Ethos, das Gesetz, etwas außen, an einer fremden Hand, einem außermenschlichen Sein Befestigtes: wir wissen, daß es nur in und durch den Menschen ist."

28. In his Whitman book of 1911, Knortz mentions that it was Whitman's friend R. M. Bucke who first suggested to him a German translation and who handed him Rolleston's manuscript. See *Walt Whitman und seine Nachahmer: Ein Beitrag zur Lite-*

ratur der Edelurninge (Walt Whitman and His Imitators: A Contribution on the Literature of the Noble Urnings) (Leipzig: Heichen, 1911), p. 62.

29. Knortz to Whitman, n.d., Feinberg Collection, Container 10, Library of Congress.

30. Rolleston to Bucke, 8 January 1885, Feinberg Collection, Container 53, R. M. Bucke papers, Library of Congress.

31. "Unsere Sprache und unsere poetischen Formen sind für ihn steif und todt geworden—Whitman verwirft letztere vollständig, und die Sprache gewinnt unter seinen Händen wieder ein seltsames neues Leben" (Walt Whitman, *Grashalme: Gedichte* [KR], ed. and trans. Karl Knortz and T. W. Rolleston [Zurich: Verlags-Magazin Schabelitz, 1889], p. vii).

32. "Souveräner Verächter aller Regeln der englischen Grammatik."

33. See Harry Law-Robertson, *Walt Whitman in Deutschland*, p. 16.

34. Monika Schaper, *Walt Whitmans "Leaves of Grass" in deutschen Übersetzungen*, p. 40.

35. Rolleston to Whitman, 9 September 1884, in Frenz, "Karl Knortz," p. 94. That this is not the whole truth is evidenced by the reply of Cotta, the most renowned German publisher of the period. Cotta declined because "we do not publish translations from living languages, a fact which you can gather easily from our list of publications" (Cotta to Rolleston, 25 July 1884, in Autoren-Copierbuch III, 14 January 1884–6 April 1885, p. 304, Deutsches Literaturarchiv, Marbach).

Of course, the presentation of *Leaves of Grass* as victim of the German police state appealed to the preconceived notions of Whitman, who had faced the power of the state himself several times. According to Traubel, Whitman fully believed Rolleston's account: ". . . it is typical history—especially that possible encounter with the German police" (*With Walt Whitman in Camden*, vol. 1, p. 18, entry for 8 April 1888). Just like their American counterparts, German Whitman disciples had a strong inclination toward martyrdom and a love of conspiracy theories, a legacy which was passed on to Johannes Schlaf—and his opponents.

36. Knortz to Whitman in an undated letter from New York, probably between 1885 and 1887: "Dr. Bucke, from Canada, who yesterday spent an hour at my house and whom I had a pleasant conversation with, left with me Rolleston['s] translation of your poems. . . . How many hours does it take from N.Y. to Camden? I should like very much to spend a few hours with you, and if you have no objections I shall make a trip to your city at my earliest convenience" (Feinberg Collection, Container 10, Library of Congress).

37. William O'Connor to William Sloan Kennedy, 9 April 1886, Whitman Collection, Special Collections, Van Pelt Library, University of Pennsylvania.

38. Frenz, "Introduction," in *Whitman and Rolleston*, p. 11.

39. The English original is lost; this is a retranslation from the German: "Ich billige Ihren Versuch, einige meiner Gedichte in deutscher Sprache wiederzugeben. Ich hatte in der That, so übermüthig die Aeußerung auch klingen mag, nicht nur mein eigenes Vaterland im Auge, als ich jenes Werk verfaßte. Ich wollte den ersten Schritt thun, um einen Cyclus internationaler Gedichte in's Leben zu rufen. Das Hauptziel der Vereinig-

ten Staaten von Amerika ist das gegenseitige Wohlwollen der ganzen Menschheit, die Solidarität der Welt. Was hier noch mangelt, kann vielleicht durch die Dichtkunst geleistet werden, durch Gesänge, ausstrahlend aus allen Ländern der Welt. Diesen Ländern in Amerika's Namen einen herzlichen Gruß zu schicken, hatte ich auch in meinen Gedichten vor. Und lieb, recht lieb wird es mir sein, Zulaß und Zuhörerschaft unter den germanischen Völkern zu gewinnen."

40. Knortz and Rolleston were well aware of the pioneering translations by Freiligrath and Strodtmann and mentioned them in their contributions. For the majority of the German audience, however, this Whitman translation represented a new beginning.

41. Knortz, *Whitman und seine Nachahmer*, p. 63: "Daß das Werk von den Zeitungen unbarmherzig durchgehechelt werden würde, dessen war ich sicher; zu meinem größten Erstaunen aber war das Gegenteil der Fall. Die meisten Kritiker sahen darin eine bedeutsame Leistung."

42. Ernst Ziel, review of *Grashalme*, trans. Knortz and Rolleston, *Blätter für literarische Unterhaltung* 26 (June 1889), 406: "Seine Rhythmen haben etwas Wildes, Ungezähmtes, etwas vom Brausen des Meeres. Von Amerika, dem großen freien Amerika, gehen alle seine Gedanken aus; auf Amerika richten sie sich alle zurück."

43. Julius Brand [Julius Hillebrand], review of *Grashalme*, trans. Knortz and Rolleston, *Gesellschaft* 5 (1889), 1818: "Aber wer sich reinbaden will in den Niagarafluten dieser grandiosen Poesie[. . .], wer lieber durch Urwaldgestrüpp als durch englische und französische Gärten wandern will, wer mit einem Wort noch Sinn hat für *Elementarpoesie*, der lese und studiere den Walt Whitman" (emphasis in original).

44. Ziel review, p. 406.

45. Brand review, p. 1818: "Hinterwäldler mit den nervigen Armen und der stolzen Brust." The term "backwoodsman" shows the literary context in which Whitman was read. Whitmanites themselves never referred to Whitman as a "backwoodsman." This is the influence of Cooper and, even more so, Charles Sealsfield, an Austrian-American author.

46. Ibid.: "eine Litteratur, pedantisch, geglättet, krankhaft lüstern, anempfunden, neurotisch-hysterisch."

47. Ibid.: "Sie sitzen zu viel. . . . Das giebt körperliche und geistige Rückgratsverkrümmung."

48. Ernst Ziel, "Walt Whitman," *Die Gegenwart* 35 (1889), 356: "Werden diese vollsaftigen Früchte von den Fluren des freien Amerika sich Herzen gewinnen in dem waffenstarrenden Lande Bismarck's? Wer weiß es? . . . Zwischen Walt Whitman und der alternden Kultur Europas liegt der Ocean—ein Ocean liegt auch zwischen Walt Whitman's verblüffender Ursprünglichkeit und dem blassen Conventionalismus, dem wir seit Urväterzeiten her auf Kanzel und Katheder, im Amtskleide wie im Schlafrocke huldigen: Walt Whitman weiß nichts von akademischer Schulung, nichts von weltmännischer Bildung, nichts von der dreisten Lüge unseres gesellschaftlichen Lebens und dem gedankenlosen Aufgehen alles persönlich Eigenartigen in modernes Schablonen- und Uniformenthum."

3. JOHANNES SCHLAF

1. Bliss Perry, quoted in Gay Wilson Allen, *The New Walt Whitman Handbook* (New York: New York University Press, 1975), p. 14. For a detailed account, see my article "Collaborators in the Great Cause of Liberty and Fellowship," *Walt Whitman Quarterly Review* 5/4 (1988), 16–26.

2. Traubel to Schlaf, 16 June 1904, Johannes Schlaf Archiv, Querfurt.

3. The Schlaf library includes a poetry volume by Crosby, *Swords and Plowshares* (New York: Funk and Wagnalls, 1902).

4. Ernest Crosby is also prominently mentioned in Knortz's *Walt Whitman und seine Nachahmer.*

5. Crosby to Schlaf, 8 April 1906, Johannes Schlaf Archiv, Querfurt. Amalie von Ende is discussed in the next chapter.

6. See the translation of Schlaf's "Kinderland" in the *Conservator* 14 (April 1903), 20f. (trans. Amalie von Ende). Concerning Schlaf's recognition by the fellowship, see also A. v. Ende, "Walt Whitman in Germany," *Conservator* 14 (January 1904), 167–169 and 183–185; and Paul Harboe, "Johannes Schlaf on Walt Whitman," *Conservator* 17 (June 1906), 58f.

7. H. B. Binns to Schlaf, 5 November 1905, Johannes Schlaf Archiv, Querfurt.

8. Bazalgette to Schlaf, 18 January 1907, Johannes Schlaf Archiv, Querfurt (original in French).

9. Bazalgette to Schlaf, 27 January 1907, Johannes Schlaf Archiv, Querfurt (original in French).

10. This theme is discussed in the section on Schlaf's creative reception of Whitman's works in chapter 11.

11. Bazalgette to Schlaf, 29 March 1906, Johannes Schlaf Archiv, Querfurt (original in French).

12. Johannes Schlaf, "Walt Whitman," *Freie Bühne für den Entwickelungskampf der Zeit* [*FB*] 3 (1892), 978f.

> Meine Arbeit für heute ist gethan. Die Dämmerung kommt. Müde und betäubt von meinen Schreibereien lehne ich aus dem Fenster und sehe, wie die Sonnenlichter drüben an den hohen Fassaden allmählich verlöschen.
>
> Und da, nach dieser Lektüre und dieser Arbeit, spür' ich, wie eingeengt wir leben, versteh' und empfind' ich unser ganzes Elend.
>
> Weit hinunter erstreckt sich die Straße mit dem Gekribbel und dem Lärm ihres Verkehrs, verliert sich nach beiden Seiten in Dunst und in dem verwirrenden Getriebe der Nebenstraßen. Oben ein schmales, karges Stück Himmel, umwölkt und verschmutzt von dem aufsteigenden schwülen Brodem, von Staub und Essenqualm. Hinter den Fenstern drüben, die ganze lange Straßenzeile hinab, hinunter, neben, über und unter mir, von allen Seiten ein enges, sich drängendes, förderndes und hemmendes Beieinander und Durcheinander zwischen den grauen Steinmassen. Und wie hier, so breitet es sich stundenlang im Kreis und weit in das Land hinaus.

13. "Die unzähligen Fäden, durch die unser Leben, Fühlen und Empfinden mit ihren unendlichen Wundern verknüpft ist, scheinen zerschnitten, und wir sind allein,

allein mit uns, mit allem nur, was wir mit unserm trennenden Urteil 'menschlich' nennen, allein mit uns, der Mensch mit dem Menschen, in der flirrenden Unrast dieses engenden Beieinander und seinem nervenzerfressenden, verwirrenden Durcheinander."

14. "Und alle Raffinements der zu Jahren gekommenen Kultur können uns nicht über unsere große Kardinalkrankheit hinwegbringen, an der wir erfolglos und mit allen möglichen Heilmitteln herummedizinieren, der Religionslosigkeit oder, wenn man will, der Kraftlosigkeit, der Atrophie des Empfindens."

15. "Aber wie wollen wir einander helfen, wenn der Zusammenhang, in dem wir mit allen Lebendigen in allen Nähen und Fernen stehen, vielleicht für unsern Verstand vorhanden, für unser Empfinden aber nicht *lebendig* ist?"

16. Johannes Schlaf, "Vorwort," in Walt Whitman, *Grashalme*, trans. Johannes Schlaf (Leipzig: Reclam, 1907), p. 9: "eine Differenziertheit und Sensibilität der Empfindung und des Wahrnehmens, eine Subtilität und ein intimes Unterscheidungs- und Feststellungsvermögen nicht nur der äußeren Erscheinung, sondern gerade ihren seelisch-geistigen Reaktionen und Wechselbeziehungen gegenüber, das völlig erstaunlich, bewunderungswürdig und unvergleichlich ist, und das gleichsam einen sechsten Sinn für die Grundwirklichkeit und Identität alles Seins bedeutet."

17. Schlaf quotes in German from Knortz and Rolleston. Throughout my study, translated passages are given in Whitman's original quoted from the *Reader's Edition.*

18. "Wie wird uns zu Mut!—Als würde alles das, was in meilenweiten märchenhaften Fernen lebt, was wir als *Gegensatz* zu unserem Leben hier empfinden, was wir kennen und doch nicht verstehen, lebendig mit seiner frischen Schönheit."

19. "Die jauchzende Ohnmacht gegenüber einer neuen, unendlichen Fülle an- und eindringender Wahrnehmungen"; "Wie seltsam! Wie wirklich!"

20. "Der selige, kräftige Tumult eines lebendigen inneren Werdens ist darin."

21. "Wir haben das Einzelne, Getrennte hinter uns, das uns verwirrte und ängstigte. Elend und Glück, Armut und Reichtum, alle die unbegreiflichen Gegensätze, die uns in unsrer Enge quälten: nichts können sie uns mehr anhaben und aufdringlich uns den Zusammenhang der Dinge verdunkeln. Oder doch: es ist alles da: aber alles an seinem Platz, eingeordnet und erlöst mit seinem Zwiespalt in den mächtigen Rhythmus des ewigen Kreislaufs alles Geschehens und aller Erscheinungen."

22. Johannes Schlaf, "Mein Verhältnis zu Walt Whitman" (My Relationship to Walt Whitman), *Die Lese* 3 (1912), 437: "Doch da begegnete ich, gerade zu einem Zeitpunkt, wo diese innerste Vereinsamung am unerträglichsten zu werden drohte, dem Dichter der 'Grashalme.' "

23. Johannes Schlaf, "Vom *Guten Grauen Dichter*" (About the Good Gray Poet), *Sozialistische Monatshefte* 8/2 (1904), 828: "Es ist wunderbar, die sympathetischen Kräfte, die aus seinen Gesängen auf einen übergehen, mit einer seelischen Heilkraft, wie zum Beispiel ich für meine Person sie ausser von einigen Büchern der Bibel und Goethes *Dichtung und Wahrheit* nur eben noch von Walt Whitmans Dichtung erfahre."

24. Ibid.

25. Johannes Schlaf, review of Karl Knortz, *Walt Whitman, der Dichter der Demo-*

kratie, 2nd ed. (Leipzig: Fleischer, 1899), *Literarisches Echo* 2 (1899–1900), col. 66: "es ist nicht zu viel gesagt, wenn ich ihn verehrungswürdig nenne wie einen der großen Religionsverkünder der Vorzeit, und wenn ich sage, er steht da, hochragend, segen- und lebensspendend wie der erste Dichter-Seher eines dritten Evangeliums."

26. Johannes Schlaf, *Walt Whitman* (Berlin: Schuster und Loeffler, 1904), p. 52.

27. "Plagiarism" in translations is different from plagiarism in creative works. Schlaf had come to know and appreciate Whitman through Knortz and Rolleston's translation. Therefore it is only natural that he incorporated large parts of this translation into his own.

28. See Harry Law-Robertson, *Walt Whitman in Deutschland*, pp. 22–24; Edward Allan McCormick, *Die sprachliche Eigenart von Walt Whitmans "Leaves of Grass" in deutscher Übertragung*, pp. 48f.

29. Monika Schaper, *Walt Whitmans "Leaves of Grass" in deutschen Übersetzungen*, pp. 61ff.

30. Johannes Urzidil, "Nachwort" to Walt Whitman, *Grashalme*, trans. Johannes Schlaf (Stuttgart: Reclam, 1968), p. 233: "Er [Schlaf] glaubte in den *Grashalmen* vor allem ein entschiedenes monistisches Empfinden zu erkennen. Die Grundakkorde von Kameradschaft, Liebe und Demokratie, der Wunsch Whitmans nach freier Gleichberechtigung der Geschlechter und eine Art der Sensibilität, die von fernher an Friedrich Nietzsche gemahnte, waren die dynamischen Bewegungskräfte für Schlafs Übersetzungen. Er spricht von Whitmans 'neuem Pathos', und in dieser Prägung ertönt bereits das Signal des aufsteigenden literarischen Expressionismus."

31. Gustav Janouch, *Gespräche mit Kafka: Aufzeichnungen und Erinnerungen* (Frankfurt/M.: Fischer, 1961), p. 186: "Er hat die Betrachtung der Natur und der . . . Zivilisation zu einer einzigen berauschenden Lebensempfindung zusammengeschlossen." This Whitman commentary is dealt with at greater length below.

32. Crosby to Schlaf, 8 April 1906, Johannes Schlaf Archiv, Querfurt.

33. Rudolf Wacker was an expressionist painter of some importance. After his return to Austria, he became the only Austrian representative of the Neue Sachlichkeit style in painting.

34.

Verehrter Herr Schlaf!

Ich muß Ihnen mitteilen, daß hier jemand ist, der sich Ihnen unendlich dankbar fühlt!—Vergangenen Sommer kam mir Ihre Übertragung der "Grashalme" in die Hände. Was mir seither Walt Whitman geworden ist, welches Glück es für mich bedeutet, daß er eben hier in mein Leben eintrat, kann ich unmöglich in ein paar Worten aussprechen. Gleich so nahe u. lieb wurde er mir, es war, als hätte ich gerade auf diesen Menschen gewartet. Auch mir ist er die umfangreichste "Bestätigung," und wird m. ganzes Leben der Führer sein (so folge ich ja nur dem Leben selber!)—Ich habe auch meine Freunde u. Frauen in Deutschld. zu ihm gewiesen und lese ihn hier meinen Kameraden vor.—Daß sich seine Gemeinschaft ausbreitet u. daß wir Ihnen, der uns die Pforte in das neue Reich geöffnet hat, dankbar sind, hier Ihnen zu sagen drängte mich!

4. KARL FEDERN AND WILHELM SCHÖLERMANN

1. Concerning the life of the now forgotten Amalie von Ende, see the autobiographical summary in Franz Brümmer, Biographies II, A. v. Ende, in the Staatsbibliothek Preußischer Kulturbesitz, Berlin. Cäsar Fleischlen, poet, critic, and editor, calls her an "unflagging champion of our German literature in America" ("Über Amalie von Ende," ms. at the Deutsche Literaturarchiv, Marbach). See also Walter Grünzweig, "Das 'literarische Wien': Idiosynkrasie und Kult: Über Amalie von Ende," *Das Jüdische Echo* 38/1 (October 1989), 181–193.

2. Amalie von Ende, "Hat Amerika eine nationale Litteratur?" *Das literarische Echo* 1 (1898–1899), col. 163.

3. Ibid., col. 166.

4. Ibid.

5. Amalie von Ende, "Walt Whitman in Germany," *Town and Country* 56/16 (29 June 1901), 11.

6. Ibid.

7. Ibid., p. 12.

8. Amalie von Ende, review of Federn, *Essays zur amerikanischen Litteratur, Das literarische Echo* 2 (1899–1900), col. 1670.

9. Amalie von Ende, "Whitman in Germany," p. 12.

10. Theodor Achelis, "Whitman-Übertragungen," *Das literarische Echo* 7 (1904–1905), col. 120: "Er [Whitman] ist inmitten der neuromantischen Verweichlichung und gefühlsmäßigen, bis zum Raffinement getriebenen Verzärtelung ein Vertreter stärksten Lebensgenusses."

11. Theodor Achelis, "Walt Whitman," *Die Gegenwart* 33/17 (1904), 264: "faden Scheinsweisheit des ausgemergelten Aesthetenthums . . . wie es sich . . . so widerwärtig in unserem modernen Leben breit macht."

12. Karl Federn, "Walt Whitman," in Karl Federn, *Essays zur amerikanischen Litteratur* (Halle: Hendel, 1899), p. 120: "Von Formlosigkeit zu reden muß man sich hüten. Walt Whitmans Dichtungen sind durchaus rhythmisch und oft voll Musik, und wer versucht, seine Gedichte in völliger Prosa wiederzugeben, wie Knortz und Rolleston es gethan, der ist wie einer, der uns durch das Textbuch allein den Genuß einer Oper vermitteln wollte."

13. Walt Whitman, *Grashalme*, trans. Karl Federn (Minden i. W.: Bruns, 1904), p. 3.

14. Wilhelm Schölermann, "Zur Einführung," in Walt Whitman, *Grashalme*, trans. Wilhelm Schölermann (Leipzig: Diederichs, 1904), p. vi.

15. Ibid., p. iv.

16. Ibid., p. x.

17. Wilhelm Schölermann, "Walt Whitman," *Deutsche Welt* 7/14 (1904), 196.

18. Ibid.

19. Schölermann, "Zur Einführung," p. x: "Parademarsch im Kugelregen bei klingendem Spiel."

20. Ibid., p. 1.

21. Ibid., p. 3.

22. Schölermann, "Walt Whitman," p. 213: "den albernen Yankee doodle [*sic*]."

23. Schölermann, "Walt Whitman, p. 215: "Wenn ihn [den Genius der Erfüllung des zwanzigsten Jahrhunderts] Europa haben soll, muß er auf germanischem Kulturboden geboren werden."

5. FRANZ BLEI

1. Walt Whitman, *Hymnen für die Erde*, trans. Franz Blei (Leipzig: Insel, 1914).

2. See Monika Schaper, *Walt Whitmans "Leaves of Grass" in deutschen Übersetzungen*, pp. 88f.

3. Franz Blei, Whitman entry in his *Das grosse Bestiarium der modernen Literatur* (Berlin: Rowohlt, 1922), p. 71: "Der Große Pan, nie gestorben, weil unsterblich, er allein unter den Göttern, wenn auch oft Zeiten lang verschwunden in den tiefsten Grotten der Erde."

6. GUSTAV LANDAUER

1. Kurt Wolff to Landauer, 14 June 1916, in *Kurt Wolff: Briefwechsel eines Verlegers, 1911–1963*, ed. Bernhard Zeller and Ellen Otten (Frankfurt/M.: Fischer, 1980), p. 242.

2. Landauer to Wolff, 15 June 1916, ibid.

3. Ibid.

4. Ibid.

5. Gustav Landauer, "Walt Whitman," in Gustav Landauer, *Der werdende Mensch: Aufsätze zur Literatur* [GL], ed. Gerhard Hendel (Leipzig and Weimar: Kiepenheuer, 1980), pp. 85–97.

6. Walt Whitman, *Gesänge und Inschriften: Übertragen von Gustav Landauer* (Songs and Inscriptions: Translated by Gustav Landauer), (Munich: Wolff, 1921).

7. Concerning the significance of mysticism for Landauer, see Ruth Salinger Hyman, *Gustav Landauer: German Jewish Populist and Cosmopolitan* (Ann Arbor: University Microfilm, 1978; Ph.D. thesis, CUNY, 1975).

8. "Daß der Mensch in seinem Ich, in seiner *Geistigkeit*, die ganze Welt trägt, daß die Welt nur eine unendliche Fülle von Mikrokosmen ist" (emphasis added).

9. "Keine vage, im Allgemeinen verschwimmende Menschenliebe; sie soll vielmehr, wie die Liebe, die die Familie gegründet hat, vom Geiste der Ausschließlichkeit beseelt sein, sie soll bestimmte Menschen, Männer mit Männern, Frauen mit Frauen und natürlich auch Männer mit Frauen zu neuen sozialen Gruppen zusammenschließen."

10. "Übermaß an Wohlstand, 'Geschäft,' 'Weltlichkeit,' Materialismus"; "das Reich der Zukunft, der noch nicht fertigen, sondern erst zusammenwachsenden, anschließenden Volksgemeinschaft"; "ein früher Vorläufer eines amerikanisch-perikleischen Zeitalters."

11. "Ein freies Volk tätiger Menschen, die alle Hemmnisse des Kastengeistes hinter

sich gelassen, alle Gespinste überjährter Vergangenheit durchbrochen haben; jeder auf seiner Scholle oder in seinem Handwerk, an seiner Maschine, ein Mann für sich selbst."

12. "Nur ein großes Volk . . . kann große Dichter haben; aber vorher muß die Poesie es sein, die das große Volk gestaltet, 'künstlerischen Charakter, Geistigkeit und Würde' ihm verleiht."

13. "Der Dichter also, der Walt Whitman in seinem Gefühl von sich selbst und seiner Aufgabe sein will, ist Priester, Prophet, Schöpfer. Daß er außergewöhnliche Gewalt auf sein Volk und die geistige Macht seines Volkes—und derer, die in fremden Völkern als einzelne zu seinem Volke gehören—ausgeübt hat und weiter übt, ist sicher."

14. *Gesänge und Inschriften*, p. 43.

15. This is also shown by his letter to President Wilson prior to the U.S. entry into the war. See Gustav Landauer, "Friedensvertrag und Friedenseinrichtung," in Gustav Landauer, *Rechenschaft* (Berlin: Cassirer, 1919), pp. 198–204.

16. Gustav Landauer, "Der Krieg" (1911), in *Rechenschaft*, p. 21: "Möge die Kriegsdrommete ein Ruf der Sammlung sein für alle die, die innerlich aus dem Staate, aus dem Reich der Gegensätze zwischen den Staaten ausgetreten sind. Mögen sie sich klar machen und auch nach außen hin dokumentieren: diese Zwecke sind für unsern Geist tot: sie binden unser Inneres nicht mehr; wir sahen längst andere Möglichkeiten der Verbindung der Menschen zum Volk; der Verbindung der Völker untereinander."

17. In 1919, a Whitman volume entitled *Der Wundpfleger* containing pacifist poetry translated by Landauer and Civil War prose translated by Ivan Goll was published by the leftist Swiss publisher Rascher.

18. Walt Whitman, "Wende dich, Freiheit," *Plan* 1 (October 1945), 3.

7. MAX HAYEK

1. Walt Whitman, *Ich singe das Leben*, trans. Max Hayek (Vienna: E. P. Tal, 1919); and Walt Whitman, *Gesang von mir selbst*, trans. Max Hayek (Leipzig and Vienna: Wiener Graphische Werkstätte, 1920).

2. Franz Diederich, "Ein Beispiel Kriegsdichtung," *Die Neue Zeit* 33/1 (1915), 374: "In der deutschen Arbeiterpresse wurde in diesen Kriegsmonden mehrfach eine Versreihe aus Walt Whitmans 'Grashalmen' gedruckt. Nur wenige Zeilen lang, aber in der Wirkung stark. Whitman ist aber auch der Dichter, dessen Stimme zurzeit den Anspruch auf besondere Geltung fordern darf."

3. Franz Diederich, ed., *Von unten auf! Ein neues Buch der Freiheit* (Up from Below! A New Book for Freedom), 2 vols. (Berlin: Vorwärts, 1911; 2nd edition 1920). The anthology contains three pieces by Whitman: "The City Dead-House," "Trickle Drops," and excerpts from "Pioneers! O Pioneers!"

4. Diederich, "Ein Beispiel Kriegsdichtung," p. 373: "Der jähe Sprung des blutigen Weltschreckens aus dem Schemenreich im Frieden geschauter Visionen in die nacktgrellste Wirklichkeit hat alle Welt vor die Schicksalsfrage geschleudert, wie es anzustellen sei, trotzig aufrecht zu bleiben. Den besten Weg weist auch hier die Antwort, daß

ein Hauptverhüllen und Abwenden nichts helfen kann, daß es vielmehr darauf ankommt, dem Schlimmsten mutig ins Auge zu schauen."

5. Ibid.: "Wir dürfen nie den Elementarsatz unserer Kampfbewegung vergessen: wir sind nicht da, um bloß zu verneinen. Wir verneinen, um aus dem Gegensatz desto stärker auf Bejahung dringen zu können."

6. Ibid., p. 374: "wie er die gräßlichste Wirklichkeit bezwingt, indem er ihr fest ins Auge sieht."

7. Ibid., p. 375: "er griff nicht zur tötenden Kriegswaffe, als Lazarettpfleger trat er in die Reihe der Kämpfenden."

8. See "Hayek, Max" entry in *Jahrbuch der Wiener Gesellschaft: Biographische Beiträge zur Wiener Zeitgeschichte*, ed. Franz Planer (Vienna: Planer, 1929), p. 235.

9. "Nie hat ein Mann mit gewaltigerm Glauben an den Menschen und die Menschlichkeit gelebt als dieser große Amerikaner. Und die blutgetränkte Erde hat ihm das Licht seiner Seele, dieses immer neu hoffende, unerlöschliche, göttliche Licht nicht zu trüben vermocht."

10. Anon., "Walt Whitman," *Vorwärts*, 27 March 1917 ("Unterhaltungsblatt"): "Vor 25 Jahren, am 27. März 1892, hat einer der edelsten Geister Amerikas die Augen geschlossen, einer, der, das dürfen wir mit Sicherheit annehmen, die heutigen Vorgänge in den Vereinigten Staaten auf das stärkste gemißbilligt hätte. . . . ihm wäre die Hinterhältigkeit, Zweideutigkeit und Unaufrichtigkeit der jüngsten amerikanischen Politik tief zuwider gewesen." Whitman actually died on 26 March.

11. Ibid.: "die 'Grashalme' waren und blieben ein Mißerfolg, und nur ganz langsam wuchs das Verständnis für diesen originellen Dichter, der noch heute nicht zu den 'Lieblingen' des amerikanischen Publikums zählt, und wohl auch nie zählen wird."

12. *Vorwärts* had traditionally been critical of the official party line regarding the war. In November 1916, however, critical journalists lost their job and the paper assumed a much more "moderate" line.

13. Max Hochdorf, review of *Gesang von mir Selbst*, trans. Max Hayek, *Sozialistische Monatshefte* 27/1 (1921), 418: "Er [Whitman] ist die wirkliche Wahrheit, nicht irgendwelche Kenntnis, die aus der Beobachtung stammt, sondern das Erfassen der Dinge von innen. Daher schwinden vor ihr die äußeren Kategorieen."

8. HANS REISIGER

1. Hans Reisiger, "Wie ich zu Walt Whitman kam," *Neue Zürcher Zeitung*, 1 March 1923.

2. Hans Reisiger, "Vorwort," in Walt Whitman, *Grashalme: Neue Auswahl*, trans. Hans Reisiger (Berlin: Fischer, 1919), pp. 7f.:

> Deutschland ist beschattet von den Bergen des Hasses und der Rachgier, die sich an seinen Grenzen türmen. Wie Gletschermoränen schiebt sich dumpfer Materialismus übermütiger Feinde in sein Land. Irdischem Boden und stofflichen Gütern gilt es. Die flüssig gewordenen Schichten seiner eigenen Bevölkerung wälzen sich vernichtend gegeneinander. Die tiefe Sehnsucht nach Weltglück und Weltgerechtigkeit wühlt nur erst Schlamm auf, auf dem die Morgenröte einer edleren Zukunft

noch kaum einen Widerschein findet. Verschüttet ist tausendfach das Tor, durch das noch je diese seit Anbeginn in blutigen Krämpfen zuckende Welt rein, ruhevoll, vergeistigt und göttlich erschien: das Tor der einzelnen Seele! Mitleid, Erschöpfung, Kleingläubigkeit, Haß, Hunger, Furcht sind die Steine, die es so tausendfach verrammt haben. . . .

Walt Whitman wage ich hier in diesem umdüsterten Augenblick aufs neue mit den Lauten deutscher Sprache zu beschwören, obwohl er vielen unter uns schon so vertraut ist wie Licht und Luft.

Immer und ewig wird das Ziel alles irdischen Ringens die Neuschöpfung des Menschen sein. Und wo anders liegt das Paradies dieses neuen höheren Menschen immer wieder als im eigenen Ich? Erst aus solcher Zeugungskraft in sich selber kann das wahre Mitfühlen strömen. "Sei ein Mann für dich selbst und ein Kamerad deinen Mitmenschen"—das ist der Satz, den Whitman über das Gemeinleben der Menschen schreibt. Feurige, zweckbefreite, selbstlose und doch im edelsten Sinn selbstsüchtige und seelenbegierige Kameradschaft, die er pflanzen will "dicht wie Bäume entlang den Strömen Amerikas," eine solche stolze Demokratie selbstbewußter Geister und anziehungsfroher Leiber ist es, die wir heißen Wunsches auch aus allen Qualen und Fiebern Deutschlands erflehen."

3. See Hauptmann's letter to Ernst Hardt of 7 February 1919, in *Briefe an Ernst Hardt: Eine Auswahl aus den Jahren 1898–1947*, ed. Jochen Meyer (Marbach: Deutsches Literaturarchiv, 1975), p. 108.

4. Thomas Mann, "Hans Reisigers Whitman-Werk. Ein Brief," *Frankfurter Zeitung*, 16 April 1922, p. 1. This is a slightly revised version of Horst Frenz's translation published in *Walt Whitman Abroad: Critical Essays from Germany, France, Scandinavia, Russia, Italy, Spain and Latin America, Israel, Japan, and India*, ed. Gay Wilson Allen (Syracuse: Syracuse University Press, 1955), p. 16:

Lieber Herr Reisiger!

Ich bin ganz entzückt über den Besitz Ihres Whitman-Werkes und kann Ihnen nicht genug danken,—wie ich denn auch meine, daß das deutsche Publikum Ihnen garnicht genug wird danken können für diese große, wichtige, ja heilige Gabe. Ich nehme die beiden Bände immer wieder zur Hand, seit sie bei mir sind, lese hier und dort, habe die biographische Einleitung gleich *in extenso* gelesen und nenne sie ein kleines Meisterwerk der Liebe. Wahrhaftig, lieber Herr Reisiger, es ist ein Verdienst ersten Ranges, daß Sie uns diesen gewaltigen Geist, dies strotzende und dabei tiefe neue Menschentum in jahrelanger Hingabe und begeisterter Arbeit nahe gebracht haben, uns Deutschen, die wir alt und unreif sind zugleich, und denen die Berührung mit dieser zukunftsmächtigen Humanität zum Segen gereichen kann, wenn wir sie aufzunehmen wissen. Für mich persönlich, der ich innerlich um die Idee der *Humanität* seit Jahr und Tag mit der mir eigenen Langsamkeit bemüht bin, überzeugt, daß es für Deutschland keine aktuellere Aufgabe gibt, als diesen Begriff, der zur leeren Hülle, zur bloßen Schulphrase geworden war, neu zu füllen,—für mich ist dies Werk ein wahres Gottesgeschenk, denn ich sehe wohl, daß, was Whitman "*Demokratie*" nennt, nichts anderes ist, als was wir, altmodischer, "Humanität" nennen; wie ich auch sehe, daß es mit Goethe allein denn doch nicht getan sein wird, sondern daß ein Schuß Whitman dazu gehört, um das Gefühl der neuen Humanität zu gewinnen: zumal sie viel gemeinsam haben, die beiden Väter, vor allem das Sinnliche, den "Calamus," die Sympathie mit dem Organischen . . . Kurzum, Ihre That—dies Wort ist nicht zu groß und stark—kann von unabsehbarer Wirkung sein, und ich, nicht eben sehr taufrisch für meine Person, will doch unter denen gewesen sein, die Sie wissenden Herzens dazu *beglückwünscht* haben!

Seien Sie vielmals gegrüßt von Ihrem ergebenen
Thomas Mann

5. Walt Whitman, *Walt Whitmans Werk in zwei Bänden* [HR1 and HR2], trans. Hans Reisiger, 2 vols. (Berlin: S. Fischer, 1922), vol. 1, pp. lxxf: "Und diese Lust strahlt nicht nur um das empfangende, weibliche 'Du,' zu dem dich alle magnetischen Blitze deines Leibes ziehen, sondern auch um das 'Du' des Mannes, des Kameraden, des Gefährten im 'Garten Welt'; auch zu ihm strebt der Magnet, auch ihm legst du mit tiefer Lust die Hand in die Hand oder auf die Schulter oder um die Hüfte, dem reinen, wohlgestalteten, durchgeistigten Freunde. Nur 'ätherischer' noch, 'gleichsam körperlos,' obwohl immer in der Wonne der Leiblichkeit; gleichsam das eigene Wunder der Mannheit im gleichgeschaffenen Adamsbruder liebevoll noch einmal erlebend, das 'Zeichen der Mannheit' mit ihm, im frischen Sinnbild in Waldestiefe am Sumpfrand gepflückter Kalmuswurzel, kühnen Phallussymbols, austauschend, in naturbeseeltem Rausch der All-Liebeskraft, in glühend-lächelnder Kameradschaft der hier auf Erden gemeinschaftlich Wandelnden und Fühlenden. Tiefer noch als im Empfängnistaumel des Weibes lebt hier im mitliebenden Gefährten der wache Erostraum. . . . Es hieße sich an diesen Gedichten [Calamus] versündigen, wenn man, wie eifrige Maulwürfe es versucht haben, den Eros aus ihnen hinwegdiskutieren wollte; sie sind durch und durch davon durchbebt, genau so gut, wie die stille Luft des Nachmittags vor den Toren Athens, als Sokrates unter der Platane am Bach mit Phaidros redete."

6. "Und so spüren wir erst die wahre Dämonie und Macht dieser feurig-geflüsterten Calamus-Lieder, wenn wir uns bewußt werden, daß ihr Sänger in ihnen sich aus der panischen Stille des Waldes etwas holen will, was der Lebensnerv des gesamten Gemeinschaftslebens der Zukunft und aller Staaten und Städte sein soll, der Herzschlag wahrer Demokratie, das elektrisch zwischen allen eine wahre Gemeinschaft bildenden Männern Spielende, das jeden Einzelnen aus der Verkrampftheit der Eigensucht, Parteilichkeit, Gehässigkeit und Stumpfheit Erlösende."

7. Thomas Mann, "Von Deutscher Republik," *Neue Rundschau* 33 (1922), 1103: "Eros als Staatsmann, als Staatschöpfer"; "Einheit von Staat und Kultur."

8. Anon., "Gedichte von Walt Whitman," *Der Kunstwart* 36/5 (1923), 193: "Walt Whitman ist entdeckt! Ein deutscher Dichter hat ihn entdeckt. Gespürt, geahnt, gerühmt, auf ihre Art 'übersetzt' haben ihn schon viele. Doch erst Hans Reisiger hat ihn entdeckt und erobert."

9. See Monika Schaper, *Walt Whitmans "Leaves of Grass" in deutschen Übersetzungen*, pp. 102–105.

10. Reisiger to Thomas Mann, 4 November 1946, *Blätter der Thomas Mann Gesellschaft* (Zurich), 8 (1968), 14.

9. TRANSLATIONS AFTER WORLD WAR II

1. Walt Whitman, *Grashalme*, trans. Elisabeth Serelmann-Küchler and Walther Küchler (Erlangen: Dipax, 1947).

2. Walt Whitman, *Lyrik und Prosa*, trans. Erich Arendt and Helmut Heinrich (Berlin: Volk und Welt, 1966).

3. Arendt translated only the poetry; the prose selections are by Helmut Heinrich.

4. Whitman, *Lyrik und Prosa*, trans. Arendt, p. 62.

5. Walt Whitman, *Tagebuch* (Diary), ed. Eva Manske, trans. Götz Burghardt (Leipzig: Reclam, 1985).

6. Walt Whitman, *Grashalme*, trans. Georg Goyert (Berlin: Blanvalet, 1948); Henry Seidel Canby, *Walt Whitman: Ein Amerikaner*, trans. Georg Goyert (Berlin: Blanvalet, 1947).

7. Monika Schaper, *Walt Whitmans "Leaves of Grass" in deutschen Übersetzungen*, p. 132.

8. Walt Whitman and Vachel Lindsay, *Manhattan und Illinois*, trans. Max Geilinger (Herrliberg and Zurich: Bühl, 1947).

9. Walt Whitman, *Walt Whitman: Ein Kosmos*, trans. Else and Hans Bestian, collages by Eric Gand (Schwifting: Schwiftinger Galerie-Verlag, 1985).

10. See Walt Whitman, *Ich rufe Erde und Meer an*, trans. Susanne Schaup (Freiburg/B.: Herder, 1987), p. 28.

11. Ibid., p. 38.

12. Ibid., p. 44.

13. Ibid.

10. WHITMAN IN GERMAN LITERATURE

1. Walter Bauer (1906–1976), a writer strongly concerned with social issues, wrote poetry, autobiographical novels, and travelogues. In 1952, he emigrated to Canada; he died in Toronto. Whitman was indeed one of Bauer's intellectual ancestors.

2. Tucholsky to Bauer, 8 December 1930, Deutsches Literaturarchiv, Marbach.

3. Oskar Loerke, "Eine neue Whitmanübersetzung" (review of Whitman, trans. Reisiger), *Neue Rundschau* 30 (1919), 1278: "Nachdem man gerade in jüngster Zeit ganze Chöre technisch und geistig von Whitman abhängiger Poeten gehört hat, erschrickt man bei der Wiederbegegnung mit dem Urbilde vor seiner Wahrheit. Man begreift, das bloße Erscheinen und Dasein dieser Sonne mußte Geschlechter von stillen Sängern der privaten Natur und empfindsamen Hingebung in Epigonen verwandeln."

4. Ibid.: "Dennoch gehört der riesige Umfang auch der literarischen Wirkung, der befruchtenden sowohl wie der verheerenden, zu dem Begriffe Whitman. Die Entdekkung eines so waghalsig unkonventionellen Gedichttyps wie des Whitmanschen konnte nur den Stumpfsinnigen unerschüttert lassen."

11. NATURALISM

1. Arno Holz, "Zola als Theoretiker," *Freie Bühne für modernes Leben* 1 (1890), 104.

2. For an analysis of the historical sequence of *Bewußtseinslagen* as expressed in American literature from Puritanism to Faulkner, see Jürgen Peper, *Bewußtseinslagen des Erzählens und erzählte Wirklichkeiten: Dargestellt an amerikanischen Romanen des 19. und 20. Jahrhunderts insbesondere am Werk William Faulkners* (Leiden: Brill, 1966). On the supersession of naturalism by impressionism, see pp. 77–94.

3. Johannes Schlaf, "Die Vollendung des Naturalismus," *Die Güldenkammer* 2/4 (1911–1912), 206.

4. Julius Hart, ed., *England und Amerika: Fünf Bücher englischer u. amerikanischer Gedichte von den Anfängen bis auf die Gegenwart* (Minden: Bruns, 1885), pp. 403–406.

5. Arno Holz to Eduard Bertz, 21 February 1907, in Arno Holz, *Briefe: Eine Auswahl*, ed. Anita Holz and Max Wagner (Munich: Piper, 1948), p. 169.

6. See Eberhard Hilscher, *Gerhart Hauptmann* (Berlin: Verlag der Nation, 1969), p. 90.

7. Gerhart Hauptmann, *Sämtliche Werke*, ed. Hans-Egon Hass, vol. 7, *Das Abenteuer meiner Jugend* (Frankfurt/M.: Propyläen, 1962), p. 1062. It remains unclear whether Hauptmann refers to the translation of his friend Schlaf or of his friend Reisiger: "Ein Dichtwerk, das weiterhin auf uns von größtem Eindruck war, hatte den Amerikaner Walt Whitman zum Verfasser und trug den deutschen Titel 'Grashalme.' Nicht zuletzt durch unsere Begeisterung hat es dann seinen Weg gemacht und ist in einer herrlichen Übertragung in den Bestand unserer Literatur übergegangen."

8. In recent times, there has been renewed academic interest in Schlaf. A thesis by Ingolf Schnittka, "Der Nachlaß Johannes Schlafs: Biographie, Bibliographie und Kommentar" (Ph.D. thesis, Halle, 1989), profits greatly from the access to Schlaf's papers. Another recent monograph was written by Gaston Scheidweiler: *Gestaltung und Überwindung der Dekadenz bei Johannes Schlaf: Eine Interpretation seines Romanwerks* (Frankfurt/M.: Lang, 1990).

9. Amelia von Ende, "The Poets of Young Germany," *Critic* 36 (1900), 240.

10. Schlaf was essentially "self-taught" as well. He had dropped out of the university and his later investigations into scientific matters are, although fascinating and provocative, wholly amateurish.

11. When von Ende uses the term "Whitman-cult," she is entirely serious and does not want to convey a derogatory judgment of the German Whitman movement.

12. Von Ende, "Young Germany," p. 240.

13. Johannes Schlaf, *In Dingsda* (Minden: Bruns, n.d.), pp. 41f.:

> Und meine Augen weiten sich, und meine Nüstern dehnen sich und schnaufen die Luft ein, und mir ist, als wollt' ich mit jeder Fiber das alles in mich aufnehmen, die ganze lichte, singende, weite, herrliche Welt!
>
> Und ich stammle wunderliche, wahnselige Worte vor mich hin, die ich nicht höre. Es ist nur, als flute etwas aus meiner Seele heraus, hinaus wie überströmendes Leben, überwallende Kraft.
>
> Und alles liegt unter mir, weit unten in der Sonne. . . . Wie betäubt lieg ich, und starre vor mich hin, in das kurze Gras und wage nicht seitwärts zu blicken.

14. Ibid., pp. 138f.: "Kein kluges, kaltes Beobachten: mit seinem Empfinden aufgehen mitten im Leben, es selbst werden. . . . Ganz selbst und doch seiner selbst entledigt zu sein; das ist das Pathos, mit dem einen die Welt erschüttert und sänftigt wie mit einem religiösen Schauer."

15. Albert Soergel, *Dichtung und Dichter der Zeit: Eine Schilderung der deutschen Literatur der letzten Jahrzehnte* (Leipzig: Voigtländer, 1911), pp. 641, 637.

16. Ernst Ludwig Schellenberg, "Johannes Schlaf, der Lyriker," *Xenien* 2 (1909), 217.

17. Johannes Schlaf, *Frühling* [*F*] (Leipzig: Insel, n.d. [1894]), p. 3: "Und dann lieg ich tief im Gras, in der hellen Sonne, die Hände unterm Genick, und pfeife und simuliere in den blauen Himmel und die milchweißen Frühlingswolken hinein."

18. "Ganz, ganz versunken . . . in jungem, duftendem Grün."

19. "Tiefer den Kopf ins Gras zurück."

20. "Hier lieg ich und strecke mich, ein Tunichtgut und Simulant schlimmster Sorte."

21.

> Mein Kopf liegt an deiner Brust.
>
> Und du, goldig, licht, jung, beugst dich über mich.
>
> Mit deiner linden Hand träufelst du mir Heliotrop auf die Stirn. Ich atme den süßen Duft und deinen Atem, der süßer ist als er.
>
> Mein Gesicht fühlt deinen Herzschlag, deinen ruhigen, ruhigen Herzschlag.
>
> Und Auge in Auge, tiefer immer, versinkender.
>
> Leise, leise hernieder zu mir, und leise, leise ich hinauf zu dir. Du lächelst, biegst den Kopf hintüber, und deine Hände drücken sich schwach gegen meine Brust mit schelmischem Drängen.
>
> Und nun: Lippe an Lippe. Lange . . . Zwischen halbgeschlossenen Lidern dunkelt dein Blick. Und nichts als sein Glanz und eine süße Wärme von dir zu mir.
>
> Frieden. Und aus ihm Kraft, Gedanken, Entschlüsse, lichter, immer lichter, kühner und kühner, und Erkenntnisse.

22. "Mit jedem Pulsschlag, mit jedem Beben meines Körpers, mit jeder Bewegung liebkose ich die weit und lustig gebreitete Welt. Und mich liebkosen die Käfer, die Blumen und Bäume mit Summen und Blüten und Laub, mit Farben und Düften und hundert sanften Berührungen. Der leise Wind durch Blätter und Gezweig liebkost mich . . . . Kühles, wogendes, anschmiegendes Schmeicheln."

23. "Nun macht mich mein begehrender, ahnender Sinn kleiner und immer kleiner, und nun bin ich winzig, ganz ganz winzig klein. Ich habe ein goldgrünes Röckchen auf einem runden, festen, geschmeidigen Körperchen, tripple mit sechs flinken Beinchen und habe zwei Äugelchen wie rote Rubinen."

24. "Dünne, dünne Scheide zwischen uns und einer neu erweiterten Welt neuer Wunder"; "Sämtlicher Laster und Tugenden bin ich teilhaftig. Ich habe mit Christus, dem Herrn, die Leidensnacht in Gethsemane durchlitten, und mit Buddha das innerste Wesen der Welt erkannt. Ich bin geschlechtslos, bin Mann und Weib. Schuldlos bin ich und naiv wie das reinste Kind und erfahren wie der blasierteste Roué! Ich bin Kaiser und Held und der niedrigste Sklave. Der gewandteste, gefährlichste und der blödeste, einfältigste Liebhaber, bin und habe, was ich will."

25.

Rote, warme Lichtlein glimmen fern in niedriger Enge zwischen breit geballten, schwarzen Wipfeln.

Und unter weitentfachter, goldiger Pracht wandre ich mit eiligen Füßen durch weiße Nebel den Lichterchen zu, den armen, glimmenden, heimlichen Lichterchen.

Zu dir, ma Dame! Zu dir!

26. Regarding the political dimension of Whitman's poetry, see Betsy Erkkila's *Whitman the Political Poet* (New York and Oxford: Oxford University Press, 1989).

27. "Heller scheint hier die Sonne, und heimlicher sind die Schatten. . . . Große schöne Menschen haben sich hier zusammengefunden, geschwisterlich, ein König jeder in Freiheit und in der Seligkeit weltfernen Glückes."

28. "Blatt schließt sich um Blatt und Hülle um Hülle bis in alle Unendlichkeit hinein."

29. See Johannes Schlaf, review of Julius Hart, *Die neue Welterkenntnis, Stimmen der Gegenwart* 3 (1902), 91.

30. Johannes Schlaf, *Das dritte Reich: Ein Berliner Roman* (Berlin: Fontane, 1900), p. 32: "neuere Nervenentwicklung"; "Die sich bereitenden Bürger des neuen heimlichen Reiches!"

31. Ibid., p. 57.

32. Ibid., p. 93: "Wie in einer inneren Vision . . . die vollendete Herrschaft des menschlichen Geistes über den Erdball."

33. Ibid., p. 97: "Das tausendjährige Reich war da!"

34. Johannes Schlaf, *Peter Boies Freite* [*PB*] (Leipzig: Seemann, 1903), p. 5.

35. "In seiner Bildung begriffenen Neumenschentypus, der sich von den Atavismen seiner ersten Jugendeinflüsse und von dem skeptischen Materialismus seiner späteren Entwickelungsjahre zu befreien trachtet und zu einer neuen, modern einheitlichen Weltanschauung hinstrebt."

36. "Es ist vielleicht auch eines ihrer [der Romantrilogie] Verdienste, und wohl nicht das geringste, daß sie den Typ der neuen Generation in seinem Werden und in seiner Entwickelung zeigt und diese Entwickelung bis zu einem positiven Resultate hin verfolgt, das vielleicht kein unerfreuliches ist."

37. Schlaf knew the French writers of his period well and had translated some of them into German.

38. "Sein Empfinden für sie [seine Freundin] war in diesem Augenblick wieder völlig tot."

39. I owe the important hint regarding the affinities with Huysmans and other French *décadents* to Jürgen Peper.

40. "Ah, was ist nun? Wir alle sind einsam. Jeder ist eine Welt für sich. Alles andere, wie man sich findet und abstößt, all diese Berührungen und 'heiligen Bande,' 'Treue,' Liebe u.s.w., u.s.w.: Chaos, Zufall im letzten Grunde, Chaos, Chaos!"

41. "Der ist modern, ohne Skrupel und Zweifel. Er ist ein denkender Mensch, philosophiert und reflektiert gelegentlich wie nur immer ein rechter Deutscher: aber es vermag ihm nichts mehr zu verschlagen. Er paßt in die Welt, wie sie heute ist."

42. See section 27 of "Song of Myself": "I merely stir, press, feel with my fingers,

and am happy, / To touch my person to some one else's is about as much as I can stand" (*LG*, 57).

43. "Man kann im übrigen nicht wissen, was bei solchen ungewöhnlichen *ethischen Experimenten* [emphasis added] nach anderer Richtung hin noch einmal Neues und Ersprießliches herauskommen kann! Die Menschen von morgen werden nicht mehr die von heute sein; die Ethik der Sozietät von morgen wird nicht mehr die Ethik der Sozietät von heute sein!"

44. The fact that Schlaf later seems to have moved away again from these radical views does not cancel out their significance. In a later presentation of his work, he referred to the "tendency" of the trilogy self-critically as "decadence." In his book *Whitman and Tradition: The Poet in His Century* (New Haven and London: Yale University Press, 1990), Kenneth Price devotes one chapter to "Whitman and the Novel" (Hamlin Garland, Kate Chopin, and E. M. Forster). It turns out that these English-language novelists found Whitman just as inspiring as Schlaf did and that the novels that came about as a result of the creative encounter with Whitman have affinities with Schlaf's fiction, such as the promotion of greater acceptance of sexuality and the depiction of sexually developing young women and their struggle to become full selves, to realize their identities.

45. See Johannes Schlaf, *Mutter Lise* (Berlin: Franke, n.d. [1914]), pp. 190–194.

46. "Umfassenden Blick überschauender Synthese"; "Vista über die Menschheit beinahe wie sie vormals dem Christus oder dem Buddha, wie sie in unseren modernen Zeiten Walt Whitman beschieden gewesen"; "Mangel an Ehrfurcht und eine Vorurteilslosigkeit, der doch auch wieder der Wirker modernen Freisinns, moderner Toleranz und Menschenverbrüderung: ein Mangel an Heimatsgefühl, mit seinem Hin und Her durch alle Länder, Erdteile, Völker und Nationen so überaus kulturwirkend geworden"; "Normaltyp der modernen bürgerlichen Kultur."

47. "Die Institution der neuen Elite!—Die Institution der Kraft und des Friedens, der einfachsten, naturgeeinten Erkenntnis!—Das neue Reich, die neue Heimat der sich heraussondernden Elite!"

48. "Schlank war sie und weiß wie Elfenbein. Kräftig und rund war ihr schimmernder Nacken, dessen Weiße noch leuchtender wurde durch das Dunkel des gelösten Haares. Hochgewölbt und fleischig war ihr gesunder Brustkasten. Schlank und doch kräftig die köstlich gerundeten Flanken und schlank gingen ihr die Beine von den Hüften hernieder mit schön gebogenen Schenkeln und festen herzhaften Waden."

49. "Von den Brüsten herab und an den Flanken nieder, über die weiße Bauchwölbung, an den Hüften und Schenkeln sickerten im zuckenden Zickzack kleine Rinnchen und Schnürchen aneinandergereihter Perlchen mit kurzen, ruckenden Stößen sich herabschiebend.—Auf dem blanken, fleischigen Brustkasten. . . . Aus der dunkel rotblonden Flut der Haare. . . . Und immer klarer und blanker trat die köstliche weiche Haut hervor, deren reiner und gesunder Schimmer nicht das leiseste Fleckchen, nicht die geringste Blutunreinigkeit trübte."

50. Arno Holz to Emil Richter, 20 August 1890, Staatsbibliothek Preußischer Kulturbesitz, Berlin, Nachlaß Holz.

51. Thérèse Bentzon, "Un poète américain—Walt Whitman: 'Muscle and Pluck Forever,'" *Revue des Deux Mondes*, 1 June 1872, pp. 565–582.

52. See Arno Holz's letter to Eduard Bertz, 21 February 1907, transcript in Amerika-Gedenkbibliothek, Berlin.

53. See Arno Holz, *Dr. Richard M. Meyer, Privatdozent an der Universität Berlin, ein litterarischer Ehrabschneider* (Berlin: Sassenbach, 1900), p. 48.

54. Gerhard Schulz, *Arno Holz: Dilemma eines bürgerlichen Dichterlebens* (Munich: Beck, 1974), p. 17.

55. A facsimile edition of the 1898–1899 version (cited as *Ph*) appeared in Reclam Universalbibliothek (West) no. 8549, ed. Gerhard Schulz in 1968.

56. Arno Holz, *Das Werk*, vol. 10, *Die neue Wortkunst: Eine Zusammenfassung ihrer ersten grundlegenden Dokumente* (Berlin: Dietz Nachf., 1925), p. 494.

57. Ibid., p. 501.

58. Holz, *Revolution der Lyrik* (Berlin: Sassenbach, 1899), p. 67. Holz quotes in German from Knortz and Rolleston.

59. Arno Holz, *Phantasus* (Leipzig: Insel, 1916), p. 12: "I shall never / perish! // I will always return, eternally, myriad-shapes changing / time and again! // I have always / been / from the very first beginning! // Through all cultures, / in good luck and bad luck, guilty and innocent, / through all centuries, / through all countries, / through all continents, / from heights to depths, / from suffering to lust, from joy to suffering, / stirred by all cravings, by all feelings, / shaken by all passions / as man, as woman, as child, as old man, / always dying, always reborn, / my fate / drove me, / tore and whirled me!"

60. "Seven billion years before my birth / I was a fleur-de-lis. // My roots / sucked themselves / into a star. // On its dark water / swam / my blue giant flower."

61. Reprinted in Karl Hans Strobl, *Arno Holz und die jüngstdeutsche Bewegung* (Berlin: Gose und Tetzlaff, 1902), p. 33: "Das letzte 'Geheimnis' der . . . Phantasuskomposition besteht im wesentlichen darin, daß ich mich unaufhörlich in die heterogensten Dinge und Gestalten zerlege. Wie ich *vor* meiner Geburt die ganze *physische* Entwicklung meiner Species durchgemacht habe, wenigstens in ihren Hauptstadien, so *seit* meiner Geburt ihre *psychische.* Ich war 'Alles' und die Relikte davon liegen ebenso zahlreich wie kunterbunt in mir aufgespeichert."

62. Schulz, *Arno Holz*, p. 208.

63. Josef Froberger, *Kölnische Volkszeitung*, no. 508, 2 July 1919: "Namentlich war es die Bibel, die ihn [Whitman] stark beeinflußte, der Psalmenton klingt deutlich und unverkennbar durch seine Verse. Arno Holz und alle die Modernen, die Whitman nachstreben, übersehen gerade diesen wichtigen Punkt fast regelmäßig, weshalb sie nie zum vollen Verständnis dieser aus geistiger Tiefe geborenen Dichtung gelangen können."

64. Arno Holz, *Werke*, ed. Wilhelm Emrich and Anita Holz, vol. 1, *Phantasus I* (Neuwied and Berlin: Luchterhand, 1961), pp. 7f. The translation of such a text is necessarily awkward; moreover, it is impossible to bring across the special effects in the German text. "Seven billion . . . years . . . before I was born / I was / a fleur-de-lis. // My searching roots / sucked / themselves / around a star. // From / its vaulted / waters, / flowerleafscarry, goldenarrowthreadpollen, / dreamblue / in / new, / flowing, becoming, surging, / brewing, steaming, / circling / cosmic rings / grew, / rose, kicked, / towered, split, skewered, / smoldered, scattered, sprayed, / full of secrets, powerful

secrets, / majestic secrets / mating with itself, impregnating itself, throwing shades on itself, / discreating itself, / flame ball meteorites, / comet cascades, colorful planet wreaths / generously / spreading, raining, throwing out blessings left and right, / squandering / slingshots / around it, / my / dark-metallic, halcyonic-phallic, ringing-crystallic, giant flower-scepter crown! // Still / in my / becoming human again, fully waking up again, / tumbling laughed, / tumbling rejoiced, tumbling shone / its / powerpridejoy, / its creative-power encouragement, its / confidence!"

65. "Noch einmal jung sein! Mit neuen Augen in die Welt sehn! / Ach, wer das könnte!"

66. Arno Holz, *Werke*, ed. Wilhelm Emrich and Anita Holz, vol. 6, *Die Blechschmiede* (Neuwied and Berlin: Luchterhand, 1961), p. 303: "Walt Whitman, der Yankee und 'Reformator,' / [kommt] auf einem wirbelnden Ventilator."

12. BETWEEN NATURALISM AND EXPRESSIONISM

1. Hugo von Hofmannsthal and Ottonie Gräfin Degenfeld, *Briefwechsel* (Frankfurt/M.: Fischer, 1974), p. 321 (letter dated 1 August 1915): "In den früheren Monaten war mir manchmal das Buch von W. Whitman mehr als man denken könnte daß einem ein Buch sein kann."

2. See Hugo von Hofmannsthal, "Dritter Brief aus Wien," in *Aufzeichnungen* (Frankfurt/M.: Fischer, 1959), pp. 298f. Regarding Hofmannsthal's interest in Whitman, see also Ursula Renner-Henke, "'Das schöne Gedicht auf den Vogel . . . ': Anmerkungen zu Hofmannsthals Rezeption Walt Whitmans," *Hofmannsthal Blätter* 33 (Spring 1986), 3–25.

3. For details concerning Bahr's life and writings, see Donald G. Daviau, *Der Mann von übermorgen: Hermann Bahr 1863–1934* (Vienna: Bundesverlag, 1984). I have dealt with the Bahr-Whitman relationship at greater length in "'Mit dem Phallus philosophieren': Hermann Bahr's Vision of Walt Whitman's 'Erotokratie,'" *Modern Austrian Literature* 21/2 (1988), 1–12.

4. Hermann Bahr, "Barbaren," *Die neue Rundschau* 4 (1908), 1774: "So sind jetzt wir am Werk, fast will es scheinen, Barbaren zu werden. Jene Worte klingen uns anders. Der geistige und sittliche Besitz, den unsere Väter Kultur oder Zivilisation nannten, ist uns fragwürdig geworden."

5. Ibid., p. 1781: "die Hand des Menschen ist schneller als Kopf und Herz."

6. Hermann Bahr, *Tagebuch (1908)* (Berlin: Cassirer, 1909), p. 162: "Was würde Leonardo, was würde Goethe sagen, in unsere Zeit geführt, zum Telephon, in ein Automobil, durch die Luft? Wenn aber Goethe dann den Wunsch hätte, nun auch die Werke der Dichter kennen zu lernen, um ihre Ausdrücke dieser neuen menschlichen Bedingungen zu prüfen, welche könnten wir ihm nennen? Einen, ja: Walt Whitman."

7. Bahr, "Barbaren," p. 1781: "Zwischen diesen [Maschinen] aber und dem inneren Menschen steht das Künstliche, das sie trennt, der ganze Wust von Gedanken und Gefühlen, die so wenig im inneren Menschen mehr lebendig sind als im äußeren Leben, nicht in unserer Seele und in unseren Maschinen nicht, und dies, daß unsere Seelen sich nach unseren Maschinen sehnen, welche wie sie sind, ist es, woran wir

leiden, jener Wust muß weg, nicht von der äußeren Welt wird der innere Mensch bedrängt, sie gleicht ihm, aber zwischen ihn und sie hat sich das Künstliche gestellt, die Wand von Gedanken und Gefühlen, welche den inneren Menschen wie sein äußeres Leben verleugnen."

8. Ibid., p. 1776: "[Der] neue Mensch ist schon da, man sieht sie [die neuen Menschen] nur noch nicht und er weiß es nur selbst noch nicht. Wie komisch, daß ein Mensch sich selbst nicht bemerkt!"

9. Ibid., p. 1779: "Sie [die neue Menschheit] hat wirklich etwas Barbarisches in ihrer fraglosen Unschuld. . . . Der Apfel vom Baum der Erkenntnis ist verdaut, nun weiß sie weder das Gute noch das Böse mehr, es ist ihr alles recht, sie geht wieder im Paradiese."

10. Ibid.: "ist nicht bloß ganz Auge, er ist ganz Ohr, ganz Nase, ganz Zunge, ganz Haut, dieser ganze Mensch scheint nur aus Sinnen zu bestehen. Der junge Maupassant war ähnlich, aber dann wollte sein Gehirn nachkommen, das hat ihn verstört."

11. Hermann Bahr, "Walt Whitman," *Die neue Rundschau* 30/1 (1919), 560: "Walts Erkenntnis beginnt immer als sinnliches Erlebnis, er denkt von den Augen und Ohren aus, er ist einer von den sinnlich übersinnlichen Freiern, die mit dem Phallus philosophieren, seiner Caritas geht Eros voraus."

12. See Grünzweig, "Bahr's Vision," p. 5.

13. EXPRESSIONISM

1. The reference is to Samuel Lublinski, *Der Ausgang der Moderne: Ein Buch der Opposition* (Tübingen: Niemeyer, 1976), pp. 234f.

2. Max Picard, "Expressionismus: Ein Vortrag" (1919), quoted from *Expressionismus: Manifeste und Dokumente zur deutschen Literatur, 1910–1920*, ed. Thomas Anz and Michael Stark (Stuttgart: Metzler, 1982), p. 568:

> In der expressionistischen Zeit soll ja alles anders sein. Aus dem Chaos, in dem die Dinge kaum einen Namen haben, damit sie von allem und zu allem gerufen werden können, aus diesem *namenlosen* Chaos ruft der neue, expressionistische Mensch das Ding heraus zu sich. Er ruft die Dinge bei ihrem *Namen* an: Du Wald, sagt er, und du Stadt, damit der Wald und die Stadt sich aus dem Chaos wieder auseinander ordnen.
>
> Du Mississippi, singt Walt Whitman; die Impressionisten haben nur das *alles* verbindende *Du* gehört, und Lublinski nennt Whitman in seinem *Ausgang der Moderne* einen urwüchsigen Impressionisten.
>
> Du Mississippi, singt Walt Whitman; die Expressionisten hören nur den isolierenden Namen Mississippi, und Whitman ist ihnen ein Künder des Expressionismus.
>
> Aber weder holt Walt Whitman den Mississippi zu den Dingen heran, wie der Impressionist halb sieht; noch ruft er den Mississippi aus den Dingen heraus, wie der Expressionist halb hört. Du Mississippi, nicht ruft es, sondern singt es.
>
> Charakteristisch für den Expressionismus ist also nicht, daß Walt Whitman propagiert wird, sondern was an ihm propagiert wird.

Der Expressionist liebt Whitman, weil durch den Anruf die Dinge aus dem Chaos heraus fixiert werden. Er ruft aber die gleichen Worte lauter als sie Walt Whitman gerufen, denn es ist für ihn eine größere Not, vom Chaos gehört zu werden als für Walt Whitman. Der Expressionist ruft darum laut und ist pathetisch, nicht aus einem *primären Lebensgefühl* heraus, sondern aus Zwang.

3. Chronologically and, in part, thematically, the socialist/leftist (political) reception of Walt Whitman belongs to the expressionist decade, especially because a number of expressionists were leftists. However, its specifically political orientation and its relative homogeneity make it feasible to examine the political reception in a chapter of its own.

4. Hellmuth Thomke, *Hymnische Dichtung im Expressionismus* (Bern and Munich: Francke, 1972), p. 11.

5. See Walter H. Sokel, *The Writer in Extremis: Expressionism in Twentieth-Century German Literature* (Stanford: Stanford University Press, 1959).

6. Georg Lukács speaks of the "excessive subjective *Pathos*" (p. 84) and the "hollowness" (p. 107) of the expressionist revolt ("'Größe und Verfall' des Expressionismus" (1934), in *Deutsche Literaturkritik der Gegenwart: Vorkrieg, 2. Weltkrieg, Nachkriegszeit*, ed. Hans Mayer, 2 vols. [Stuttgart: Goverts, 1971], pp. 67–122). Thomke limits the significance of his own study by stating in his introduction: "By surveying the history of German expressionism from the beginnings until its late effects in the most recent period, one will hardly get the impression that its outstanding achievements are in the area of hymnic poetry" (*Hymnische Dichtung*, p. 7).

7. Richard Hamann and Jost Hermand, "Vorwort," in *Epochen deutscher Kultur von 1870 bis zur Gegenwart*, vol. 5, *Expressionismus* (Frankfurt: Fischer, 1977), pp. 14f.

8. There are a few exceptions, such as Thomke's study of hymnic expressionism, dealing mainly with messianic expressionist poets. For Thomke, "the influence of Whitman and Verhaeren . . . cannot be excluded from the early history of expressionism" (*Hymnische Dichtung*, p. 19). Another significant contribution was made in an essay by Reinhold Grimm and Henry J. Schmidt, emphasizing the international conditions for the emergence of modern German poetry. According to this essay, the most important influence next to the French (especially Rimbaud) was Whitman: "During the heyday of the personality cult surrounding Rimbaud, adulation of Whitman was reaching ecstatic proportions" ("Foreign Influences on German Expressionist Poetry," in *Expressionism as an International Literary Phenomenon*, ed. Ulrich Weisstein [Budapest and Paris: Akadémiai Kiadó and Didier, 1973], p. 74). An unpublished essay by Daniel Brooks ("Walt Whitman and German Expressionism," unpublished graduate seminar paper, Department of Comparative Literature, State University of New York at Binghamton, 1984) should also be mentioned since it deals with Whitman's creative reception by such authors as Ernst Stadler, Ivan Goll, and Franz Werfel. His erroneous conclusion that Whitman's "influence must not have been very great" is based on his study of a very small body of works by just a few authors. But despite his erroneous conclusion, Brooks clearly recognizes the importance of the German reception of Whitman as a literary phenomenon. Finally, Helmut Gier's comparative analysis of German and French literary development in a book on Ernst Stadler emphasizes Whitman's significance in the "attempt to replace and displace symbolism" (*Die Entstehung*

des deutschen Expressionismus und die antisymbolistische Reaktion in Frankreich: Die literarische Entwicklung Ernst Stadlers [Munich: Fink, 1977], p. 168): "In contrast to symbolism, Whitman's affirmation of the value of life, his advocacy of human solidarity, and his turn toward modern reality appear as a break with established standards."

9. Arthur Eloesser, "Generationen" (1918), quoted from *Literaturrevolution 1910–1925: Dokumente, Manifeste, Programme*, ed. Paul Pörtner, vol. 1, *Zur Aesthetik und Poetik* (Darmstadt: Luchterhand, 1960), p. 251: "Walt Whitmans westliche Prärie hat sich mit dem unablässigen Gewoge breittragender Verse bis nach Prag vorgeschoben. . . ."

10. Johannes Urzidil, "Nachwort" (1968), in Walt Whitman, *Grashalme*, trans. Schlaf, p. 234.

11. Walter Mehring, "Berlin Avantgarde," in *Als das Jahrhundert jung war*, ed. Josef Halperin (Zurich and Stuttgart: Artemis, 1961), p. 34.

12. Stefan Zweig, "Das deutsche Walt Whitman-Werk," *Berliner Tageblatt*, no. 147, 28 March 1922.

13. See Reinhard M. G. Nickisch, *Armin T. Wegner: Ein Dichter gegen die Macht* (Wuppertal: Hammer, 1982), p. 24; and Martin Rooney, *Leben und Werk Armin T. Wegners (1886–1978) im Kontext der sozio-politischen und kulturellen Entwicklungen in Deutschland* (Frankfurt/M.: Haag und Herchen, 1984), p. 34.

14. See O. M. Graf's letter to Franz and Trautl Müller, 22 February 1960, in *Oskar Maria Graf in seinen Briefen*, ed. Gerhard Bauer and Helmut F. Pfanner (Munich: Süddeutscher Verlag, 1984), p. 297.

15. Otto Wittner, "Ernst Lissauer und die deutsche Lyrik der Gegenwart," *Die neue Zeit* 30/2 (1912), 995: "Die stärksten Anregungen, welche die deutsche Lyrik in den letzten beiden Jahrzehnten erfahren hat, neue Inhalte aufzunehmen, neue Formen zu suchen, kamen aber aus dem Ausland: aus Amerika durch Walt Whitman, aus Belgien durch Verhaeren. Der Amerikaner hat die Tatsachen des modernen Lebens zuerst mit der Gewalt seiner großen Seele erfaßt. Seine ungefügen Rhythmen sind wie mit der Axt zugehauen, die er als Farmer so wohl zu handhaben wußte."

16. Carl Sternheim, "Die deutsche Revolution" (1918), in Carl Sternheim, *Gesamtwerk*, vol. 6, *Zeitkritik*, ed. Wilhelm Emrich (Neuwied und Darmstadt: Luchterhand, 1966), p. 75: "Hauptsächlich bei der Firma Walt Whitman, New York, die in einem ungehemmten Christentum reißenden Absatz hatte, einem Christentum, das von seinen Bekennern nicht gerade wie das Tolstoische die eigene ständige seelische und zerebrale Läuterung verlangt, sondern mehr sich selbst und alle Welt nur leben läßt."

17. In the first scene of Brecht's *Baal* (Bertolt Brecht, *Gesammelte Werke: Stücke I*, [Frankfurt/M.: Suhrkamp, 1967], p. 6), Whitman is referred to ironically in the manner of contemporary critics:

A Young Man: How do you achieve this incredible naiveté, dear master? It is Homeric. I hold Homer to be one of several highly educated editors taking a penetrating pleasure in the naiveté of the original popular epics.

A Young Woman: You remind me more of Walt Whitman. But you are more significant. I think.

Even greater irony transpires in a dialogue between an American reporter and

Wotan in Ernst Toller's comedy *Der entfesselte Wotan* (Wotan Unbound) (Potsdam: Kiepenheuer, 1923), p. 49:

Reporter: Hello, Sir. Great opportunities for your enterprise in America. What do you think about America?

Wotan: I am a glowing admirer of hers. Camerado, this is no book, who touches this touches a man!

Reporter: O, you know Walt Whitman?

Wotan: Sir, for years I have been keeping up with the most recent world literature.

Reporter [in English]: Very interesting.

This passage even ironizes Whitman's frequently varied formula of *Leaves of Grass* as being directly expressive of a human being, a formula which was much valued by the expressionists because it supposedly broke down the barriers between art and life.

18. Stefan Zweig, "Das neue Pathos," *Das neue Pathos* 1 (1913), p. 1: "nichts als ein modulierter, kaum Sprache gewordener Schrei." The motif of the "cry" or "scream" often found in expressionist poetry originated with Edvard Munch's painting *The Scream* (1893). Munch, who lived in Germany at the time, was a great inspiration for German expressionists. His *Scream* expressing human anxieties has little to do with Whitman's "barbaric yawp" in section 52 of "Song of Myself"—however, later expressionist poets also connected moments of optimistic liberation, which were closer to Whitman than to Munch, with the motif.

19. Ibid., pp. 1f: "Jenes [Ur-]Gedicht und sein Vortrag war nicht zur Prüfung gebotene Vorzeigung eines Fertigen, ein Gerät oder ein Schmuck, schon gehämmert und ganz gefügt, sondern ein noch Entstehendes, ein im Augenblick neu Werdendes, ein Kampf mit dem Hörer, ein Ringen um seine Leidenschaft."

20. Ibid.: "Diesen innigen, glühenden Kontakt mit der Masse haben die Dichter seit der Schrift verloren."

21. Ibid., pp. 3f: "Aber eben in unseren Tagen scheint sich wieder eine Rückkehr zu diesem ursprünglichen, innigen Kontakt zwischen dem Dichter und dem Hörer vorzubereiten, ein neues Pathos wieder zu entstehen. . . . Aber die Zeit der Absonderung des Dichters von der Menge, die einst bedingt war durch die großen Distanzen der Nationen, scheint heute überwunden durch die neue Annäherung, durch die Industrialisierung der Städte. Die Dichter lesen heute wieder selbst in Sälen ihre Verse vor, in den Volksuniversitäten Amerikas, selbst in den Kirchen klingen die Verse Walt Whitmans zu amerikanischem Bewußtsein, und was sonst nur die heißen politisch bewegten Tage schufen . . . das gibt nun fast jeder Tag."

22. Ibid., p. 5: "Wer die Menge zwingen will, muß den Rhythmus ihres neuen und unruhigen Lebens in sich haben, wer zu ihr spricht, muß beseelt sein von neuem Pathos."

23. Ibid., p. 5: "*Das neue Pathos muß den Willen nicht zu einer seelischen Vibration, zu einem feinen ästhetischen Wohlgefühl enthalten, sondern zu einer Tat*" (emphasis in original).

24. *Open Road* (*Freie Straße*) was also the title of an expressionist journal edited by Franz Jung and Otto Groß. In Georg Kaiser's play *Von morgens bis mitternachts* (From Morning till Midnight), a bank clerk liberates himself by becoming a "ragged wan-

derer on the road" (in Georg Kaiser, *Werke*, vol. 1, *Stücke, 1895–1917*, ed. Walther Huder [Frankfurt/M., Berlin and Vienna: Propyläen, 1971], p. 489). Whether or not this motif derives directly from Whitman's "Song of the Open Road," which was highly popular in the German-speaking countries, does not matter: it is important that it was in the air and it proves once more how Whitmanesque motifs lent themselves to expressionism.

25. Quoted from Paul Raabe, H. L. Greve, and Ingrid Grüninger, *Expressionismus: Literatur und Kunst, 1910–1923* (Stuttgart: n.p., 1960), pp. 171f. (exhibition catalogue):

> Der neue Dichter wird unbedingt sein, von vorn anfangen, für ihn gibt es keine Reminiszenz, denn er, wie kein anderer, wird fühlen, wie wesenlos die Retrospektive auf die Literatur ist, wie unnötig das Vergnügen am Tonfall. Er wird wissen, daß sein Gedicht nicht ein Satzbild im Buche ist, sondern ein Teil, ein schwacher, unsäglich feiner Tropfen seines großen, allerbarmenden, zugewandten, überall eingreifenden Lebens, ein Blitz seines Herzens, in dem sich allein die bebende Welt empfindet.
>
> Seine Pflicht ist es, ewig aufzustehen, der weite Prediger zu sein der Koexistenz und des Todes, der allen uns gemeinsam ist. . . .
>
> O, möchten die Skribenten fühlen, wie verächtlich sie sind! Wie ihre Intellektualität Verrat und Unwahrheit ist.
>
> Mögen sie sich abkehren von dem ungeheuren Beruf, den sie nicht ertragen können. Möchten sie ahnen den Schritt des Wahren! Möchten sie fühlen, daß diese Erde Jesaia und Tolstoi getragen hat. Daß bei einem Sonnenuntergang Whitman weinend im Lazarett blessierte Brüder gepflegt hat. . . .

26. Max Brod states that Kafka listed the two-volume Whitman edition by Reisiger on a list together with other books. Jürgen Born (Wuppertal) informs me this edition appears also on a second list in Kafka's handwriting. An article by Frank Möbus on a short Kafka text entitled "Kalmus" also commands great interest ("Kalmus: Zu einer Notiz aus dem Nachlaß Franz Kafkas," *Jahrbuch des Freien Deutschen Hochstifts* [1984], 295–305).

27. Gustav Janouch, *Gespräche mit Kafka: Aufzeichnungen und Erinnerungen* (Frankfurt/M.: Fischer, 1961), pp. 185f. The authenticity of Janouch's material is questionable. For our purposes, however, this presents no problem: even if the passage should be a semitruth or falsehood (which is improbable), it describes very well the atmosphere of the expressionist understanding of Whitman. See also Hartmut Binder, *Kafka-Handbuch*, 2 vols. (Stuttgart: Kröner, 1979), vol. 2, p. 560:

> Doktor Kafka schenkte mir ein zentimeterdickes Reclam-Bändchen: das Gedichtbuch *Grashalme* des Amerikaners Walt Whitman.
>
> Dabei sagte er mir: "Die Übersetzung ist nicht besonders gut. Sie ist stellenweise sogar recht holprig. Doch man bekommt durch sie wenigstens ungefähr ein Bild dieses Dichters, der zu den größten Forminspiratoren der modernen Lyrik gehört. . . .
>
> Das Formale von Walt Whitmans Gedichten hat in der Welt einen ungeheuren Widerhall gefunden. Dabei liegt Walt Whitmans Bedeutung aber eigentlich ganz woanders. Er hat die Betrachtung der Natur und der ihr augenscheinlich ganz entgegengesetzten Zivilisation zu einer einzigen berauschenden Lebensempfindung zusammengeschlossen, weil er ständig die kurze Dauer aller Erscheinungen vor sich

sah. Er sagte: 'Das Leben ist das wenige Übriggebliebene vom Sterben.' Deshalb widmete er sein ganzes Herz jedem Grashalm. Damit hat er mich schon sehr früh bezaubert. Ich bewunderte seine Übereinstimmung zwischen Kunst und Leben. Als in Amerika zwischen den Nord- und Südstaaten der Krieg ausbrach, durch den die größte Kraft unserer heutigen Maschinenwelt eigentlich erst richtig in Bewegung kam, wurde Walt Whitman Krankenpfleger. Er tat, was heute eigentlich jeder von uns tun sollte. Er half den Schwachen, Kranken und Geschlagenen. Er war ein wirklicher Christ und deshalb—besonders uns Juden sehr nah verwandter—bedeutsamer Grad- und Wertmesser der Menschlichkeit."

[Janouch:] "Sie kennen also seine Schriften sehr gut?"

[Kafka:] "Nicht einmal so seine Schriften wie sein Leben. Denn das ist ja eigentlich sein Hauptwerk. Das, was er schrieb, seine Gedichte und Aufsätze, sind nur glimmende Aschenherde der Feuergarben eines konsequent gelebten, werktätigen Glaubens."

28. Kafka's observation that the American Civil War started the "machine world" is remarkable and proves great insight into American history and culture.

29. Meidner contributed a portrait depicting Whitman to the first issue of *Neue Pathos* (p. 19) which is used on the cover of this book.

30. Some of the most popular photographs circulating in Germany at the time show Whitman with long white hair and a wide hat.

31. Probably refers to Whitman, the "thunderer of Manhattan."

32. Ludwig Meidner, "Gruß des Malers an die Dichter" (The Painter's Salute to the Poets, 1920), in *Literaturrevolution, 1910–1925: Dokumente, Manifeste, Programme*, ed. Paul Pörtner, 2 vols. (Darmstadt: Luchterhand, 1960), vol. 1, p. 111:

> Leg den Pinsel weg, Klexer. Genug der farbentriefenden Stunden, der ledernen, schwerfälligen Leinwände. Schwing dich endlich aus der Höhle deiner Dachkammer hinauf in den Wolkenhimmel und grüße die Dichter!
>
> Heran, heran, ihr Schwadronen der Angst und Verzückung. Heran, ihr, mit den großen Hüten auf den mähnenden Häuptern. Ihr, mit knatternden Fahnen an euern Hüften; mit Wimpeln und Bändern an den Schultern. Ihr, mit den gewaltigen Beinen, Donnerer durch die Jahrtausende. Ihr Riesen-Krokodile, schwimmend, tauchend, schnaufend im Meer der Gefühle; aus euern Nasen prasseln Fontänen von Begeisterung. Ihr sperrt eure Mäuler gewaltig auf zu Liebe, Klage und bußfertigem Sinn. Ihr weißen, hochgetürmten Elephanten mit wunderbaren, beschwingten Rüsseln, die erschnüffeln, was den Menschenseelen nottut.

33. Ibid., p. 113 (emphasis in original):

> Gegrüßet du Weltdichter Goethe, du imposanter Victor Hugo und du lieber Bruder *Walt Whitman*! Du Menschheitssinger, du Allererster, Allernächster, Fackel, Herzblut und Komet der neuen Zeit! . . . Friedrich von Schiller, Kühnster, Männlichster unter den Deutschen! Herwegh, Freiligrath, Uhland! Ihr Volksdichter Desaugier und Béranger! Du Lamartine! Noch einmal walle, du Jüngling, Mann und Greis Walt Whitman! Du südlicher Mistral! Du Dichter der schäumenden Städtemeere! Verhaeren! Du, wie die weiße Sonne, Alfred Mombert: Meteor über Gebirgen, so sehr geliebt von mir und gefeiert in manchem Gemälde und vielen tönenden Blättern!

Alfred Mombert sei gegrüßt!

34. Walter H. Sokel, *The Writer in Extremis*, p. 3.

35. Carl Dallago, "Walt Whitman," *Der Brenner* 1 (1910–1911), 145: "Robust und breit veranlagt, hünenhaft und von großer Gebärde wie Millet. Dabei ein Landschaftsmensch von klarster Prägung, herangereift an großen Wassern, Wind, Wellenspiel, an den Linien von Prärieen, Steppen und Urwaldungen."

36. Arthur Holitscher, "Amerikas Literatur," *Die Aktion* 4 (1914), col. 617: "Walt, das chaotische Sinnbild seines ungeheuren, unerforschten Kontinents, die Feuersäule am Eingang eines rätselhaften neuen Zeitalters des Menschengeschlechts, der wilde Seher und besessene Johannes, diese aus der Natur über alle Zivilisation hinwegschlagende Flut, dieser wahrhaftige Tornado von einem Menschen, um sich blickendes Auge weit und sicher wie das Auge des Leuchtturms, offene Hand, in deren Höhlung die Elemente sich begatten, aufwärtshörendes Ohr, schlagendes Herz, darin das Weltgeschehn pulst, warme Riesenstirne milde niedergeneigt zur letzten Kreatur, Walt, der nie Geborene, der Unvergängliche, Anfang und Ausgang, erschütternder Ausblick in Zeiten, die kommen werden, hinaus und hinauf!"

37. Dallago, "Walt Whitman," p. 147: "Eine so große Liebe zu allen nächsten und fernsten Dingen—eine so tiefgehende Verbrüderung mit dem Wesen der Schöpfung ist kaum jemals von einem Dichter zum Ausdruck gebracht worden. Ich füge noch hinzu, bei diesem Großen wie mit Heimatgefühlen verweilend und ihn für mich erkennend: Er war der größte Sänger einer ganz Schöpfungswillen gewordenen Menschennatur."

38. Rudolf Kayser, "Die Kunst stirbt" (Art Is Dying), *Die Aktion* 1 (1911), cols. 663f:

> In Wirklichkeit ist jedoch die Kunst nicht die Erfüllung, die Synthese einer Kultur, sondern gerade ihr Jenseitiges, ihre Ueberwindung. . . .
>
> Mit heißen Händen schreibe ich: "Der neue Rhythmus hat die fliegende Kraft der intellektuellen Eroberung; die fiebernde Ekstase eines neuen Barbarentums. Fruchttragende Decadence, gebärende Agonie beschwingt ihn. Ein Anfang wölbt sich vor unseren Augen. Schon geht ein neues Schreiten über die alten Wege. Die Kunst stirbt *nicht* unter den Händen der Walt Whitman und seiner Erben. . . ."

39. Kurt Pinthus, "Zuvor," in *Menschheitsdämmerung: Symphonie jüngster Dichtung*, ed. Kurt Pinthus (Berlin: Rowohlt, 1922), p. xv. "Und immer wieder muß gesagt werden, daß die Qualität dieser Dichtung in ihrer Intensität beruht. Niemals in der Weltdichtung scholl so laut, zerreißend und aufrüttelnd Schrei, Sturz und Sehnsucht einer Zeit."

40. Friedrich Bill, "Walt Whitman," *Der Mensch* 1 (1918), 147f:

> Es war mir als müßte ich am Wege sterben. Was ich noch sah—noch immer scheut es nicht das Licht des Tages—quälte meine Augen, was ich hören mußte, verletzte meine Ohren. Das Ansinnen, das man an mich stellte, ließ mich erschauern. Mauern türmten sich vor mir auf, von jenen bejubelt, die an ihnen nicht zerschellten. Fahnen im Winde verwehten mir die Sonne. Ich wollte flüchten. Die Kräfte schwanden mir und ich sank hilflos zusammen. Da kamst Du des Weges, Walt Whitman, nahmst mich in Deine starken gütigen Arme, sahst mich mit Deinen treuen Augen an und sprachst diese Worte, an deren wunderwirkendem Balsam ich gesundete.

41. This is not true for all activists. Gustav Landauer's and Rene Schickele's efforts, much more directly "political," are considered in the section on politics.

42. Kurt Hiller, "Monolog um Franz Werfel," *Pan*, 1 August 1912, p. 1044: "Wissen Sie, weshalb ich ihn [Werfel] besonders liebe? Seines *Mitleids* wegen. Außer Walt Whitman (diesem mehr Bäurischen, mehr Gebräunten . . .) gibt es ja niemanden, niemanden, der so voll Gefühls und großer Menschenliebe wäre (unter Dichtern) wie Franz Werfel."

43. Ernst Stadler, review of Werfel, *Weltfreund*, in Ernst Stadler, *Dichtungen, Schriften, Briefe: Kritische Ausgabe*, ed. Klaus Hurlebusch and Karl Ludwig Schneider (Munich: Beck, 1983), p. 344f.: "Und doch führt aus dem Vielspältigen ein Weg immer wieder in die eigene Seele zurück, die sich im Fremden erkennt, in dem sie sich darein verwandelt. Denn hier ist mehr als bloße menschliche Anteilnahme, soziales Mitempfinden . . . hier vollzieht sich wirklich etwas wie eine geistige Transsubstantiation. Auf ihrem Grunde ist die neue und heftige Intensität des Welterlebens, deren erste Verkünder Whitman und Verhaeren waren: berauschte Propheten freilich eher als schöpferische Erfüller."

44. Ludwig Rubiner, "Der Bruder" (The Brother), in Ludwig Rubiner, *Der Mensch in der Mitte* (Berlin-Wilmersdorf: Verlag Die Aktion, 1917, p. 148.

45. See the afterword to the small Sonnenschein anthology *Die Fesseln meiner Brüder: Gesammelte Gedichte*, ed. Karl-Markus Gauß and Josef Haslinger (Munich and Vienna: Hanser, 1984); and Karl-Markus Gauß, "Der 'weltverkommene Bruder Sonka': Leben und Werk des vergessenen Dichters Hugo Sonnenschein," *Österreich in Geschichte und Literatur* 28/4 (1984), 251–263.

46. See Gier, *Die Entstehung des deutschen Expressionismus*, pp. 174–177.

47. Johannes R. Becher, *Das neue Gedicht: Auswahl (1912–1918)* (Leipzig: Insel, 1918), p. 135:

> Sieh, mein lieber Bruder Whitman . . . da schlug ich eben heute wieder Dein unsterbliches Buch auf (. . . o welch eines . . .)—und da erlebte ich, als ob ich Auge in Auge, Hand in Hand mit Dir stände—: o unendlicher, schmelzender allverbindender ewiger Kontakt! Es geschah sogar, als ob eine Unzahl von Antennen, Bündeln von Strahlen rings gleich, aus unseren Leibern hervorschössen, alle Wesen, die fernsten Dinge im Umkreis spitz berührend.
>
> Lieber Bruder Whitman—: Hoffnung, Ansporn, absolute Gesichertheit, aus der dampfenden Masse Deiner wogenden Strophenarmeen heraus bestätige ich mich.
>
> Ja, hätte ich beinahe gesagt, ich übernehme für dieses Jahrhundert Dein Kommando.

48. Ibid., p. 98: "Ja—: brüderlich Verschmelzen! / Nicht einsam, sondern *jeder* sein!"

49. Ibid., p. 120: "Orkus-Dämonen."

50. Ibid., p. 70.

51. Armin T. Wegner, *Die Strasse mit den Tausend Zielen* (Dresden, Sybillen Verlag, 1924), p. 117:

> An alle, alle, alle! An die Völker Europas und die Völker Amerikas!
> An die Steppenhorden Asiens, die Reisbauern Indiens und die Völker der Südsee!

An die steinernen Dschungeln der Städte,
An den einsamsten Kamelhirten, der in seinem Zelte betet!
Aus verschüttetem Brunnen hebe ich mein Herz und rufe euch zu: trinkt! trinkt! . . .

Laßt mich herantreten zu euch mit entblößtem Haupte, ihr Völker, die Hände berühren,
Euch in die Augen schauen, tief, tief, wie die Liebenden nach langer Getrenntheit.
Ihr Einsamen, die ihr verschüttet lagt, die das Schweigen zerbrach,
Die ihr vertrieben über die Fremdheit der Erde irrtet,
Ihr Einäugigen, ihr von Tränen geschwächten Mütter! Ihr alle, die ihr besessen und belogen wart—
O der Geruch der Leichenfelder der Erde,
Der durch das Filter eurer Herzen steigt, ihr Wiederbekehrten, ist süßer als Paradiesesduft.
Und ihr, Geliebteste, aus den Gefängnissen aller Länder,
Denen wir die Ketten vom bleichen Strunk ihrer Hände lösten,
Muß ich nicht niederknien, in Freudentränen eure Lende zu küssen?

O Arme, die den Erdball umspannen!
Liebe strahlt aus meinen zehn Fingerspitzen.
Und noch das Haar auf meinem Haupte ist Flamme der Liebe.

52. "Ein zersprungenes Gefäß der Liebe, hinzuströmen in alle Äcker der Welt."

53. Georg Kulka, "Dem Geiste Landauers," in *Der Stiefbruder: Aufzeichnung und Lyrik* (Vienna, Prague, and Leipzig: Strache, 1920), p. 64 (excerpt): "Du Uranfänglicher, du wirst uralt / Als Meister Eckehart, als Blutsfreund Walt."

54. These are versions of an imaginative "talking back" to Whitman. For an extensive anthology and a critical examination of such reception documents, see *Walt Whitman: The Measure of His Song*, ed. Jim Perlman, Ed Folsom, and Dan Campion (Minneapolis: Holy Cow! Press, 1981). The anthology does not include examples in German.

55. Arthur Drey, "Walt Whitman," *Die Aktion* 1 (1911), col. 907. The English version is an adaptation of John M. Gogol's translation published in the *Walt Whitman Review* 20/5 (September 1974), 105:

Fackelschwinger! Lodernder Titan des keuschen Urwalds!
Deine Augen küssen die Welt, und traumschmeichelnd
Fließt die weiße Sonne deiner Haare über das Meer—
Weltmensch!

Dein Herz ist zwischen den streitenden Blöcken Liebe
In aufgerissener Brust blutenden Brudergefühls—
Kinder knien augenmüde vor deiner Jünglingsseele—
Traum!

Aus deinen bleichen Tränen blinkt warmer Friede,
Und Blumen sind deiner lieben Lippen Worte—
Die wir trinken, heilenden Quell—
Wunder!

Dein Urgebäude wächst, wilderndes Gold . . .
Es breiten fromme Länder ihre grauen Hände
Zum Fang—Einsam stehst du am Saume der Welt—
Prophet!

56. See the biography by Peter Stephan Jungk, *Franz Werfel: Eine Lebensgeschichte* (Frankfurt/M.: S. Fischer, 1987), which does not contain any important references to Whitman. The most recent biography is by Norbert Abels, *Franz Werfel* (Reinbek b. Hamburg: Rowohlt, 1990).

57. Frederik Schyberg, *Walt Whitman*, p. 286.

58. Leopold Zahn, *Franz Werfel* (Berlin: Colloquium, 1966), p. 9.

59. See Lore Foltin, *Franz Werfel* (Stuttgart: Metzler, 1972), pp. 22f.

60. Abels, *Franz Werfel*, p. 26.

61. Felix Stössinger, "Der Weltfreund," *Die neue Rundschau* 23 (1912), 1778f.:

> Der moderne Dichter, der die Wirklichkeit in seine Kunst am gastlichsten aufgenommen hat, ist Walt Whitman und von ihm kommt Werfel den langen Weg, der in weitem Bogen um Verhaeren in die deutsche Lyrik führt. . . . Whitman übertrug das demokratische Prinzip seines Landes aus der Politik auf den Kosmos und berauschte sich an der Massenhaftigkeit der Dinge, deren Gleichwertigkeit er feierte. Er hatte die Kraft, die Einheit in der Vielfalt zu suchen, und sich von der Ungehemmtheit seiner Sachwollust nicht schwächen, sondern beleben zu lassen. . . . [Werfel "überholte" Whitman] indem er die Mannigfaltigkeit nicht anbetet, sondern ehrlich liebt. So zeigt sich der große Fortschritt des Individuums in der Überwindung dieses lyrischen Amerikanismus, den wir von jetzt ab ignorieren können.

62. Richard Rieß, "Franz Werfel, *Wir sind: Neue Gedichte*," *Die schöne Literatur* 14 (1913), 519: "Werfel kennzeichnet jenes kosmische Fühlen und Mitfühlen, das uns in den Gedichten des Amerikaners Walt Whitman stets so gewaltig packt. Seine leidenschaftliche dichterische Anteilnahme setzt alle Dinge und Menschen in persönliche Beziehung zu ihm selbst."

63. See Kurt Pinthus, "Werfel," *Die Aktion* 6 (1916), col. 604.

64. Johannes Thummerer, "Die Dichter des 'neuen Weltgefühls,'" *Deutsche Arbeit* 13 (1913–1914), 519.

65. Urzidil, "Nachwort," pp. 234f.: "[Whitman folgte] als erster und entschiedenster Franz Werfel (1890–1945) in seinem frühesten Gedichtband *Der Weltfreund* (1911), aber auch in seinen nachfolgenden Bänden *Wir sind* und *Einander*, und dann überhaupt mit dem dichterischen Rhythmus seines ganzen Lebens."

66. See Max Brod, "Death of a Poet: In Memoriam Franz Werfel," *Palestine Post*, 7 September 1945, p. 7.

67. See Kurt Wolff, "Vom Verlegen im allgemeinen und von der Frage: Wie kommen Verleger und Autoren zusammen?" *Sprache im technischen Zeitalter* 11–12 (1964), 903.

68. Franz Werfel to Alma Mahler, n.d., probably August 1918, Werfel Papers, Department of Special Collections, University Research Libraries, University of California, Los Angeles: "alles, was mein Wissen ist, nur in einem anderen Typus Mensch gebannt. . . . Ich hatte Walt Whitman erst viel später kennengelernt, als man schon lange behauptete, ich mache ihm nach!—Ich bin glücklich, daß diese Seele gelebt hat, in der ich so viel Bestätigung finde."

69. Franz Werfel, "thanks," *Decision*, January 1941, p. 43.

70. *World-Telegram*, 1941, n.d. (newspaper clipping).

71. Leipzig notebook, Werfel Papers, Los Angeles.

72. Speech in New York City, 1935, ms., Werfel Papers, Los Angeles. This speech is a part of the Werfel anthology *Zwischen Oben und Unten: Prosa, Tagebücher, Aphorismen, Literarische Nachträge*, ed. Adolf D. Klarmann (Munich and Vienna: Langen Müller, 1975), pp. 545f.

73. Werfel, "thanks," p. 43.

74. "Verteidigung der Strophe" (Defense of the Stanza), Hodov Notebook, 1916, Werfel Papers, Los Angeles: "sie *strömt* aus allzu hoher Fülle, um andere Gesetze zu achten als die, welche sie sich selbst gibt" (emphasis added).

75. "Verse [die] den breiten Strömen dieses Kontinents gleichen."

76. Franz Werfel, *Gesammelte Werke: Das lyrische Werk* [FWL], ed. Adolf Klarmann (Frankfurt/M.: Fischer, 1967), p. 55. In the preface, the editor, a friend of Werfel and a Werfel specialist, also emphasizes Whitman's influence on Werfel's early work.

> Bin ich nicht, wo mein Name fällt, schon nah,
> Wo ich gefühlt bin doppelt waltend da?
> Denn Existenz ist Mittel, Wirkung alles.

77. "Auch war einmal ein Tag, / da gab ein König mir die Hand."

> DIE SCHULTASCHE
> Einmal senkte jemand in mich
> eine Chrestomathie.
> Und da geschah's, da lebte ich
> Groß, wie noch nie.
> Und wie ich wissend rings geschah,
> Das Schweigen meines Wesens schrie:
> *Wir alle sind, alle sind da!*

78. See Silvio Vietta and Hans-Georg Kemper, *Expressionismus* (Munich: Fink, 1975), chapter on the reification of the self and the anthropomorphization of objects, pp. 40ff. The animation of the object world is a sign of the breakdown of human consciousness—the threatening object world of modern technological society results in a human inability to perceive and process the outside world.

79. Susa, Capernaum, and the "niggers" probably refer to young Werfel's readings; the latter term indicates no racist intention.

> Was war ich denn ein kleiner Traum,
> War Susa und war Kapernaum?
> Ein Held, der wild mit Niggern rang,
> Und eine alte Frau,
> Die nachts ins Wasser sprang?
> Und immerfort bin ich ein Ort,
> Bin Sternenwind und -tier
> Und bin Ihr alle vier.

80. Thummerer, "Die Dichter," p. 519. Other reviewers consider this expansion of self the most characteristic quality of Werfel's poetry.

81.

Was in und über mir ist, sprach verschmitzt:
"Du bist es selbst, was nimmer du besitzt,
Und nennst es: Wein, Greis, Mitzi, Rosen!

Bist eins mit ihm und wirst es nie verstehn,
Du liebst, und liebst dich selbst als Irgendwen.
O du Gestalt des ewig Wesenlosen!"

82. See Martin Buber, "Vorbemerkung über Franz Werfel," *Der Jude* 2 (1917–1918), 1.

83. Franz Werfel, *Zwischen Oben und Unten*, p. 546: "hat uns in völlig neuen Formen die *allumfassende* Weite seines kosmischen Kameradschaftsgefühles gelehrt."

84. Eva Cassirer, "Franz Werfel: Wir sind: Neue Gedichte," *Die Frau* 21/5 (1914), 297: "Von Liebe erfüllt ist er [Werfel, Werfels Gedichte] der Ort, in den die Welt eingeht, um in ihrem wesentlichen Leben wiederzuerstehen, die alte Frau, die Spielerinnen der nächtlichen Damenkapelle, der Mörder und der Kanarienvogel und die alte Schultasche. In ihm ist alles verknüpft und ist in ihm in Gott verknüpft."

85. Julius Kühn, "Der Dichter und das All: Drei Studien" (The Poet and the Cosmos: Three Studies), "III. Der Dichter und Gott (Franz Werfel)" (The Poet and God, Franz Werfel), *Weimarer Blätter* 2/5 (May 1920), 233: "Das Leben zeigt uns Umblikkenden heute ein tausendfaches *Neben*einander. Die Jugend [Werfel] möchte—aus tiefstem Drang—dieses Nebeneinander durch das Miteinander überwinden: im ersten Erleben der Liebe."

86. Kurt Pinthus, "Erinnerungen an Franz Werfel," in *Der Zeitgenosse: Literarische Portraits und Kritiken von Kurt Pinthus. Ausgewählt zu seinem 85. Geburtstag am 29. April 1971* (Marbach: n.p., 1971), p. 82: "This was an address, a call, which had not been heard since Walt Whitman's poetry in America. This was not a mood, but a voice ['nicht Stimmung sondern Stimme']. Everybody knows that nobody since has equaled this voice in power and musicality." Parts of this analysis of "An den Leser" have been previously published in my article "Inundated by This Mississippi of Poetry: Walt Whitman and German Expressionist Poetry," *Mickle Street Review* 9/2 (1988), 51–63.

87.

AN DEN LESER

Mein einziger Wunsch ist, Dir o Mensch, verwandt zu sein!
Bist Du Neger, Akrobat, oder ruhst Du noch in tiefer Mutterhut,
Klingt Dein Mädchenlied über den Hof, lenkst Du Dein Floß im Abendschein,
Bist Du Soldat oder Aviatiker voll Ausdauer und Mut.

Trugst Du als Kind auch ein Gewehr in grüner Armschlinge?
Wenn es losging, entflog ein angebundener Stöpsel dem Lauf.
Mein Mensch, wenn ich Erinnerung singe,
Sei nicht hart, und löse Dich mit mir in Tränen auf!

Denn ich habe alle Schicksale durchgemacht. Ich weiß
Das Gefühl von einsamen Harfenistinnen in Kurkapellen,
Das Gefühl von schüchternen Gouvernanten im fremden Familienkreis,
Das Gefühl von Debutanten, die sich zitternd vor den Souffleurkasten stellen.

Ich lebte im Walde, hatte ein Bahnhofsamt,
Saß gebeugt über Kassabücher und bediente ungeduldige Gäste.
Als Heizer stand ich vor den Kesseln, das Antlitz grell überflammt,
Und als Kuli aß ich Abfall und Küchenreste.

So gehöre ich Dir und allen!
Wolle mir, bitte, nicht widerstehn!
Oh, könnte es einmal geschehen,
daß wir uns, Bruder, in die Arme fallen!

88. Robert D. Faner, *Walt Whitman and Opera* (Philadelphia: University of Pennsylvania Press, 1951); Adolf D. Klarmann, "Musikalität bei Werfel" (Ph.D. thesis, University of Pennsylvania, 1931).

89. Franz Werfel, Hodov Notebook, Werfel Papers, Los Angeles: "Hier sei auch etwas zu der rein rhythmischen Prosa gesagt: zu der Poesie, die jede räumliche Gebundenheit verschmäht, und sich von den Gesetzen des Atmens beherrschen läßt. Sie hat, wenn ich nicht irre, ihre Väter in Walt Whitman, der sie aus der biblischen Form heraus erneuert hat. Sie ist unumstößlich, wenn sie ihrer Aufgabe treu bleibt: der Prophetie."

90. See especially Whitman's "Crossing Brooklyn Ferry" with its gradual movement toward the reader (section 1 to sections 7–8, where a union with the reader is achieved).

91. I do not wish to present a one-dimensional view of Whitman as a poet of unrelieved optimism. There is a change from the pre-Civil War optimism to the postwar Whitman of reduced expectations and chastened spirits. What I am comparing here is the two poets at the optimistic best. The difference is still telling and significant.

92. Letter to Hayek, Werfel Papers, Los Angeles: "Wer meine Bücher kennt, weiß, daß diese Tugenden [der Menschen- und Weltfreundschaft] als schmerzlich zu erkämpfendes *Sehnsuchts-Ziel* gesetzt sind und daß nirgends behauptet wird, daß ich oder ein anderer Mensch sie erfüllen."

93.

Der Wanderer wirft sich ins Gras
Ich bin müde, so marschmüd,
Ich bin schwer, so schön schwer.
Nicht müd bin ich, nicht schwer,
Nur marschmüd und so schön schwer.
Ich weiß, das kommt daher:
Die Erde liebt mich Reinen inniglich
Und reißt mich fest und fest an sich.

94.

O Tanzlokale am Ufer, o Brüder, o Dampfer, Fährhaus, Erd und Himmelsgeleit!
Ich bin ein Geschöpf!—Ich bin ein Geschöpf!
Und breite die Arme weit . . .

95. See letter to Alma, n.d., above: "Im übrigen alles, was mein Wissen ist, nur in einem anderen Typus Mensch gebannt, in einem Bärtigen, einem atlantischen Farmer! Das ist die Demokratie, der Sozialismus, die Menschenliebe als *Seelenwissen*, wie ich

an sie glaube. . . . Erwacht, todbewußt, genußedel, mit einer männlich väterlichen Ironie begabt, die aus dem erhabenen Erlebnis der Einheit kommt."

96. Edwin H. Miller, *Walt Whitman's Poetry: A Psychological Journey* (Boston: Houghton Mifflin, 1968), p. 12. For a discussion of Whitman's internal contradictions, both biographically and in his *oeuvre*, also in the light of the differences between European and American Whitman criticism, see Klaus Poenicke, "'The Test of Death and Night': Pose und bewältigte Wirklichkeit in Whitmans *Leaves of Grass*," in *Amerika: Vision und Wirklichkeit*, ed. Franz H. Link (Frankfurt/M. and Bonn: Athenäum, 1968), pp. 171–197.

97. See Justin Kaplan, *Walt Whitman: A Life* (New York: Bantam, 1982), especially pp. 64ff.

98. "Obwohl diese Gedichte noch *tief dort unten* stehn, wo die Wahrheit *eben erst zu atmen beginnt*, scheinen sie mir für die Menschen dennoch wichtig zu sein, weil sie Sendung haben. Sie reden in mancherlei Gestalten nur von einem. Von dem *permanenten Existenzbewußtsein, das ist Frömmigkeit*" (emphasis added).

99. Detlev W. Schumann, p. 204. "Enumerative Style and Its Significance in Whitman, Rilke, Werfel," *Modern Language Quarterly* 3 (1942), 204.

14. BEYOND EXPRESSIONISM

1. Tucholsky wrote a number of Whitman parodies. For a summary, see Hans-Werner Am Zehnhoff, "Walt Whitman und Kurt Tucholsky: Ein parodistisches Dienstverhältnis," *Arcadia* 22/1 (1987), 30f. Some of the German poetry dealt with in this chapter has been published and analyzed in my article "'Teach Me Your Rhythm': The Poetics of German Lyrical Responses to Whitman," in *Walt Whitman: The Centennial Essays*, ed. Ed Folsom (Iowa City: University of Iowa Press, 1994), pp. 226–239.

2. Theobald Tiger [Kurt Tucholsky], "Die fünf Sinne," *Die Weltbühne* 32 (11 August 1925), 225. Tucholsky frequently used "Ignaz Wrobel" as pseudonym. "Walt Wrobel" then is Tucholsky turned Whitman—or the other way around.

DIE FÜNF SINNE

Fünf Sinne hat mir Gott, der Herr, verliehen, mit denen ich mich zurechtfinden
darf hienieden:
Fünf blanke Laternen, die mir den dunkeln Weg beleuchten;
bald leuchtet die eine, bald die andre—
niemals sind alle fünf auf dasselbe Ding gerichtet . . .
Gebt Licht, Laternen—!

Was siehst du, Walt Wrobel—? . . .
ich sehe neben dem unfreundlichen Mann am Schalter die kleine schmutzige
Kaffeekanne, aus der er sich ab und zu einen Zivilschluck genehmigt . . .
ich sehe den ehrenwerten Herrn Appleton aus Janesville (Wisconsin) auf der
Terrasse des Boulevard-Cafés sitzen, lachende Kokotten bewerfen ihn mit
Bällchen, er aber steckt seinen hölzernen Unterkiefer hart in die Luft . . .

Das sieht mein Gesicht.

Was hörst du, Walt Wrobel—?
Ich höre den Küchenchef in der französischen Restaurantküche rufen: "Ils marchent: deux bifteks aux pommes! Une sole meunière!" Und vier Stimmen unter den hohen weißen Mützen antworten: "Et c'est bon!" . . .
Das hört mein Gehör.

Was schmeckst du, Walt Wrobel—?
Ich schmecke die untere Kruste der Obsttorte, die meine Tante gebacken hat; was die Torte anbetrifft, so hat sie unten ein paar schwarze Plättchen, da ist der Teig angebrannt, das knirscht im Mund wie Sand . . .
Das schmeckt mein Geschmack. . . .

Fünf Sinne hat mir Gott, der Herr, verliehen, mit denen ich mich zurechtfinden darf hiernieden:
Gesicht, Gehör, Geschmack, Geruch, Gefühl.
Fünf Sinne für die Unermeßlichkeit aller Erscheinungen.
Unvollkommenheit ist diese Welt, unvollkommen ihre Beleuchtung. . . .

Gebt Licht, Laternen!
Stolpernd sucht mein Fuß den Weg, es blitzen die Laternen.
Mit allen fünf Sinnen nehm ich auf, die können nichts dafür: meist
ist es
Schmerz.

3. See Thomas Mann, *Gesammelte Werke*, vol. 3, *Der Zauberberg* (Frankfurt/M: S. Fischer, 1960), pp. 477f.

4. Thomas Mann's use of Whitman has been investigated in a number of small studies. See Joel A. Hunt, "The Stylistics of a Foreign Language: Thomas Mann's Use of French," *Germanic Review* 32 (1957), 19–34; Joel A. Hunt, "Mann and Whitman: Humaniores Litterae," *Comparative Literature* 14 (1962), 266–271; and Henry Hatfield, "Drei Randglossen zu Thomas Manns *Zauberberg*," *Euphorion* 56 (1962), 365–368.

5. See Robert K. Martin, "Walt Whitman and Thomas Mann," *Walt Whitman Quarterly Review* 4/1 (Summer 1986), 4–6. Martin also points out the Whitman affinities in the final section of *Der Zauberberg*.

6. Ernst Waldinger, *Musik für diese Zeit: Ausgewählte Gedichte* (Munich: Weismann, 1946), p. 85.

7. See Susanne Araas-Vesely, "Gertrud Kolmar's Response to Walt Whitman," *Walt Whitman Quarterly Review* 7/2 (Fall 1989), 87–90.

8. In *Literaturmagazin* 5, *Das Vergehen von Hören und Sehen: Aspekte der Kulturvernichtung*, ed. Hermann Peter Piwit and Peter Rühmkorf (Reinbek: Rowohlt, 1976), p. 136.

DEIN SELBST KANN ICH NICHT SINGEN
(Für Walt Whitman)

Du singst das Selbst, du Sänger und vollkommner Krieger,
und dein Gesang, unadressiert, trifft einen Toten.
Töne, die sich verfangen

in deinen zartesten Halmen,
verknoten sich nicht im alten Widerspruch,
den du, Präriegras kauend, geknüpft hast
aus Eile und Gebein.

SCHREIBEN spottet der Technik deines Handgelenks:
im Goldenen Schnitt hast du nie gesungen.
Wer dich heut berührt, berührt ein Buch,
das sich bewegt in den Händen rühriger Leichen.

"Demokratisch" spreche ich, wenn du willst, gelassen aus,
aber meine Physiologie hat keine Sohle.
  Statt dessen schieße ich schon wieder,
und der Knall, der entsteht, ist der Gesang
auf die Krümmung deines schreibenden Fingers
  (o wie er mir schmeichelt).

Dasselbe alte Lachen.

Verkünde nicht, was nach dir kommt:
dein eignes Finale ertrank in den Akkorden.
Wissen, was es heißt, schlecht zu sein,
macht uns nicht besser.

Sänger, du hast Blasen an den Lippen!

9. Gabriele Eckart, "To Walt Whitman," in *Ich nenn euch mein Problem: Gedichte der Nachgeborenen*, ed. Bernd Jentzsch (Wuppertal: Hammer, 1971), pp. 154f.:

AN WALT WHITMAN

auf der suche nach metren bin ich dir
                    begegnet, Walt Whitman.
ich weiß, lebtest du heute und hier,
du würdest singen in endloser erstaunung—
die gigantischen themen in hymnen
                    erschließen,
du würdest
  singen von den wogenden zügen, die die
                    städte durchschreiten,
    jubelnd im beifall der hellen fassaden,
  singen von den millionen gesichtern,
    gerötet von begeisterung
    hoch darüber fahnen vom blute
                    gefallener Kämpfer,
  singen von den riesigen kombines, die wie
                    silbervögel
    über die ackerfurchen eilen,
  singen von den studenten auf den bänken
    der endlosen kastanienallee,

die nächsten hundert jahre berechnend,
singen vom lila flieder, der die kinder
beschattet,
sie kennen nicht Lincoln, doch bauen
im sande
raketen und schlösser, die keine
illusionen bleiben,
singen vom atmen der städte,
die ins all hineinwachsen,
singen von den menschen auf ihren flachen dächern
hoch oben, die der sonne winken mit roten tüchern,
singen von den blumenüberfluteten wiesen,
die die liebenden tragen.
doch du bist tot, Walt Whitman,
deshalb sei mein Lehrer; lehr mich deine rhythmen!
ich singe statt deiner!

10. See Grünzweig, "'Teach Me Your Rhythm,'" pp. 226–228.

11. Roland Kluge, "Der oft schon totgesagte Geist Walt Whitmans," *Neue Deutsche Literatur* 32/5 (May 1984), 105f.:

DER OFT SCHON TOTGESAGTE
GEIST WALT WHITMANS

In diesen mittleren Jahren   diesen
Jahren der Reife
Da unerschöpflich zu sein scheint die
Zeit
Und wie in Berge von Weizenkörnern
Meine Hände in sie hineingreifen

Traf ich auf dich   auf deine
Stimme traf ich   unzähmbare
Dort
Wo der Rauch ist und das Rollen der
Städte
Wo Menschen aneinanderstreifen
Tauschend ihre Elektrizität

Masse liebst du   Substanz
Zwischen Zähnen zu kauen   zu erschmecken
Körper   zu umschlingen mit tiefsten
Atemzügen   Glänzender
Anwalt unserer Fähigkeiten zu lieben
Ein Niagara   nicht zu überschreien oder
Niederzuzischen

Wie mit Donner erfüllen die Herden der Bisons
Amerikas Ebenen

Ergreifst du den Kontinent von Küste zu
Küste Geist
Umbrandet die Kapitolinischen Hügel
In entfernteste Zitadellen der Macht
Schmettern die Ozeane
Gischt deiner Worte

Den Kosmos begreifend als Großen
Camerado
Im namenlosen Grashalm wie im
Unerschöpflichen Sperma der
Galaxis vernehmend den gleichen
Gesang
Quillst du noch aus der abgerissenen
Pflanze
Unbesiegliche Wolfsmilch

15. WHITMAN AND THE MARXISTS

1. Schlaf, "Vom *Guten Grauen Dichter*"; see chapter 3, note 23 above.

2. Stefan Großmann, "Der Dichter der neuen Welt" (The Poet of the New World), *Arbeiter-Zeitung* (Vienna), 27 July 1905.

3. Richard Scheid, "Ein amerikanischer sozialistischer Dichter," *Die Gleichheit*, 22 July 1907, p. 127.

4. M. R. v. Stern, "Der Kollektivismus Walt Withmans [sic]," *Berliner Tageblatt* ("Zeitgeist" supplement), no. 8, February 1907.

5. Henriette Roland-Holst, "Sozialismus in der amerikanischen Poesie," *Die Neue Zeit* 26/1 (1908), 39: "In Walt Whitman haben wir denjenigen amerikanischen Dichter genannt, in dessen Schöpfungen alle Strömungen jenes vorproletarischen Sozialismus, welcher aus der Begeisterung für die Demokratie und aus dem Zutrauen zu ihren Wirkungen geboren wurde, den stärksten und großartigsten Ausdruck finden. . . . Und zwar nicht jener europäischen Demokratie, die auf jedem Schritte gehemmt, eingedämmt, deren Entfaltung zurückgehalten wurde durch alte Traditionen und starke Reste reaktionärer Klassen."

6. Ibid., p. 40: "konnte die Demokratie jene großartigen Ausblicke auf eine dämmernde Ferne eröffnen, in der sie selbst allmählich in den Sozialismus hinüberzuschillern schien."

7. Ludwig Ullmann, "Hermann Bahr über Walt Whitman," *Der Merker: Österreichische Zeitschrift für Musik und Theater* 2/5 (October-December 1910), 225:

> Er [Bahr] endete seine Ausführungen mit der Feststellung, daß Whitman der Verherrlicher des Begriffes der Organisation, der Sänger des Wortes "Genosse" gewesen sei. . . .
>
> Den Abend beschloß Bahr mit der Rezitation einiger Dichtungen Whitmans . . .

deren im besten Sinne antikonventionelle Tendenz . . . von diesem Publikum stürmisch bejubelt wurde.

8. The term does not appear in *Leaves*, but occurs eight times in the prose works, mostly in political or military contexts.

9. Such an aesthetics, of course, hardly ever existed. The further development of "working-class literature," up to the vague formula of "socialist realism" in East European socialist countries, certainly did not show any such anticonventional characteristics.

10. Clara Zetkin (1857–1933) was a leading leftist Social Democrat and later became a prominent member of the Communist Party.

11. The poem, with the German title "Der Brief" (The Letter), was published in *Die Gleichheit*, no. 10, 1915, pp. 39f.

12. Walt Whitman, *Der Wundarzt: Briefe, Aufzeichnungen und Gedichte aus dem amerikanischen Sezessionskrieg* (The Wound-Dresser: Letters, Notes, and Poems from the American War of Secession), ed. René Schickele, trans. Gustav Landauer and Iwan Goll (Zurich: Rascher, 1919).

13. Franz Diederich, "Ein Beispiel Kriegsdichtung," *Die Neue Zeit* 13/1 (1915), 378.

14. Max Hayek, "Walt Whitman, der Dichter der Demokratie: Zu seinem 100. Geburtstag—31. Mai," *Der Kampf* 12/9 (31 May 1919), 344: "Walt Whitmans Zeit ist erst jetzt gekommen. Er ist der Dichter des heutigen Tages, er ist der Dichter der Jahre, die sich nun entfalten."

15. Max Hayek, "Walt Whitman," *Donauland* 3/5 (1919–1920), 434: "*En masse*, es ist das Wort der Demokratie. Kein Staat ist geringer als der andere, keine Rasse schlechter als die andere, kein Mensch zuletzt besser als der andere. Auch die untersten werden heraufkommen und die zuhinterst stehen, werden nach vorne kommen. Alles Erschaffene ist göttlich, nichts ist unvollkommen."

16. Hayek, "Whitman," *Kampf*, p. 344: "die Bibel der Demokratie, ihr mächtiger Odem ist es, der durch diese gewaltigen Aussprüche und Verkündigungen weht, der Gedanke der Gleichberechtigung und Gleichwertigkeit aller Menschen und Rassen, keine weniger göttlich als die andere, der demokratische Gedanke in seiner rein menschlichen, zeitlosen Kraft ist es, der uns da mit unvergleichlicher Herrlichkeit vorgetragen wird."

17. Großmann, "Der Dichter der neuen Welt": "Die Religiosität des Konfessionslosen, die Liebe des neuen Heiden, die jubelnde Lebenslust des gottlosen Erdenträumers braust in seligen Chören durch seine Schöpfungen."

18. Karl Fischer, "Was Dichter über Frauen denken" (What Poets Think about Women), *Vorwärts* ("Frauenstimmen" supplement), 4 September 1924.

19. Heinz Eisgruber, "Walt Whitman, der Sänger der Kameradschaft" (Walt Whitman, Singer of Comradeship), *Arbeiter-Jugend*, no. 10, 1 October 1927, pp. 238f.: "Ja, du bist Walt, der große, starke Lebensbruder, der Zukunftsfrohe, der Daseinsbejahende, der vorwärtsschreitende, schaffende Sohn der Welt!"

20. *Jungsozialistische Blätter* 5/8 (1926).

21. Walt Whitman, *Ich singe das Leben*, trans. Max Hayek (Vienna: E. P. Tal, 1919); Walt Whitman, *Gesang von mir selbst*, trans. Max Hayek (Leipzig and Vienna: Wiener Graphische Werkstätte, 1920).

22. Some aspects of Whitman's presence in Social Democratic Party life are discussed in a fine article by Anna Jacobson, "Walt Whitman in Germany since 1914," *Germanic Review* 1 (1926), 132–141. Jacobson was very well acquainted with the atmosphere of a period which is difficult to reconstruct today.

23. See Program for "Vortrag Arbeiter-Dichtung," Heilbronn, Germany, 5 November 1926.

24. Erich Knauf, "Walt Whitman, ein Kosmos: Zum 30. Todestag des Dichters," *Freiheit*, 26 March 1922.

25. See Helga Lumer, "Zur Rezeption der Literatur der USA in der deutschen kommunistischen Presse (1918–1933)" (Ph.D. thesis, Humboldt University, Berlin, 1978), p. 78. The poem appeared in the issue of 27 September 1921.

26. Anatoly Lunacharsky, "Whitman und die Demokratie," in A. L., *Das Erbe*, ed. and trans. Franz Leschnitzer (Dresden: Verlag der Kunst, n.d.), pp. 232–234.

27. Johannes R. Becher, "An Europa," in *Das Neue Gedicht: Auswahl (1912–1918)* (Leipzig: Insel, 1918), p. 69.

Aber unermüdlich und immer wieder geht
  Whitman, lange ein Einzelner, einen hymnischen
  Päan, gleich einem jener fahrbaren Schutzschilde
  Vor sich herschiebend, gegen der noch kriegerischen
  Nationen—hah!—ungezählte Kanonenmündungen an!
(—!Ihr aber, Dichter des Verfalls! . . .
Aus dem Behälter euerer Werke goß
Sich stilisierte Fäule. Blank
Schraubt Eiter-Mond sich Korridor der Adern hoch.

28. Ibid., p. 117: "Ordnen wir uns, ein für alle Mal: o herrlichste, ruhmreichste der Taten, als Bewußte, als Gläubige unter: disziplinieren wir uns willentlich. En masse: welch ein Wort: welch ein Zauber! Welch ein Zauber! Welch ein Strömen, welch ein Wort: en masse! . . . Angliedern wir uns!"

29. Johannes R. Becher, *Vorwärts Du Rote Front* (Frankfurt/M: Taifun, 1924), pp. 122: "Aus zwei Ländern schlagen steil die Leuchtfeuer empor, sie leuchten dir, Deutsches Volk, auf deinem Marsch. Aus Amerika. Aus Rußland. . . . aus dem anonymen 150-Millionen-Rußland der Arbeiter und Bauern, aus dem Rußland Lenins, aus dem Rußland Gorkis. . . . [Und . . .] aus dem Amerika Whitmans und Sinclairs, und, ich wage es zu behaupten, aus dem 'Chaplin-Amerika.' Aus dem Amerika, dem kraftäugigen, stahlhäutigen, elektrischen Amerika, das einst das technisch vollendetste Bollwerk der Erde sein wird, beherrscht von den werktätigen Massen."

30. *Ein Blick in die Welt: Heimabend zur Weltjugendwoche* (Berlin: Neues Leben, 1947), p. 41: "der große Freiheitsdichter Amerikas." This booklet appeared as part of a series used for political youth work, the Kleine Bücherei der Freien Deutschen Jugend: Heimatabend-Heft. For the copy of this publication, I am indebted to Eberhard Brüning (Leipzig).

31. Anton Methyn, "Walt Whitman," *Sonntag*, no. 22, 6 June 1948: "Die bürgerliche Gesittung hat individuelle Konfessionen, auch wenn es Bekenntnisse zu den abwegigsten Lastern waren, stets ohne Entrüstung von der Literatur akzeptiert. Ungemütlich

wird es ihr immer erst dann, wenn sich der Autor mit seinem Wort einer Wirklichkeit bemächtigt, für die die Tonangebenden das Recht der Verschleierung beanspruchen. Sobald an die Stelle der literarischen Konfession das Bekenntnis zu den Realitäten der Welt tritt, sobald das 'ich' des Dichters für das 'wir' des Lesers gelten soll, wird die öffentliche Hypokrisie mobil. Sie hat Whitman bis ins Greisenalter verfolgt."

32. Anneliese Gabrisch, "Der Sänger der Demokratie: Zum 60. Todestag Whitmans, des Dichters der 'Grashalme,'" *Börsenblatt für den Deutschen Buchhandel* (Leipzig) 119/13 (29 March 1952), 219.

33. Hans Petersen, "Nachwort," in Whitman, *Lyrik und Prosa*, trans. Erich Arendt and Helmut Heinrich (Berlin: Volk und Welt, 1966), p. 537: "Was häufig als tiefenpsychologische Beschäftigung eines Egozentrikers mit dem eigenen Ich interpretiert wurde, ist in Wirklichkeit der Ausgangspunkt für die Entdeckung der Welt, des Weltalls, der Unendlichkeit von Raum und Zeit und des Menschen, die als pantheistische Einheit begriffen werden."

34. Gabrisch, "Der Sänger," p. 219: "Von der 'absoluten Poesie,' der Kunst um der Kunst willen, wußte Whitman freilich wenig. Er dichtete, um die Menschen für ein besseres Dasein zu begeistern, sie für seine Idee zu entflammen."

35. Kahlo, "Walt Whitman zum Gedenken," *Sonntag*, 3 July 1955: "er verfaßte eigens für die Jugend eine Erzählung, 'Evans, der Trunkenbold.' Whitman, der vortreffliche Schulmeister, wollte mit seinen Werken nutzen. . . . Whitman [wollte] in jedem Gedicht etwas Moralisches, d.h. für die Menschheit Nutzbringendes darstellen."

36. A. R. [Achim Roscher], "'Ein Kosmos, Manhattans Sohn . . .' Zum 100. Geburtstag des Erscheinens der 'Grashalme' von Walt Whitman," *Neue Deutsche Literatur* 3/8 (1955), 72f.: "die amerikanische Demokratie war jung wie er, als er zur Feder griff. Der Liberalismus hatte noch revolutionäre Leidenschaft und Lebenskraft; Revolution, Menschenrechte, Freiheit, Ablehnung der Klassenunterschiede—all das machte die Tradition aus, die Whitman später 'die gute alte Sache' nannte."

37. See Maurice Mendelson, *Life and Work of Walt Whitman: A Soviet View* (Moscow: Progress, 1976), p. 310. This claim is authenticated by William Harrison Riley, an American anarchist who knew Marx personally.

38. Friedemann Berger, "An der Wiege der modernen Literatur: Zum 150. Geburtstag des amerikanischen Dichters Walt Whitman," *Neue Zeit*, no. 126, 1 June 1969, p. 4.

39. Kuba [Kurt Barthel], "Er schrieb für Millionen: Wladimir Majakowski zu seinem 20. Todestag," in *Kritik der Zeit: Der Sozialismus—seine Literatur—seine Entwicklung*, ed. Klaus Jarnatz (Halle: Mitteldeutscher Verlag, 1970), p. 238: "Denn wie das Gedicht Walt Whitmans, des Sängers des jungen bürgerlichen Amerika, den individuellen Menschen zum Inhalt hat, wird bei Wladimir Majakowski, dem Auftrag der jungen Arbeiterklasse entsprechend, die neue Gesellschaft zum Inhalt aller seiner Gedichte."

40. *Neue Deutsche Literatur* 2/5 (1954), 138f.

41. Karl-Heinz Wirzberger, "Einhundert Jahre 'Leaves of Grass,'" *Zeitschrift für Anglistik und Amerikanistik* 4 (1956), 87: "träge . . . Völlegefühl satter amerikanischer Bürger."

16. THE ANARCHIST WHITMAN

1. *Der arme Teufel* was a European successor to a German-American journal of the same title. The first run of the journal appeared in Detroit, a publication edited by Robert Reitzel (1849–1898), German-American theologian and social activist.

2. *Der arme Teufel* 1/1 (1902), 8.

3. This was the first publication of this poem in German; it was not republished (retranslated) until after World War II!

4. Anon., no title, *Freie Jugend*, official publication of the Föderation der revolutionären Jugend deutscher Sprache (Federation of German-speaking Revolutionary Youth), 1/12 (1919):

Sein inbrünstiges Rufen sollt auch ihr, deutsche
Jugend, zu hören bekommen,
so wie 1853 seine Landsleute, Nordamerika.
Dieser Mann tat den Mund auf, ohne dazu die Er-
laubnis einer Behörde zu haben.
Er schrieb und druckte seine "*grünen Halme*"
(Titel seines Werkes) ohne Schulexamen, ohne ge-
prüft zu sein von Professoren.
Aus dem *Leben*, nicht aus Büchern ist er weise
geworden, durch sich selbst.
Zimmermann und eines Zimmermanns Sohn, wie
Jesus
brennend von Liebe zu *allen* und zu *allem*, wie
Jesus
ein Kämpfer gegen *alle* Beherrschung.
Feind des Staats: aus Liebe zur *Ordnung* unter
den Menschen.
Feind der Kirche: aus Religion und Gewissen.
Nur *eine* Autorität will er für den eigenen Men-
schen: das eigene Gewissen.
Wie's auch nie eine andere Autorität gegeben hat.
Nicht zur Zeit Jesus, der nach Jerusalem ging, um
sich kreuzigen zu lassen.
Nicht zu Karl Liebknechts Zeit, den unsere Kriegs-
knechte erschlugen,
die große Heldentat der deutschen Republik.

5. N., "Blut oder Geist?" (Blood or Spirit), *Freie Jugend* 1/12 (1919): "Kommunismusten! Wir wollen das Notwendigste! Es ist uns ernst! Mit Ideen spielt man nicht, man kämpft um sie. Wir wollen dasselbe."

6. Ibid: "Aber: Euer Weg ist die Waffe! Euer Weg ist die Diktatur! Das ist Blut! Das ist Macht! Gegen Blut, gegen Macht habt Ihr gekämpft! Jetzt geht es um Blut zur Macht. . . . *Einer muß zuerst auf Blut und Macht verzichten, wenn Blut und Macht aus der Welt sollen.* Zur Waffe greifen ist eine ganz elende Schwäche. . . . Haßt nicht, *liebt*!

Liebe zeugt Liebe! Haß zeugt Haß! Aefft nicht den anderen nach. *Seid* frei! Nicht Blut, sondern Geist!"

7. Advertisement for the *Neue Erde* regularly published in the *Freie Jugend* in 1919: "für den raschesten und vollständigsten Aufbau der sozialistischen Gesellschaft auf freiester Grundlage."

8. *Neue Erde* 1/15 (20 June 1919), 247. The quote is taken from M. E.'s (Max Ermer's) introduction to Hermann Bahr's article on Whitman entitled "Der gute graue Dichter vom fischförmigen Paumanok," pp. 247–250: "Ein Vorahner des brüderlichen Lebens, einer grossen, fühlenden, übernationalen Menschengemeinschaft, ein Liebender zu allen Dingen, auch zu den schmerzlichen."

9. See Hermann Bahr, *1919* (Leipzig, Vienna, and Zurich: E. P. Tal, 1920), pp. 187f. (diary entry for 1 June 1919).

10. Wandervögel and Freideutsche were members of youth movements in the early twentieth century. See chapter 20.

11. Leberecht Migge, "Das grüne Manifest" (The Green Manifesto) 1/12 (31 May 1919), 195f.:

> Ich sehe:
> *das Grüne Land der Jugend, der Gesundheit und*
> *des Glücks,*
>   Das frische, jungfräuliche Land.
> Aber, Bürger und Bürgerinnen,
> dieses schönere Dasein kommt nicht von selbst: Es muß errungen werden!
> Jeder einzelne muß (mit sich selber) kämpfen.
> Jeder einzelne muß (seine eigene Zukunft) bauen.
> Jeder einzelne muß (seinem Nächsten) helfen,
> *Helfen, Bauen, Kämpfen!*
>
> Kommt ran
>   Ihr starken Einzelgänger
>   Ihr Freiesten der Naturmenschen
>   Ihr Jüngsten der Wandervögel und Freideutschen
>   Ihr Beweglichsten der Spieler und Sportler
>   Ihr Erfolgreichsten der Schreber und Landleute
>   Ihr Lustigsten der Musikanten
>   Ihr Künstler, Denker und Dichter
> faßt an:
> Schafft neues Dasein. Schafft neue Kraft. Rettet euer Land!
> Schaffe Mut, Deutscher, noch ist nichts verloren.
>   Dein Volk wird leben,
>   Dein Volk wird steigen,
>   Dein Volk wird führen.
>   *Hoch*
> Die neue Daseinsidee der Deutschen, die neue allgemeine Generalidee:
>   *Das Land!*

17. WHITMAN ON THE RIGHT

1. E. L. Wulff, "Walt Whitman: Eine Skizze," *Der Alte Glaube* (Leipzig) 10 (19 February 1909), col. 540. The biblical quotation is from Romans 13:1: "Es ist uns schlechterdings unmöglich, diesen revolutionären Posaunenstößen Whitmans noch weiter nachzugehen, wie wir auch seine demokratische Gesinnung nicht teilen. Jede Revolution bedeutet einen Verstoß gegen das Bestehende, das Reale. . . . Wenn Whitman sagt: 'Widersetzt euch viel und gehorchet wenig!' so sagt die Schrift dagegen . . . 'Jedermann sei untertan der Obrigkeit, die Gewalt über ihn hat; denn es ist keine Obrigkeit ohne von Gott, wo aber eine Obrigkeit ist, ist die von Gott verordnet.' . . . Und es ist uns doch sehr fraglich, ob man diesen wilden Kämpfer gegen göttliche und menschliche Ordnung mit ernsthafter Miene als den größten Dichter seit Goethe verherrlichen darf. Denn wo bleibt bei Whitman der veredelnde Zweck der Dichtkunst?"

2. Samitasa [Willy Schlueter], "Walt Whitman, ein germanischer Lebensdeuter" (Walt Whitman, a Germanic Life-Interpreter), *Der Hammer* 3/1 (1904), 269:

> Bei levitischer Klugkoserei ist für ein deutsches Herz nichts zu holen. Propheten-Rhytmen [sic] müssen wiederum durch die Gauen [*sic*] gehen.
>
> Wie dumme Schuljungen standen wir vor den Akademikern und ließen uns einreden, über das Denken zu denken, das sei Weisheit und sonsten nichts. Nein, unser Geist ist ein Lebenserfassungs-Werkzeug, dem Kämpfen und Lieben ist er zugewandt.

3. Ibid.

4. Paul de Lagarde (1827–1891) was one of the ideological precursors of German fascism. An extreme antiSemite and antidemocrat, he taught the superiority of the German "master race."

5. *Der arme Teufel* 3 (13 December 1904), 5: "Das will ich allerdings gern gestehen, daß ich . . . die Zeit für ein heroisches und freies Jung-Germanentum im Geiste Emersons, Walt Whitmans und Lagardes . . . erfüllt halte. . . . Die Hauptsache ist, daß Verantwortungsmenschen, Mitbauer an einer freudigen Zukunftsrasse Raum gewinnen, daß nicht die intellektualistische Vergreisung, die heut so gern als Wissenschaftlichkeit sich gebärdet, den neuen Balder-Mut ertötet."

6. Quoted in Harry Law-Robertson, *Walt Whitman in Deutschland*, p. 84. Lersch goes on: "He is a Führer-type, through and through, and his intuitive prescience is so great that he has included our time in his poetry as well as a time still further off in the future" (85).

7. Heinrich Kästner, "Walt Whitman, der Künder eines neuen Menschentums" (Walt Whitman, the Prophet of a New Humanity), *Der Volkserzieher: Blatt für Deutschtum auf christlicher Grundlage* 37 (May 1933), 90: "Den Weg, gekennzeichnet durch Maschinen, Technik und Kapitalismus, auf welchem sich noch heute die Menschheit befindet, verließ bereits im vergangenen Jahrhundert ein Mensch von jener seltenen Größe, der Jahrhunderte der menschlichen Entwicklung überschlug und zum Künder kommender Geschlechter wurde."

8. Ibid.: "Whitman verleiht dem Menschen wieder einen offenen Sinn für alles

Lebendige und gibt ihm Kraft zu einem starken Dasein, zum Leben und zum Tode. Zutiefst hat dieser Einmalige die Göttlichkeit des bewußten Seins erfühlt, aus welchem der Mensch einen Diener seiner Lebensbedürfnisse gemacht hat."

9. Ibid.

10. Ibid., p. 90: "Wir glauben an ein vollkommenes Menschengeschlecht, das ein Einzelner vorlebte."

11. Hans Flasche, "Deutscher Geist in angelsächsischer Geschichtsphilosophie (Walt Whitman)," *Deutsche Vierteljahrsschriften* 17 (1939), 426: "*Zum anderen aber ist es die überaus starke Betonung [bei Whitman], das unmittelbare Spüren aller Vitalwerte, die Natur, Volk, Rasse, Blut, Boden als wichtige Kräfte erscheinen läßt. So weiß Whitman den Eigenwert der Persönlichkeit gar hoch zu schätzen, aber er stellt sie sogleich mitten in die Gemeinschaft eines Volkes hinein*" (emphasis in original).

12. Ibid., pp. 426f.: "Mann und Frau dürfen nicht in der punktuellen Enge ihrer Individualität verharren. Sie müssen sich immer bewußt sein, daß sie Ahnen, daß sie Glieder einer langen Kette sind, daß sie Kinder zeugen und gebären und so rassische und völkische Werte erhalten sollen. Zu den höchsten Rassewerten, die weitergegeben werden, gehören Tapferkeit, Heldenmut und Heroismus. Denjenigen, die für ihr Vaterland das Leben gaben, gebührt insbesondere einmütige Dankbarkeit. Aus ihren Gräbern steigt Energie zu neuen Taten empor. Das Andenken an die Söhne, die ihr Blut für die Heimat vergossen, ist heiligstes Erbe eines Volkes, heiliger noch in bestimmter Hinsicht als nationale Literatur und Kunst."

13. Anon. [Josef Winckler], "Kunst und Industrie" (Art and Industry), *Quadriga* (Fall 1912), 70: "Arme-Leute-Poesie."

14. Karl Bröger, "Bekenntnis," in Karl Bröger, *Aus meiner Kriegszeit: Gedichte*, 2nd ed. (Nuremberg: Fränkische Verlagsanstalt, n.d.), p. 33:

Immer schon haben wir eine Liebe zu dir gekannt
blos wir haben sie nie bei ihrem Namen genannt.
Herrlich zeigte es aber deine größte Gefahr,
daß dein ärmster Sohn auch dein getreuester war.
Denk es, o Deutschland.

15. Hans Hermann Schulz, *Das Volkstumserlebnis des Arbeiters in der Dichtung von Gerrit Engelke, Heinrich Lersch und Karl Bröger. Ein Beitrag zur Morphologie des Problems* (Würzburg: Triltsch, 1940), p. 29: "Durchbruch des Arbeiters zum Volk."

16. See ibid., pp. 29–40. The German term is "Mythos der Arbeit."

17. "Ein freier Deutscher kennt kein kaltes Müssen: /
Deutschland muß leben und wenn wir sterben müssen!"

18. The motto is a translation of Whitman's "inscription" "Thou Reader" (*LG*, 15). In German, the motto reads:

In dir, Leser,
pulst Leben, Stolz und Liebe
genau wie in mir.
So seien auch dir diese Lieder geweiht.

19. Heinrich Lersch, *Mensch im Eisen: Gesänge von Volk und Werk* [*MiE*] (Berlin and Leipzig: Deutsche Verlagsanstalt, 1925), p. 58:

Kohlen auf die Glut, hoch lodere, Prächtige! Schmiedesonne,
gehe auf!
Lodere höher, Flamme! Friedensfeuer!
Scheine, leuchte, wärme, Werk-Liebesglut!
Leuchtturm, nach dem wir unsern Kurs einstellten
Solange wir, schiffbrüchige Soldaten, im Blutmeer irrten auf dem schwanken Hoffnungskahn.
Lohe empor, goldene Leuchte des Werktags! Du Osterkerze,
Licht nach den langen Karwochen des Kriegsgolgatha;
Abend- und Morgenstern! Trost nach durchwachter Nacht;
Du bist die Feuersäule, die den Weg ins Gelobte Land weist.
Flamme! Ernährerin, du reifst die Ähren auf unsern Feldern, die der Bauer gesät.
Flamme! Verzehrerin aller Unreinigkeit Tod, Tod aller schlechten Gedanken;
Wie die wilden Tiere dich meiden in der Urwaldnacht,
So meiden die bösen Gedanken den Schmied, wenn er in deinem Lichte steht!
20.
Laßt uns wohnen bei den Elementen
Feuer, Wasser, Luft, Erde, bei den Symbolen des tätigen Lebens:
Feuer! Amboß! Hammer!
Segen! Segen! Segen!
Unsere Kinder werden Jünglinge, Mädchen,
Brüderlich-Schwesterlich.
Sie werden die Heimat entdecken und dahinter die Erde.
Sie werden ihre Kraft entdecken, erwecken und in die Freiheit staunen . . .
Sie werden eines Tages, die mutigen Jungen,
Gegen die Maschinen, die Motore, gegen uns
Die alten Hämmer erheben, die Herrschaft der Maschinen zu zerschlagen,
Daß die Seelen wieder frei.
21.
Wir schmieden.
Der junge Geselle und ich.
Der Junge zieht das Gestänge des Blasebalges. Hinauf, hinab gehn seine mädchenhaften[!] Arme.
Ich stehe und besorge das Feuer . . .
Der Junge und ich sehen in die Flamme hinein. Sehen nicht um uns, nicht neben uns, bis er den Kopf wendet und in mein Gesicht blickt.
Ich sehe auch ihn an. Wir sagen nichts und lächeln. Denn jeder fühlt eine Freude aufsteigen.
Freude, die von der roten Flamme ausgeht und in unsre Herzen sinkt. Wie ein Geheimnis, von dem wir beide nur wissen, ein Geheimnis, das uns bindet. Das Freundschaft wortlos entzündet, tatlos vermehrt. Freundschaft der Freude, die von der Flamme stammt. Wir sehen wieder ins Feuer hinein, der Junge und ich, und schweigen. Aber wir wissen beide, daß wir aus diesem Feuer glücklich sind.

22\.

Meine Arbeiter sind meine Freunde.
Sie wollen keinen andern Meister als mich.
Ich teile ihre kleinen und großen Sorgen. Bin Pate bei ihren Kindern und Trauzeuge bei ihren Hochzeiten.
Ich höre ihre Meinungen und freue mich, wenn sie mir einen neuen und schönen Gedanken vermitteln.
Aus den Geheimnissen ihrer Herzen empfange ich alle Mysterien der Erdenschaft.

Ich brauche die Bücher nicht mehr.
In ihrem Leben spielen die gewaltigsten Dramen, und ihre Schicksale sind reine und wahrhaftige Romane. Das Versegeklapper der Lyriker ist Geschwätz, wenn ich mir von meinem jungen Gehilfen erzählen lasse, wie er die Sonntage heimlich mit seiner jungen Geliebten vertut.

23\.

Jedes Ding in der Welt ist vollkommen: die Sonne, die Sterne, der Baum, das Tier, der Grashalm, und das Ganze ist vollkommen an sich.
Wie darf ich mir erlauben einzig unvollkommen zu sein?
Unvollkommener als irgendein anderer Teil der Schöpfung?

Nichts ist notwendig.
Aber eins ist notwendig: daß ich glücklich bin!
Daß ich glücklich bin und singen kann bei meiner Arbeit.

24\.

Er war siebenunddreißig Jahre, in Amerika geboren,
durch alle Berufe gegangen, als Vagabund um die Erde gewalzt,
hatte mit Indianern, Negern, Insulanern
gelebt und arbeitete jetzt nur ein paar Wintermonate
in der fernen Stadt als Sportlehrer.
Ich übergab mich ihm nach langem Widerstreben und bat ihn,
daß er meinen Leib gesund mache.

25\.

Und ich ward doch sein Kamerad.
Er lehrte mich meinen Leib, den alten Adam,
lehrte mich die Gesetze des Leibes.
Und ich sah: Es waren die gleichen Gesetze von allen ewigen Dingen; von Meer und Wolke, Sterne und Blume, Tier und Stein, von Mensch und Erde: Die allmächtigen Gesetze von Frühling und Herbst, Sommer und Winter, die unerschütterlichen Gesetze von Kommen und Vergehen, Leben und Sterben. Und er lehrte mich, der

> große Kamerad, die Ströme fühlen, die
> auf ihrem Wehn und Atmen den Kosmos
> tragen, lehrte, mich einordnen in die le-
> bendige Welt; und ich ward inne der
> Kraft, die diese Erde, die Sonnen und
> Sterne bewegt; aus der sich in ewiger Ge-
> burt alles Lebendige erneuert.

26.

Ein Kind, entdeckte ich von neuem mich selbst!

Prangender schwoll im Frühherbst noch einmal die Wiese, Musik wurde Rauschen des Wasserfalls, abendliches Kreisen der Sterne. Und im großen Atem der Welt atmete, hob und senkte ich mit.

27. See Dietrich Strothmann, *Nationalsozialistische Literaturpolitik: Ein Beitrag zur Publizistik im Dritten Reich*, 2nd ed. (Bonn: Bouvier, 1963), pp. 222, 226.

28.

> Wir befreien das Weib aus erstickendem Dunst der
> Küchen,
> erlösen aus Magdniedrigkeit, Kochtopfverantwortung
> das Weib zur Mannesgespielin[!],
> Zur Mutter der Kinder, zur Schwester der Menschen.
> Völker befreien wir
> von Nahrungsangst und Raumbedrängnis.
> Siehe, sie kehren heim die Geknechteten, Entmenschten,
> die Volkscharen, zu nichts als Paria verdammten, heim
> kehren die Völker nach Osten, woher sie kamen.

29. See Gudrun Heinsen Becker, "Karl Bröger—ein Beispiel für die Publikumsgebundenheit der Arbeiterdichtung" (Ph.D. thesis, Rice University, 1973); and Gerhard Müller, *Für Vaterland und Republik: Monographie des Nürnberger Schriftstellers Karl Bröger* (Pfaffenweiler: Centaurus, 1986).

30. Karl Bröger, "Walt Whitman's Werk deutsch!" *Frankfurter Zeitung*, 3 December 1922, section "Gute Geschenkliteratur":

> Walt Whitmans Werk ist ein starker innerer Trost und eine noch stärkere Hoffnung. Das durchaus männliche Wesen dieses Pioniers neuer Welten verscheucht den Nebel erheuchelter und verlogener Literatenliteratur, der dick und dumpf über unsrer Zeit liegt. Es bricht aus Whitmans Werk ein Glanz, der die dunkle Gegenwart überstrahlt. Was Demokratie sein wird, wenn das Wort aus seiner begrifflich politischen Bedeutung gelöst und mit allen Fasern des lebendigen Menschen ergriffen ist, dafür stellt Walt Whitman ein überwältigendes Beispiel auf. Die besten Tugenden einer männlichen Zeit, die wieder kommen müssen, wenn die Welt lebenswürdig sein soll, beschwört der amerikanische Seher herauf: Kraft zum Größten wie zum Kleinsten, offene Sinne für den Augenblick und seine unvergänglichen Werte, Liebe, die ins Nächste wie ins Fernste greift, Kameradschaft in einem uns zunächst leider verlorenen Geiste!
>
> Wir brauchen heute Bücher, aus denen die Kraft quillt, dem Zeitenlauf unser Dennoch entgegenzustellen. Walt Whitmans Werk ist eine solche Quelle.

31. Karl Bröger, "Der blühende Hammer," in Karl Bröger, *Der blühende Hammer: Gedichte* (Berlin: Arbeiterjugend-Verlag, 1924), pp. 8f.:

DER BLÜHENDE HAMMER

Da!—an dem kahlen, gedrehten Schaft
wirkt eine geheime Wunderkraft.
Ein Keimen, ein Treiben, die Zweige sprossen,
gleich sind die ersten ins Blatt geschossen,
und im obersten Wipfel gebettet liegt
schon die erste Blüte, vom Wind gewiegt.
Die zweite, die dritte ist aufgegangen,
bald ist das ganze Geäste behangen
mit roten Rosen, die grüßen weit
hinein in die feiernde Frühlingszeit . . .

Um den blühenden Hammer, Hand in Hand,
stehn die schaffenden Brüder aus Stadt und Land.
Sie kommen alle, das Wunder zu sehn,
und jubelnd hört man die Kunde gehen:

"Jetzt blüht der Hammer in unsrer Hand!
Frei herrscht die Arbeit im freien Land!"

32. Schulz, *Das Volkstumserlebnis*, p. 12: "seherische Vorausnahme der Maifeiern, wie sie das Dritte Reich aus Parteihaß und Totschlag heraus zu lauterer Arbeitsfreude verwirklicht hat."

33. Ibid. From the "Führerrede," 1 May 1923: "eine Verherrlichung des nationalen Wissens gegen den internationalen Zersetzungsgedanken."

34. Karl Bröger, "Phallos: Gesänge um den Mann," *Die Tat* 12 (1920–1921), 118–123 (118).

35. Klaus Mann, "The Present Greatness of Walt Whitman," *Decision* 1 (April 1941), 22.

36. Friedrich Sally Grosshut, "Walt Whitman," *Orient* 3/12 (19 June 1942), 23: "Erhoben hat sich Amerika, die athletische Demokratie, das Finale zu verwirklichen, der Freiheit zu helfen. Die Freiheitsstatue grüsst die Schiffe, die Flieger, die die amerikanische Küste verlassen, den verbündeten Voelkern und Ländern in der gemeinsamen Sache beizustehen. Aus dem Droehnen der Fabriken und Werften, dem Haemmern der Schiffsmaschinen, dem Donner der Flugzeugmotore toent Walt Whitman's unsterbliches Lied. Das Lied von menschlicher Groesse, inbrünstiger Liebe zum Leben, das Lied vom Ordnungswillen und Aufbau einer sieghaften kuenftigen Demokratie."

18. THE GERMAN SIXTIES

1. Günter Grass, letter to W. Grünzweig, 16 December 1987.

2. Günter Grass, "*Dich singe ich Demokratie*": *Loblied auf Willy* (Neuwied and Berlin: Luchterhand, 1965), p. 3:

Ich habe noch nie Wahlreden gehalten und verspüre seit Wochen etwas mir Neues:

Lampenfieber. . . . Geholfen hat mir ein amerikanischer Kollege: Walt Whitman. Er lebte von 1819 bis 1892, trug einen wallenden, biblischen Bart, verfügte über Atem, der von der Ost- zur Westküste, von Long Island bis Kalifornien reichte, und hinterließ das Buch "Grashalme." Endlose, jeden Landstrich und jeden Beruf, den einzelnen und die Masse berührende Gesänge, die den Vereinigten Staaten von Amerika eine poetische und bis heute gültige Verfassung gegeben haben. Walt Whitman, ein Lincoln der Sprache. Jemand, der die Demokratie besungen hat. Mut und Humor ließen ihn sagen:

"O, was für Themen, Gleichheiten! O göttlicher Durchschnitt!"

Walt Whitman soll unser Podest sein. Auf ihn gestützt, als Bürger zwischen Bürgern, gilt es, den Mund aufzumachen: "Dich singe ich, Demokratie!"

Dieses Motto, mit dem meine Freunde und ich eine aufregende Reise beginnen, habe ich dem folgenden Walt-Whitman-Zitat abgewandelt: "Für dich dies von mir, o Demokratie, dir zuliebe, ma femme. Für dich, für dich zwitschre ich diese Lieder."

3. Grass, letter to Grünzweig: "Meine ersten Wahlkampfreden habe ich wenige Wochen vor Beginn meiner ersten Wahlkampfreise im Sommer 65 aus ziemlicher Distanz in Amerika entworfen. In jenen Jahren hatte ich, neben gewiß vielen anderen Vorlieben, auch ein intensives Leseverhältnis zu Walt Whitmans episch ausladenden Gedichtpanoramen. So war es naheliegend für mich, seine Anrufung der Demokratie zum Motto zu nehmen; gewiß spielte auch die politische Absicht eine Rolle, der rechten Anbiederung an die USA zu widersprechen und gleichzeitig dem plumpen Anti-Amerikanismus Paroli zu bieten."

19. HOMOSEXUALITY

1. My investigations for this chapter are deeply indebted to Hans-Joachim Lang (Hamburg), especially his two articles on Bertz: "Eduard Bertz vs. Johannes Schlaf: The Debate on Whitman's Homosexuality in Germany," in *A Conversation in the Life of Leland R. Phelps, America and Germany: Literature, Art and Music*, ed. Frank L. Borchardt and Marion C. Salinger (Durham, N.C.: Duke University Press, 1987), pp. 49–86; and "*Das Sabinergut* von Eduard Bertz: Ein vergessener Amerikaroman," in *Wege amerikanischer Kultur: Ways and Byways of American Culture*, ed. Renate von Bardeleben (Frankfurt/M.: Lang, 1989), pp. 143–158, published in English translation in *Gissing Journal* 29/3 (July 1993), 1–16.

2. Magnus Hirschfeld, "Petition an die gesetzgebenden Körperschaften des deutschen Reiches behufs Abänderung des §175 des R.-Str.-G.-B.," *Jahrbuch für sexuelle Zwischenstufen* 1 (1899), 241.

3. See Lang, "Bertz vs. Schlaf," pp. 65*n*f.

4. Ibid., p. 50.

5. Eduard Bertz, "Walt Whitman: Zu seinem siebzigsten Geburtstag," *Deutsche Presse* 2 (June 1889), 177: "Als den höchsten Gewinn meines Aufenthalts in Amerika, ja als eins der glücklichsten Ereignisse meines Lebens betrachte ich die Bekanntschaft mit den Schriften des eigenartigsten und tiefsten aller amerikanischen Dichter. Wenn

der Menschheit ganzer Jammer mich anfaßt, wenn weder ein profanes noch ein heiliges Buch mir den inneren Zwiespalt lösen will, so darf ich nur einen der Bände des alten, ewig jungen Walt Whitman aufschlagen, und ich fühle, wie von jeder Seite eine Kraft ausgeht, die mich freudig durchdringt, eine gesunde, frische Lebensfülle, die elektrisch dem starken Herzen dieses geistigsten Naturmenschen entströmt. . . . Ich liebe ihn."

6. Bertz to Whitman, n.d. (mentioned under Traubel's entry for 28 June 1889), in *With Walt Whitman in Camden*, vol. 5, *April 8–Sept. 14, 1889*, ed. Gertrude Traubel (Carbondale: Southern Illinois University Press, 1964), pp. 330f.

7. Bertz to Schlaf, 12 November 1897. I have published Bertz's available Whitman correspondence in "Adulation and Paranoia: Eduard Bertz's Whitman Correspondence (1889–1914)," *Gissing Journal* 27/3 (July 1991) 1–20; and 27/4 (October 1991), 16–35. Hereafter these letters are quoted giving the name of the addressee, date, issue, and page numbers. The passage from Schlaf's letter is in 3:11f. Text of the German original:

> Was Sie von dem Dichter sagen, las ich mit Teilnahme, nur über Ihr Wort, seit Freiligrath habe sich bei uns in Deutschland kaum wieder jemand um Whitman bekümmert, empfand ich leises Bedauern. . . .
>
> Denn einer hat sich seit Freiligrath doch mit unzweideutigen Worten zu Whitman bekannt, und zwar ich selbst.

8. See Lang, "Bertz vs. Schlaf," p. 62. Bertz also had great praise for Schlaf. In a review of a translation of Whitman's early stories in *Literarische Echo* 3 (May 1901), cols. 1079f., he wrote: "Johannes Schlaf's introduction is a precious addition [to the book]. Schlaf has done much to heighten Whitman's popularity in Germany. Emphatically he stresses that this 'first great genius of a new monistic religion' could counterbalance Nietzsche's detrimental influence on German literature and one has to agree with him." Later on, Bertz would put it much differently.

9. Traubel mentions this offer in his report to the *Walt Whitman Fellowship* for 1904: "Léon Bazalgette, Paris, and Edward Bertz, of Berlin, have written the Secretary that they could very extensively add to the Continental scope of the work, if their contributions were desired" (*Walt Whitman Fellowship Papers* [Philadelphia: n.p., 1904], p. 7).

10. Eduard Bertz, "Walt Whitman. Ein Charakterbild" (Walt Whitman: A Character Sketch), *Jahrbuch für sexuelle Zwischenstufen* 7 (1905), p. 164: "denn nichts ist so sehr geeignet, das Vorurteil zu beseitigen und einer gerechten Beurteilung Bahn zu brechen, wie die Erkenntnis der Tatsache, daß viele von den Größten der Menschheit diese Anlage besaßen und dadurch nicht im mindesten gehindert wurden, ihren Mitmenschen mehr zu nützen als Tausende und aber Tausende von Normalen."

11. Eduard Bertz, *Whitman-Mysterien: Eine Abrechnung mit Johannes Schlaf* [*WM*] (Berlin: n.p., 1907), p. 12.

12. Bertz, "Charakterbild," p. 166.

13. Ibid., p. 177: "Und eine Gleichstellung Whitmans mit diesem Idealbilde [Jesus Christus] zeugt von einer an das Pathologische streifenden Überspanntheit."

14. Ibid., pp. 192f.

15. See ibid., pp. 192f.

16. To Schlaf, any "scientific" literature on Whitman had to be suspicious. In one article he exclaimed: "May God keep us from having Whitman-scholars for as long as possible!" ("Mein Verhältnis zu Walt Whitman," *Die Lese* 3 [1912], 436).

17. See Johannes Schlaf, *Walt Whitman Homosexueller? Kritische Revision einer Whitman-Abhandlung von Dr. Eduard Bertz* (Minden: Bruns, 1906), pp. 25f.

18. "Durch ein systematisches Studium der 'Grashalme' war es mir zur zweifellosen Gewißheit geworden, daß er [Whitman] in seinen Kalmusliedern und den verwandten Gedichten eine pathologische Anomalie des Liebestriebes zum Ausdruck bringt. Zu meinem Schmerz hatte ich dies erkannt."

19. A report on the annual meeting of the committee in 1919, which included a visit to Potsdam, stated that the participants "were welcomed by our long-standing friend, the author Eduard Bertz" (*Jahrbuch für sexuelle Zwischenstufen* 19/20 [1919–1920], 180).

20. "Es liegt eine sittliche Gefahr darin, wenn Fanatiker aus einer pathologischen Gefühlsweise ein Evangelium, ja eine Religion machen und die normale männliche Jugend mit solchen Irrlehren vergiften. Deswegen habe ich nachdrücklich betont, daß bei der Klärung dieses Punktes das größte öffentliche Interesse in Frage steht, '*weil Unheil und Verwirrung dadurch angerichtet wird, wenn die ungesunde Idee als die gesunde und erlösende kursiert.*' "

21. Bertz to Rivers, n.d., 4:29: "There cannot be the slightest doubt, I think, that society is morally justified in protecting its *youth* against being debauched, as well as in preventing any *public* breach of modesty."

22. See W. C. Rivers, *Walt Whitman's Anomaly* (London: George Allen, 1913), pp. 4f. Rivers mentions Bertz's works favorably. The sale of the booklet was "restricted to Members of the Legal and Medical professions" (title page) and was the first publication in English dealing exclusively with Whitman's homosexuality. Like Bertz, Rivers attempted to provide "scientific" evidence.

23. Bertz to Rivers, 12 March 1913, 4:16.

24. Bertz to Rivers, 29 March 1913, 4:20.

25. "Schlaf tut gelegentlich so, als ob bei Whitman und seinen Anhängern gar kein Grund vorgelegen hätte, irgendetwas zu bemänteln. Aber der Grund ist ganz offenbar. Die Whitmaniten als Partei, als Sekte, wissen ganz genau, daß das Zugeben der homosexuellen Erklärung ihrer Sache in Amerika tödlich sein würde, und das wußte schon Whitman selbst."

26. Bazalgette to Schlaf, 22 November 1905, Johannes Schlaf Archive, Querfurt (original in French).

27. Bazalgette to Schlaf, 10 December 1905, Johannes Schlaf Archive, Querfurt (original in French).

28. Ernest Crosby to Traubel, 8 April 1906, Johannes Schlaf Archive, Querfurt.

29. Henry Bryan Binns to Schlaf, 5 November 1905, Johannes Schlaf Archive, Querfurt.

30. Ibid.

31. Triumphantly, he communicated to Rivers that Apollinaire had told him "that *Bazalgette is himself homosexual*" (8 February 1914, 4:26). He also suspected that the former Whitmanite and translator of some of Whitman's prose Otto Eduard Lessing

"was entrusted, by the German publisher of Binns' biography, with the task of writing about me in a leading German Review *with the express purpose of tearing my book to tatters*" (12 March 1913, 4:17).

32. See Holz to Bertz, 21 February 1907, in Arno Holz, *Briefe: Eine Auswahl*, pp. 170f.

33. Johannes Schlaf, unpublished diary, vol. 1, p. 188, entry for 7 July 1908. I am obliged to Ingolf Schnittka (Halle) for the communication of this entry: "Ich träumte in letzter Nacht überaus lebhaft, ich ginge mit dem bejahrten Walt Whitman Arm in Arm in einer großen Stadt. Das war ein unsagbar schönes Glücksgefühl. Das Gefühl seines herrlichen Manneskörpers, durch den eingehängten Arm hindurch. Ein unsagbares unmittelbares Gefühl von Wohlgefallen, Ruhe, unbegreiflichsten Gestilltseins. Das glückselige und heilige Gefühl eines vollkommenen Menschen mit völlig harmonischem inneren Gleichgewicht."

34. See Eduard Bertz, *Der Yankee-Heiland: Ein Beitrag zur modernen Religionsgeschichte* [*YH*] (The Yankee-Messiah: A Contribution to Modern Religious History) (Dresden: Reissner, 1906), pp. ixf.

35. Cesare Lombroso's *Genie und Irrsin* (*The Man of Genius*, originally published in 1887) was widely known in Germany. On the basis of Whitman's poetry as well as his biography, Lombroso concluded that the author was "positively insane" (*Genie und Irrsinn in ihren Beziehungen zum Gesetz, zur Kritik und zur Geschichte* [Leipzig: Reclam, n.d.], p. 333). Max Nordau agreed with Lombroso with regard to insanity but denied Whitman genius. Filled with hatred, he wrote: "Without doubt, Whitman was insane. But a genius? This would be hard to prove. He was a vagabond and a depraved debauchee and his poems contain outbursts of erotomania. . . . He owes his reputation to bestial, sensual pieces which drew the attention of all American lechers" (Max Nordau, *Entartung* [Degeneration], 2 vols. [Berlin: Duncker, 1892], vol. 1, p. 358). In spite of the early dates of these attacks, they seem to have done relatively little harm to Whitman's reputation. For Nordau, Whitman's works were important documents for his thesis of a "degenerate art" ("entartete Kunst," p. 505)—a concept which later assumed central importance in Nazi ideology.

36. See Jürgen Peper, "Heuristische Epoché statt mimetischer Totalität: Zur Ich-Analyse in der Literatur des späten 19. Jahrhunderts," in *Die Modernisierung des Ich: Studien zur Subjektkonstitution in der Vor- und Frühmoderne*, ed. Manfred Pfister (Passau: Rothe, 1989), pp. 22–35.

37. O. E. Lessing, "Die Whitman-Legende," *Allgemeine Zeitung* (Munich), no. 63, 15 March 1907, p. 500: "Die 'leidenschaftliche Liebe von Mann zu Mann,' von der Whitman das Heil der Zukunft erwartet, hat einen durchaus erotischen Charakter. Verdankt nun auch Whitman seiner abnormen Veranlagung, seinem feminin rezeptiven Empfinden wesentliche Vorzüge künstlerischer Art, so wird er andrerseits dadurch aus der Reihe der 'Erzieher der Menschheit' ausgeschlossen. Mit dieser Tatsache muß sich die Whitman-Propaganda abfinden."

38. Landauer, "Der Streit um Whitman," *Das literarische Echo* 9 (1906–1907), col. 1529.

39. Anon., review of *Yankee-Heiland, Nation*, 21 February 1907, p. 179. According to Bertz, the article was authored by Amalie von Ende (see letter to Rivers, 29 March 1913, 4:19).

40. Anon., "The 'Feminine Soul' in Whitman," *Current Literature* 41 (July 1906), 53.

41. A. von E. [Amalie von Ende], "Whitman in Germany: Edouard Bertz Now an Apostate from the Whitman Cult—A Bitter Arraignment of the Camden Poet," *New York Times Saturday Review*, 9 March 1907, p. 146.

42. Ibid.

43. Léon Bazalgette, *Walt Whitman: The Man and His Work*, trans. Ellen FitzGerald (Garden City, N.Y.: Doubleday, 1920), p. 220.

44. See Betsy Erkkila, *Walt Whitman among the French*, pp. 199f.

45. Guillaume Apollinaire, "Funérailles de Walt Whitman racontées par un témoin," *Mercure de France* 102 (April 1913), 658f.

46. Robert K. Martin, *The Homosexual Tradition in American Poetry* (Austin and London: University of Texas Press, 1979), p. 7.

47. Ibid., p. 6.

48. See John C. G. Röhl's introduction to *Philipp Eulenburgs politische Korrespondenz*, 3 vols. (Boppard/Rhein: Boldt, 1976), vol. 1, pp. 35–49.

20. WANDERVOGEL AND NUDISTS

1. Karl Federn translated Whitman's "birds of passage" "Wandervögel." The literal German translation would have been "Zugvögel."

2. Walt Whitman, *Gesang von der offenen Landstraße*, trans. Hans Reisiger, woodcuts by W. Tegtmeier (Lauenburg/Elbe: A. Saal), 1921.

3. Karl August Wittfogel, "Das Treffen in den Glauer Bergen," *Freideutsche Jugend* 4 (August 1918), 291f.

4. Hans Blüher, *Wandervogel: Geschichte einer Jugendbewegung* (Charlottenburg: Blüher, 1921).

5. Herbert Grünhagen, "Der zukünftige Mensch," *Vivos Voco* 2 (1921–1922), 523. The book with the three seals is the small Reclam edition of Whitman's works which accompanied Grünhagen his whole life long and which he passed on to subsequent generations of his family.

> Ich saß ganz allein nachmittags auf meinem Büro. Die Sonne schien. Es war ganz still. Ich war der endlosen Diskussionen, Versammlungen, des ganzen theoretischen Krimskrams müde. Im Winter hatte ich Weininger gelesen. Weininger, der, aus Gram über sich und seine Zeit, zertritt, was er heilig nennen möchte. . . . Da plötzlich klappte sich dieses dreifach versiegelte Buch vor mir auf, und ein Strom von Freude und Ahnung ging durch mein Blut. Die Gehirnkrämpfe, Zweifel und Dunkelheiten schnurrten zusammen, blieben liegen, irgendwo ganz weit unten, eine große und starke Hand riß mir allen Kleiderplunder vom Leibe und allen Gedankenplunder von der Seele, ich wurde ganz nackt. So hob sie mich in die Luft und hielt mich auf ihrer breiten robusten Fläche. Da lag ich, der Kopf fiel zurück, die Beine sanken herunter, kein Krampf war mehr in den Gliedern. Und ich schlürfte durch Mund und Haut Sonne und Wind.
>
> So ungefähr war es. Und seitdem kam das Buch nicht oft mehr aus meiner Tasche. Oft klappt es wieder zu, die Worte tönen ganz aus weiter Ferne, ich taste und

finde ihn doch nicht. Aber wer diese Luft einmal geatmet hat, kann nie wieder ganz zurückfallen in die andere Zeit; Romantik und Neuromantik, Klassizismus und Naturalismus, Maschine, Gehirn, Technik, Mache, Fieber und Kälte, Zweifel und Krampf nehmen ihn nie wieder ganz in Besitz. Die Zivilisation rast draußen vorbei. Hast, Ungeduld, Propaganda, Schlagworte, Beleidigung, Druck machen ihn nie wieder ganz blind.

6. Ibid., p. 527.

7. Ibid.

8. Franz Rinskofer, "Walt Whitman," *Die Freude: Monatshefte für freie Lebensgestaltung* 4/7 (July 1927), 333f.:

So wird ihm [Whitman] Natur zur Grundlage aller weiteren Beziehung zur Umwelt, Prinzip aufbauenden Lebens, der "Verwirklichung" schlechthin. Seit Rousseau und Goethe hat niemand mehr Natur so tief erlebt wie Whitman. . . . Jede ihrer Erlebnismöglichkeiten wird bis zum Grunde ausgekostet. Da bieten z.B. Luft und Wind sich an, ein ewig wechselndes Spiel von Empfindungsmöglichkeiten. Die sollen nun genossen werden; denn Whitman ist in die Atmosphäre "verliebt":

"Zum Hügelhang am Wald will ich gehn, ohne Kleidung will ich sein, nackt;
Rasend bin ich danach, mit ihr in Berührung zu kommen."

Whitman ist ein starker Genießer und blieb es sein Leben lang. Eine Tagebuchaufzeichnung verrät uns, worin für ihn Genuß eigentlich besteht: Er hat z.B. das "Hochgefühl der Nacktheit" entdeckt und definiert es als das Bewußtwerden eines "inneren Gemeingefühls, das uns mit Erde, Licht, Luft, Bäumen usw. verbindet." Eine Philosophie des Genusses blitzt auf. Genuß als höchste Bewußtheit der Empfindungen, Steigerung seelischer Keimanlage.

CONCLUSION: A GERMAN "WHITMANN"

1. See the introduction.

2. Switzerland, a country with a functioning democratic society, fewer material problems, and a more pragmatic approach to the "ills of society," must be excluded here. In fact, owing to their exceptional social and political status, the Swiss have contributed relatively little to the German-language reception of Whitman. Schabelitz's radical publishing house, which undertook the publication of the first edition of *Leaves*, is an exception to the rule.

INDEX